YOUR ADOPTED DOG

Everything You Need to Know about Rescuing
and Caring for a Best Friend in Need

Shelley Frost and
Katerina Lorenzatos Makris

The Lyons Press
Guilford, Connecticut

An imprint of The Globe Pequot Press

The Lyons Press is an imprint of The Globe Pequot Press

10 9 8 7 6 5 4 3 2

Printed in the United States of America

Designed by Sheryl P. Kober

Library of Congress Cataloging-in-Publication Data

Frost, Shelley and Makris, Katerina Lorenzatos.
Your adopted dog : everything you need to know about rescuing and caring for a best friend in need / Shelley Frost and Katerina Lorenzatos Makris.
p. cm.
ISBN-13: 978-1-59921-047-6
1. Dogs. 2. Dog adoption. 3. Dog rescue. I. Makris, Kathryn. II. Title.
SF427.F785 2007
636.7'0887—dc22
2007020776

The authors will donate a portion of their proceeds from this book to animal protection and rescue organizations.

Dedicated to:
Gretchen Wyler, the loving godmother of animal rescue;
Kathryn Mennone, who had the idea for this book;
dogs and the people who protect them.

ACKNOWLEDGMENTS

With deepest gratitude to Christopher Ameruoso; Carmen Hinojoza Atilano, DVM; Susan Barnes; Gavin and the Bowlby family; Jane Brown; Christine Eastus; David J. Eagle; Scott A. and April Apperson Farrell; Ken Foster; Bret Frost; Kevin Frost; Lilly Golden; Cathleen T. Hall, M.S.; Allison and Roy Harrison; Dr. James P. Hendrix; Sheryl Jaehne; Dr. Jim and Mrs. Helen Kambosos; Colleen Kessler; Jeff Lerner; Zanna Magoula and family; Alec, Stella K., and Stuart Makris; Mardeene B. Mitchell, Dr. Rex O. Mooney and family; Alexandra Paul; Laura Rennert; Nancy Ruff; Kevin Sielky; Anna Maria Simpson; the Sterling/Simpson family; Julian and Jean Spooner; Linda Young; Donna Wolosin; the staff of The Humane Society of the United States, including Kathy Bauch, Wayne Pacelle, Nancy Peterson, and Jen Tait; and all the rescuers and dogs who contributed their inspiring stories to this book.

WITH THANKS TO OUR
CONSULTANTS AND CONTRIBUTORS

Veterinary

Don Conkling, DVM
Masson Veterinary Hospital
San Bruno, CA

Carolyn Cupp, MS, DVM
Liberty, MO

David M. Munson, DVM
Foothill Animal Hospital
Lake Forest, CA

Paul Richieri, DVM, MS
Melrose Veterinary Hospital
Vista, CA

Writing/Editing

Meera Lester

A. Bronwyn Llewellyn

Dog Rescue

Rita Martinez, CPDT
Vizsla Rescue Fund, Inc.
Vizsla Club of Northern California

JP Novic
Executive Director
Center for Animal Protection &
Education (CAPE)

Behavior/Training

Barbara O'Connor

Mal Lightfoot
Director and CEO
San Bruno Dog Obedience School
San Bruno, CA

Contents

Foreword by Alexandra Paul

I grew up with adopted animals. To purchase a pet from a pet store or breeder seemed silly when there were so many wonderful dogs and cats in nearby shelters waiting for homes. Our dogs, Dividend and Twiggy (who was very thin when we adopted her but who soon literally outgrew her name) were the most loving dogs ever, and my dad used to say if you adopt a dog from a shelter, you have a loyal friend for life. They know you rescued them from an uncertain fate and they love you forever in return.

Nowadays, there are even more dogs that need rescuing, so buying one from a breeder or pet store is not only a waste of money, it is encouraging overpopulation among dogs. And buying from a pet store often means supporting "puppy mills," the factories that churn out puppies from mothers that spend their lives in small cages and horrible conditions.

It has been a while since I have had a dog. I would want to be home more than I am now, to be with them and to take them out for frequent breaks. I would worry about them being lonely and uncomfortable. My mom had strict rules with our dogs—when we lived in the city, they were exercised an hour a day. I grew up feeling that having a dog is a major commitment.

But I still get to enjoy and help needy pets. After Hurricane Katrina I was in Mississippi volunteering for a few days at the Best Friends Animal Society's rescue compound. I think that taking care of the rescued animals there—just cleaning and feeding and petting—was some of the most important work I've done.

You bought this book probably because you have just rescued a dog. Or are thinking of doing so. Thank you. Thank you for giving a loving home to an innocent animal. Thank you for opening your heart to a creature who had been lost and forgotten before you came along. Thank you for seeing the soul, and not just looking for perfect breeding, when you picked your dog. You will be rewarded many times over with love and loyalty from a wonderful companion.

Dividend and Twiggy and my shelter kitty, Hallie (who is sitting on my lap purring as I write this), thank you too.

Alexandra Paul
January 25, 2007
Pacific Palisades, California

BIO NOTE: In 1997 the United Nations commended actress Alexandra Paul for her environmental activism. In 1999, she won the International Green Cross award. Over the years Alexandra has had one rescued dog and six rescued cats. She will not use any products tested on animals, and has been a vegetarian since age fourteen.

Alexandra and Corelli.

Introduction by Katerina Lorenzatos Makris

Unknown to my husband, while visiting Greece without him, I'm sharing my room with a handsome young guy. A lanky redhead, Corelli mercifully lets me sleep all night but demands playtime several times a day.

Yes, this is betrayal. Yes, this endangers my marriage. Our house is already occupied by seven other friends who "followed me home." But the combination of Corelli's mischievous charm and intense need are too much to resist. Come what may, I'll be taking him back to the United States. The only question is whether to tell my husband before we arrive, after, or, with luck, never.

Beyond the husband hurdle, there's the matter of all the money, energy, and time I'm spending on this little fling. I had vowed to kick the habit. It's especially foolish to give in to the compulsion in Greece, where I've come to deal with a family emergency.

Yesterday, after shelling out the equivalent of $200 for Corelli's blood tests, shots, and medications, I questioned my sanity. I'll pay his plane fare, too. Is this the behavior of a sensible person? Anyone who has ever let a Corelli into his or her life must ask the same question. And there are untold thousands of us all over the world.

The last thing I need is an additional responsibility. But the night I arrived, here on the island of Kefalonia, Corelli came bounding out of the darkness to greet me, a total stranger, as if he'd been waiting all his life. He tried, to the best of his bone-thin ability, to "help" me with my bags, dragging one of them across the street into the bushes before I'd noticed.

Corelli was a beach bum. He made his living all summer here at this quiet cove by charming tourists out of their *souvlakia*, or sometimes just snatching snacks out of their hands. He frequently raided the rubbish bins, strewing trash all over the sand so as to pick out whatever might be worth ingesting.

For the most part, he was tolerated; sometimes befriended and adored. Word is he was invited to spend a few nights in some of the hotel rooms. But also, sometimes, he was slapped and kicked, and there was a rumor that he might get poisoned.

Now it's chilly November and the tourists are gone. I'm still here because of my elderly aunt and uncle. If I hadn't come, and if I weren't taking him home, what would Corelli do after the season ended? He's resourceful, but the cove is deserted all winter, and in the nearest villages, miles away, folks don't always take kindly to homeless hobos.

For him, at this point, I'm the only hope. Hundreds of tourists passed through the cove all summer and left him behind. I want to be like them. It's smarter and far more convenient.

That brings me to wonder—why do this? Is it really *his* need I'm driven to meet? Or do *I* need *him*? Why compromise my time, finances, and, not the least, my marriage?

For rescue addicts like me, there's no high that tops saving a life. Getting a starving bum off the streets provides a heady hit. It's power. For one shining moment, you take command of this haphazard world and do a little good. Most of life is impossible to fix. To find some tiny part that you can improve is intoxicating.

There—it's the dirty little secret behind rescue. It's not always so much about the rescuee as about the rescuer.

When Corelli dives into a bowl of chow, he trembles with joy. When I invite him for a walk, he whirls in delight. When he rests his head on my knee, he sighs. His simple pleasures are enough to make me forget, for a moment, the problems in this world that I am not powerful enough to fix, like the ones that have called me to Greece.

I'm sending his photo around to everyone I know. Maybe this little hunk will get lucky, and there will be a pair of loving arms waiting for him at the airport. Maybe *I'll* get lucky enough to deliver him into those loving arms forthwith, so that my husband will have a pair of his own waiting for me.

I'll hold off a bit before breaking the news to my long-suffering mate. After all, as they say, the husband is always the last to know.

Postscript

After arriving in California, Corelli kept himself busily underfoot in our home for a few months while I worked on this book. He endlessly pestered me, my husband, and the seven resident dogs to play. Thanks to Vizsla Rescue of Northern California, he joined his wonderful new forever family, the Navarros, on Mother's Day, 2007. As they drove away, my husband, to whom, happily, I remain married, cried even more than me.

That night we received this email update from Marco Navarro: "Corelli was the perfect traveler. He and our two kids slept most of the way home. Lorraine felt very special on this Mother's Day with all three of her children sleeping peacefully in the back seat. Thank you for preparing Corelli to be this wonderful companion."

A couple of weeks later this message came in: "All of us have noticed how much more loving we are with Corelli in our home. It has always amazed me how much happier a family is when a four-legged love sponge is part of the household."

We did, indeed, get lucky.

Introduction by Shelley Frost

"Can we really adopt another dog?" I asked myself over and over again. Whenever the subject came up, my husband, Kevin, would get a serious look on his face and say, "Shelley, do whatever you need to do." Sounded like a yes to me. Bret, my twelve-year-old son, enthusiastically argued for naming rights and predicted our need to stock up on tennis balls because the new dog would definitely want to play fetch. Poor Abby, our eight-year-old, nonfetching terrier mix, had no clue that her life as an only dog was about to be forever changed.

We've never had two dogs at a time. And since our yard is small, walks throughout the day are critical. Two dogs would mean two collars upon which to attach two leashes, without forgetting to grab two poop bags. Well, I thought, there was no getting around the fact that I do have two hands, so, why not?

I had been volunteering for dog rescue groups for years, watching dogs come from the streets and, hopefully, go into new homes. It was time that we opened our home and our hearts to another dog with nowhere else to go.

Yet I was losing sleep. How would our one-year-old cat, Stevie, react? Abby has always believed she is the only one of her species allowed in our house. Would she ignore the new dog, causing a divided household? Would our new dog be a cat-chasing, barking, chewing, escape artist? I was almost to the point of deciding that I could not risk the happiness of my family, when Bret came running upstairs, calling for me to hear his latest news. He had decided that our new dog's name would be Kellie. Kellie . . . she was out there, and she needed us.

I began my online search for Kellie and quickly became overwhelmed by the enormous numbers of dogs needing homes. I filled out adoption forms and questionnaires and had numerous phone interviews. Then my friend, JP Novic, founder of the Center for Animal Protection and Education (CAPE) in Santa Cruz, California, forwarded me the photos of several dogs recently rescued from an animal shelter in Juarez, Mexico.

In one week these dogs were going to be placed in a minivan and driven twelve hundred miles to an animal shelter near my home. JP encouraged me to consider the border collie mix. I am a dog fanatic who believes all dogs are marvelous creatures, but the idea of adopting a border collie worried me. They're known for herding and nipping. Nope, we needed another, perhaps younger version of Abby—a dog whose idea of entertainment was being positioned under a human hand for hours at a time.

So I downloaded the photos and opened them up, one by one. Each face was adorable— cute noses, bright eyes, happy smiles. Then I double-clicked on the last photo icon, and there was Kellie. Border collie ears, black, and alert. White stripe down her nose. A huge, toothy smile. Bent whiskers springing cockeyed from her muzzle.

On my kitchen floor, a new ceramic bowl had been placed next to Abby's. She had sniffed the bowl and then looked at me with questioning eyes. I hoped and prayed the answer would be to her liking, because I was looking at her new sister.

On the day of Kellie's rescue, a veterinarian, Dr. Carmen Hinojoza Atilano, witnessed a speeding car hit a small black-and-white dog. She picked up Kellie's injured body and took her off the streets. Dr. Atilano volunteers at a spay-and-neuter clinic operated by Compassion Without Borders (CWOB), a nonprofit organization founded to alleviate the suffering of companion animals around the world. There, on Kellie's first day in her "new" life, she was treated for her injuries and later spayed.

My friend JP was the matchmaker between my family and Kellie. Over the years, CAPE has collaborated with several animal organizations in rescuing hundreds of dogs out of Mexico and placing them into new homes here in the United States. JP says, "In a country with so many animals that have very few options, we were compelled to help. We work very hard not to compete with dogs in our local shelters that are hoping to be adopted. The dogs we rescue from Mexico are usually small dogs that are hard to find in shelters in our community. I'd rather people adopt the small, rescued Mexican dogs instead of buying a small dog from a breeder."

My little immigrants from Mexico (Abby is from a dog shelter in Mexico City) prove that a dog is a dog no matter in what street, city, and country he or she was made homeless. But when people meet Kellie and Abby and hear about their past, I am often peppered with questions. Were they put into quarantine? (No.) Why didn't you adopt from a shelter here? (Why did *you* buy *your* dog from a breeder?) Do they speak Spanish? (Maybe—ask them a question.)

I believe that all dogs have visions and thoughts and memories. If only they could tell us about them. But they can't, so I have taken the liberty of helping Kellie express herself in narratives of her story throughout this book. I apologize to her if I got it wrong. If only I spoke Spanish . . .

An Interview with
Albuquerque Mayor Martin Chávez

Imagine having the power to improve the lives of millions of companion animals. Many government officials have such power, and, slowly, some are beginning to use it. One of them is the mayor of Albuquerque, New Mexico. During his election campaign, Martin Chávez promised to work for the protection of pets in his city. In 2006, his promise became law. A new ordinance requires all cats and dogs older than six months to be microchipped and spayed or neutered. Steep fees are charged to pet owners who wish to let their animals reproduce. Dogs cannot be chained longer than one hour a day. To enforce the new law, Mayor Chávez hired additional animal control officers to patrol the streets, ensuring that more animals will receive assistance.

Today, Albuquerque's previous euthanasia rate of one thousand pets per month has dropped to half. City shelters now adopt out more animals than they kill.

From city hall in Albuquerque (with his rescued dog, Dukes, at his side), Mayor Chávez spoke by phone with author Shelley Frost.

Mayor Chávez and Dukes

Shelley: Is everything we're reading about you in the news correct?

Mayor Chávez: All the good things are correct.

Shelley: Great, because we are really excited about what you guys are doing and we hope you run for president someday.

Mayor Chávez: Yeah, right. No, I think I'll run for the border.

Shelley (laughing): Can you tell me about Dukes's adoption?

Mayor Chávez: Dukes comes from our Eastside Animal Services shelter, and he's about two years and two months old.

Shelley: What was his story? Why did he end up there?

Mayor Chávez: He just was abandoned. I think somebody brought him and his siblings in. They could not take care of them. He was just a little puppy.

Shelley: Were you looking to adopt when you found out about him?

Mayor Chávez: I was looking to adopt, looking for about three months, and every time I'd go over there I'd take a look, kind of just taking my time to find the right puppy.

Shelley: What happened when you saw him?

Mayor Chávez: We connected. You know, as every pet owner knows, we just connected. He's my dog.

Shelley: Tell me about his state visits or his city visits where he's with you at meetings.

Mayor Chávez: He's in the office all the time. He comes to work every day. He's the best-known dog in the state. He's done commercials for spay and neuter and adoption. He's had a billboard for adoption and spay and neuter. He has his own TV show called *Dukes' Rescue 311*. It's on Comcast Cable, an idea we got from Salt Lake City, but we improved on it. It has an intro from Dukes with his story, then after that it features all the animals we have in animal care for adoption. We have a trainer hired who works with the dogs and she says things like, "This is Angel, and Angel is two years old," and just a snippet on each of the animals.

Shelley: So has it shown to really work so far as adoptions go?

Mayor Chávez: Our adoptions have doubled. This allows us to get a much better grip on euthanasia as well.

Shelley: So Dukes is like an ambassador, helping other dogs in the same predicament he was in.

Mayor Chávez: Yeah, and Dukes goes with me to a lot of my press conferences—not all of them anymore because we always take a rescue dog from the shelter to the press conferences so they can get adopted. So when the media and cameras see the dogs, they are drawn to them. At these press conferences, very rarely do we not get our dogs adopted out.

Shelley: How did you get interested in animal protection?

Mayor Chávez: I've always had pets, and when I first got out of law school I had a yellow Lab who was a digger and a runner. He'd get out. He got out one time and was picked up by the city. I went at 4:30 in the afternoon to pick up my dog, and they said, "Sorry, the cash register is closed, come back tomorrow." So I said, "Well, you make sure he's here. I'll be back tomorrow morning." So the next morning on his pen, there was a slip of paper that was stamped "Medical Research." And it was stamped "Medical Research" *over* the note that said "Do not destroy—owner will be here in the morning to pick him up." So they basically euthanized him. I went back to my office and drafted a complaint for like $2 million, since I was a lawyer, and filed suit, and of course found out that in New Mexico pets are chattel. You don't get damages for pain and suffering since they are property. So I just settled for $200, but that wasn't what it was about.

Since then I've always had pets. And my marvelous communications officer, Deborah James, who is an animal activist, sees every animal as a unique, sentient being, and she has definitely infected me.

Shelley: Describe your relationship with Dukes.

Mayor Chávez: He's my dog. He's my best friend. He's the one who, no matter what kind of mood I'm in, is always in a good mood. Whether I've been good or bad he always thinks I'm good. He sleeps at the foot of my bed. He's a big dog and takes all the covers. When you hear his sounds at night it means everything is OK. Those few times when he's not with me, for example, if I have to go out of town, and I wake up in the middle of the night and he's not there, it's just not the same.

Shelley: You've been quoted as saying, "We can't be a complete city as long as we euthanize animals."

Mayor Chávez: I think I said euthanize *adoptable* animals. Because not every animal we get in the shelter is adoptable. Some are very ill, have injuries, and some have, frankly, temperament issues, so there is unfortunately a need for some euthanasia. But the euthanasia of adoptable pets is just sinful. Albuquerque today really is a unique city. *Forbes* magazine ranked us as the number-one city in the country for business or career. We are one of the best cities for bicycling, art, travel, tourism, you name it. All those are important to any mayor, but there's also that human side, the compassionate side, and we have failed in great measure in that.

Shelley: Politically, how is advocating for animals helping or hurting you?

Mayor Chávez: That's been a really interesting thing because it has been a tremendous help, unexpectedly so. What I've found—and I did not fully appreciate this before—is that passion for animals has no party boundaries and no income boundaries. It just cuts across the board. All walks of life have this very special passion for animals and companion pets. In the election I had the support of the animal activist community, and we did something that has never been done. We pulled all of the animal licenses and we sent each one of them a postcard from Dukes saying, "Vote for my dad—he's done all these things for us." It was kind of cute, and it ended up on the front page of the newspaper. In fact, one of my opponents was very upset, mostly because he hadn't thought of it. It was a direct appeal from an animal enthusiast to other animal enthusiasts.

Shelley: We saw that the American Kennel Club considers your new law to be a draconian measure. How do you respond to someone who's on the other side, who feels spay and neuter should not be enforced?

Mayor Chávez: Well, the ordinance we have in place takes a pretty big hit at breeders. I don't fully support that part of the law. That was the sponsor and me disagreeing a little bit, for the following reasons: one, I'm not into breeding. I don't fully get this idea why you want to put a dachshund with a Chihuahua to see what happens, you know? I've had purebred dogs in the past and they are wonderful pets. But I like the mutt variety—personal preference. What I'm trying to address in Albuquerque, desperately, is overpopulation and euthanasia of adoptable pets. And in addressing that problem in Albuquerque, I don't see the professional breeders as the problem for that particular issue. They don't like the law. I'm not fully on board with that part of the law. What I see are the backyard breeders and the puppy mills and irresponsible owners who don't have their dogs spayed and neutered as the ones contributing to this problem of pet overpopulation. And so we've really gone after the puppy mills, and there are no longer any backyard breeders or puppy mills [in Albuquerque]. Hope that's not too convoluted. It's just that I'm a pragmatist. Let's go after the overpopulation problem. I don't need to fight with the breeders right now.

Shelley: They are very well organized and they have the AKC behind them.

Mayor Chávez: They [breeders] are not my cup of tea, but I'm trying to address a specific problem. And that's why, in a statewide law we have pending in the legislature, we are kind of removing the breeders from that fight, because we want to fight the fight that we need to fight to actually address the problem. Then we can get more specific down the road.

Shelley: My final question is about the upcoming Mayor's Annual Dog Ball.

Mayor Chávez: It's the silliest thing you've ever seen. It's people with their pets, everyone dressed up. Dukes will be wearing a tuxedo. People will have all their dogs out. The money goes to a spay and neuter program for low-income citizens. And it is just a hoot. There's very nice food for the grown-ups, and some special things made for the dogs. We bring the Girl Scout troops in so they can walk the dogs for those who need a break during the doggie ball, and there's music and dancing. People dance with each other, they dance with their dogs. It's really pretty silly, but it's just a hoot.

Shelley: Do you give a speech or an intro?

Mayor Chávez: Oh yes, I thank everyone for coming. And Dukes will probably have something to say. We'll have to send you the intro to *Dukes's Rescue 311*. It has him presiding at city meetings and things. Kind of cute.

It is true that whenever a person loves a dog he derives great power from it.

—Old Seneca Chief

YOUR ADOPTED DOG

1.
Why Dogs Need to Be Rescued
The Epidemic of Pet Overpopulation and Mistreatment

Kellie: An Outside Life

Look at that! It's a torn-up piece of rubber! Hey, I can pick it up and throw it in the air! Chase it! Paw it! Fun! I wish I could eat it.

I am starving! Something smells delicious. Perfect! Tables full of people eating. I'll just sit by my favorite garbage can and wait for something tasty to . . . YELP! Oh, that hurt! Something whacked the back of my head! Run fast! Faster! Ahhhh—that car almost wiped me out! I guess they don't stop for little dogs like me.

Every year in the United States, three million to four million dogs and cats are euthanized. Some people might consider those animals lucky compared to the untold millions who die annually from causes related to abandonment, neglect, and abuse.

This book is a guide for the legions of individuals who struggle to help dogs in need. In this chapter we'll take a look at why that need exists.

> Although the world is full of suffering, it is full also of the overcoming of it.
>
> —Helen Keller

Dogs Aren't the Only Ones

Many other companion animals in need, such as cats, livestock, birds, reptiles, and rodents, are also cared for by shelters—if they're lucky—or worse—and deserve our help.

AN OUNCE OF PREVENTION . . .

The horrors of dog and cat overpopulation can be reduced dramatically through widespread neutering or spaying of companion animals. For both males and females, it's a relatively routine surgery that removes the reproductive organs, and as a side benefit, improves the animals' long-term health and safety. Communities that have adopted public policies to promote spay/neuter programs have seen drastic declines in the numbers of unwanted pets relinquished to shelters or roaming the streets. Such programs save lives as well as taxpayer dollars. Spay/neuter is an ounce of prevention worth tons of cure. For a complete description of this procedure see chapter 2, p. 9.

So Many Dogs, So Few Homes

Many factors contribute to dog overpopulation. Of these, perhaps the single biggest factor is biology. Females can have two litters of puppies per year. Litters average from about six to ten pups each. Theoretically, in six years, a breeding pair and their offspring can produce tens of thousands of dogs.

There are nowhere near enough homes for such great numbers. Overpopulation leads to neglect and abuse of owned animals. Dogs are plentiful, and thus in the eyes of many, easy to replace. Overpopulation also leads to euthanasia when jam-packed animal shelters run out of kennel space.

Adding to the Problem

About one out of every four dogs in shelters is a purebred, and many of the others had a purebred parent. Most of the purebreds were originally purchased as puppies—for hundreds or even thousands of dollars. Contrary to popular assumption, a high price tag does not protect these dogs from being thrown away. By churning out more and more puppies every year, some breeders add significantly to the problem of dog overpopulation.

There are different types of breeders. Rescue organizations and government agencies describe them in various ways. We'll define them in three main categories: commercial, backyard, and accidental.

Commercial breeders bring puppies into the world for profit or as a hobby. They operate at various levels of activity. Some might be dog show enthusiasts who selectively breed just one female to another breeder's male once every couple of years, carefully re-searching genetic histories and adhering to strict canine club standards. The puppies that don't seem to measure up are sold as pets. At the opposite extreme are large commercial outfits operating entire kennels full of dozens, or more, of dogs, creating hundreds of puppies annually. Those that maintain unsanitary, unsafe, and inhumane conditions are often referred to as *puppy mills*. Another player in the breeding industry is the broker or wholesaler who trades, imports, and otherwise profits from buying and selling quantities of purebred pets.

Backyard breeders have purebred pets that they decide to breed for various reasons. Perhaps they believe they can make money from selling the puppies. Some might consider their dog to be an extraordinarily beautiful specimen whose bloodline should be perpetuated. Or maybe they adore their pet so much that they want to produce more just like it in order to own facsimiles of that pet in the future. In any case, backyard breeders tend to be relatively casual in their breeding strategies and not heavily involved in researching genetic histories or conforming to dog-club standards.

The term *accidental breeders* speaks for itself. These pet owners have nonspayed and nonneutered animals that mate randomly and opportunistically, either among themselves or perhaps with the neighbors' dogs or homeless strays. Perhaps the owner has taken measures to prevent mating, such as building a fence or trying to keep their pooch indoors. But when those measures fail—and they usually do—the result can be litter after litter of puppies. An unaltered dog will breed. Unless the dog lives in the tower of Rapunzel, chances are that it will find a way to mate. The drive to breed is powerful, and canines have crafty ways of circumventing things like doors, gates, and fences. For example, it is not unusual for dogs to mate through a chain-link fence!

Caring breeders, whether they are of the commercial, backyard, or accidental variety, take responsibility for their actions. They recognize that because they are the ones who, either through intent or neglect, brought living beings into the world, they are responsible for the animals for life.

Caring breeders sell only to buyers whom they are confident will give the animal a safe, loving home. Caring breeders give more consideration to the dog's future health and happiness than to making money. They follow screening procedures similar to the ones we've outlined in chapter 10 for placing a rescued dog in a "forever" home. Caring breeders have all buyers sign a contract containing elements similar to those in chapter 10, requiring that if the new owner cannot or does not wish to keep the animal, he or she will return the dog to the breeder. The breeder might also offer an incentive, such as a refund of all or part of the purchase price, to encourage the new owner to bring the dog back rather than allow it to end up in a neglectful home or in a shelter or abandoned on the street.

Even in litters bred by show enthusiasts, only one or two puppies might be of "show quality." It is pointless to breed the others. Caring breeders offer a rebate on the purchase price of spayed/neutered pets, or offer other incentives like free training or grooming for buyers who get their purchased puppies spayed/neutered.

The caring breeder follows up for years after the adoption to check on the dog's status. This might involve phone calls, e-mails, or home visits.

Caring breeders rescue more dogs than they breed. If they have the time, energy, facilities, and money to breed animals, they should be able to devote some of those same resources to fostering and placing dogs in need.

Yet when all is said and done, even the most caring, responsible breeders still add to the problem. Every dog bred and sold takes up space in a potential adopter's home.

Born to Roam?

Some twelve thousand years of domestication and selective breeding have turned wild canines into pets. Our human ancestors bred them to depend on us. Therefore, dogs cannot fend for themselves when they are lost or abandoned. They cannot survive in the wilderness or off the haphazard kindness of strangers in urban areas.

Some of the bad things that happen to dogs who are on their own include:

- getting hit by cars
- starving
- falling ill
- being poisoned (sometimes on purpose)
- being used for medical research
- being used for target practice
- being used in satanic rituals
- being tortured by psychopaths who are "practicing" before they move on to humans

Born to Love

Perhaps the worst thing for a dog is loneliness. All canine species, from domesticated dogs to dingoes to wolves, are highly social. They crave and seek companionship. Most pooches especially enjoy human companionship. Thousands of generations of breeding have made them need and love us.

No matter how neglectful or even violent owners may be, many dogs will not try to leave them. Most dogs can't or won't defend themselves against abuse, but instead react with submissiveness. They cower and try to forgive. Animals who do fight back are often abused even more cruelly, abandoned, or killed.

The phrase *man's best friend* came about for good reason. It's not often in life that we find the unconditional devotion that is given by our canine companions. Their wholehearted desire to accompany, comfort, and protect us is a unique and precious gift.

> Dogs have given us their absolute all. We are the center of their universe. We are the focus of their love and faith and trust. They serve us in return for scraps. It is without a doubt the best deal man has ever made.
>
> —Roger Caras

For People's Sake

Rescuing dogs is showing concern for fellow humans as well.

Shelter workers, animal control officers, and other rescuers pay a high emotional price for the difficult jobs they do. It's especially harrowing for those who work in euthanasia rooms.

Homeless dogs pose a variety of hazards to people. Out on the streets, they can be road hazards and cause accidents. They can attack livestock and pets. They can become vicious toward passersby.

The presence of stray dogs is detrimental to a community's image. It is often a sign that the local government lacks the resources or the will to correct the problem.

Supply and Demand

The most important need that dogs have right now is to be more highly valued. Preventing unwanted births with spay/neuter will help accomplish this. Right now dogs are, by and large, considered throwaways. Even in the eyes of the law, dogs have little worth beyond their monetary replacement value.

The "E" Word

While awareness and practice of spay/neuter is spreading, what do we do with the many unwanted dogs we already have right now? Euthanasia is a four-letter word to some people. Shelters that practice it often draw disapproval.

A more popular option is to find homes for unwanted dogs. If each of the 115 million households in the United States took in one homeless dog, pet overpopulation—at least for the moment—would disappear. But, realistically, that's never going to happen. For the time being, millions of pets roam the streets or suffer under neglectful or abusive owners.

Waiting.

A NECESSARY EVIL?

Many dedicated people involved in pet rescue object to terms like *euthanasia* and *putting an animal to sleep*, seeing them as misleading euphemisms. They maintain that this publicly funded practice in thousands of shelters around the country is nothing short of sanctioned slaughter.

In the original Greek, euthanasia means "good death." Is that what we are giving to millions of pets every year? For animals that are physically healthy and behaviorally stable, it's certainly a premature and tragic death. But in the United States, shelters are required by law to kill animals in a humane, painless way, usually by lethal injection. That's a better death than the ones suffered by countless other pets that are abandoned or abused.

Terminology aside, in almost everyone's opinion it's shocking that a country with the resources and ingenuity of ours must resort to destroying "excess" animals.

Every Drop Fills the Bucket

Many citizens cannot tolerate dogs suffering and do everything they can to alleviate it. There are currently more than four hundred rescue groups in the United States listed on the Internet, and some four thousand to five thousand animal shelters. Most of the people who staff these organizations are volunteers.

The help provided by these Good Samaritans might seem like a drop in the bucket. So what if we personally save one or two or even a hundred dogs, when there are still millions who desperately need help? That's a logical argument, but the urge to help is not always logical. For many animal lovers, it's hard to resist responding to the pain and suffering of a dog in the here and now.

This book is intended to help those people. Rescuing a dog in need can be difficult and time consuming. It can take a high emotional and financial toll. It can stress the rescuer's relationships with their spouse and other family members, affect job performance, and even have an impact on the rescuer's health.

Yet the rewards can be enormous. And, anyway, some of us have no choice. We have to do something.

This book aims to make life a little easier for those who cannot turn away.

The greatness of a nation and its moral progress can be judged by the way its animals are treated.
—Mohandas Gandhi (1869–1948)

Dennis and friends.

and it was pretty clear how close he was with his brother, Duke. My wife, Holly, said, 'They're small—let's rescue two.'"

How could two adorable purebred toy poodle puppies need to be rescued?

According to Kris King, founder of Poodle Preserve, purebred dogs are on the receiving end of plenty of neglect and abuse. She remembered the anger she felt upon hearing of Fabio and Duke's situation: "Six puppies were living in the basement of a house, locked in a dog crate for five and a half months. A friend of mine, who convinced the homeowner to give them up, stood on the front porch and could smell this horrible odor coming through a crack in the door."

Happily Ever After True Story Number One:

Duke and Fabio

• •

Retired firefighter Dennis Polito was at the controls of his Piper Malibu twenty-five thousand feet above the desert plains of central Nevada. He was headed to Colorado where he was going to meet and take home a curly-haired poodle puppy named Fabio. But one and a half hours into his flight, the weather turned ugly. Dennis's small plane bounced from one air pocket to the next. He had to return home to the San Francisco Bay Area, poodleless.

Months later, as Dennis sat comfortably on his couch with Fabio nestled in his lap, another small curly-haired body squirmed for affection. Dennis said, "If it wasn't for the bad weather that day, I might have just adopted one doggie. But after that flight, I received more pictures of Fabio

Kris's friend brought the crate of poodle pups to Poodle Preserve. "We opened the door to the crate and suddenly had a pack of wild, furry little beasts on our hands!" Having never felt the touch of a human hand, the puppies were riddled with fear and fleas. They had never been outside, so their awareness of where to eliminate was simply wherever they were standing. And that was usually on top of each other. She described taking them outside on cold Colorado mornings: "It was like a rodeo of catching six unsocialized poodle puppies and trying to train them how to sniff and urinate."

Inside the house the puppies sought security by hiding and huddling together, scuttling out of arm's reach. "Gradually, the bolder ones ventured out. I would scratch them a bit under the chin and talk to them softly in a high-pitched voice. Then I'd ignore them. This made the puppies want more." By introducing them to toys, brushing, and even vaccinations, Kris was drawing them into a world of normalcy.

One day as she watched them play, Kris knew they had left their dark days behind. "I saw them do the psycho run! That's when young dogs fly in circles just as hard as they can. It is the most rewarding thing, watching them discover joy."

Kris listed the puppies on her Web site and on Petfinder.com. And it was late at night, after searching page after page for a poodle to adopt, that Holly and Dennis, about ready to give up, clicked on the last page where Fabio's brown eyes looked into theirs as if to say, "I don't mind an airplane ride, just get me to your house!"

A commercial flight did just that. Dennis and Holly went to the freight area at San Jose International Airport, and picked up the crate containing Duke and Fabio. Dennis remembered seeing the pups for the first time: "Duke, being the front man that he is, leaped out to meet us. Fabio saw his brother's enthusiasm and eventually came out, too."

The two puppies had further acquaintances to make upon arriving at their new home. Two big sisters, rescued toy poodles Betty and Chou Chou, formed a receiving line at the front door.

Asked how having two more family members has changed Dennis's life, he said, "Fabio and Duke will be dead asleep, but if I get up to walk to another part of the house, they will leap up and follow me."

Eventually Dennis took Fabio and Duke up in the Piper Malibu for their first flight. Betty and Chou Chou, experienced airplane passengers, curled up and napped on their leather seats. As for Duke and Fabio? "They just thought they were riding in the car like we always do. Me at the controls and both of them on my lap."

Update on Dennis Polito:

On Sunday, February 18, 2007, Dennis landed his plane at the Hayward Executive Airport in Hayward, California. His flight had originated in El Paso, Texas, where, at the request of the Center for Animal Protection and Education (CAPE), he picked up his passengers, Moncho Camblor and Christi Payne of Compassion Without Borders. Several other passengers boarded the airplane as well—ten dogs, all recently rescued in Juarez, Mexico. Now safely in California, all ten would be fostered and placed into forever homes through CAPE. Scratching the head of Pablito, a gray poodle who seemed well-rested after the flight, Dennis said, "Everything went smoothly. I'm ready to plan another trip to rescue more of these guys."

2.
What You Can Do for Dogs Right Now
Help All Dogs by Taking a Few Basic Steps

Kellie: Cars Are Faster Than Dogs

All morning the little girl and I played a game. She ducks left, I dodge right, she claps her hands, I bow, tail wagging very fast. People smile when they see me do my air-circles. I haven't eaten in so long that I'm feeling a little lightheaded. Okay, just one more game of chase, then I've got to stake out my garbage can for some chow. Dodge right, dodge left, spin three times, and run that way!

Loud screeching sound. I'm turning to look. Too late. It's a car!

I can't move. Arms are around me. My body can't dodge or spin or run. I open my eyes. A lady is putting a bowl of food next to me. Who's it for? Should I take a bite? She's staring at me. I'll just wait until she goes away. Oh, but it smells so good! She's putting food into my mouth? And my tail is wagging.

Charity begins at home. The best thing you can do for all dogs right now is to make sure you don't add to the problem of pet overpopulation. Here's how.

I am only one,
but still I am one.
I cannot do everything,
but still I can do something,
and I will not refuse to do
the something I can do.

—Helen Keller

A Routine Operation— Spay/Neuter

Spay or neuter all dogs in your care. These are routine, safe surgeries that remove the reproductive organs to prevent breeding. In this way, you can ensure your pooch won't create more puppies to stand in the long line of those already waiting for homes.

You might believe that if you take the right precautions, you can avoid spaying or neutering your pets. Yet unless you live in an underground bunker, you can bet that your unaltered dog will foil your most clever attempts to keep it from breeding. When it comes to the mating urge, dogs are ingenious at defeating our best efforts. The easiest, healthiest, and only certain way to prevent a contribution to pooch overpopulation is to take your dog in for this beneficial procedure, described below.

A Guide to Spay/Neuter

The vet gives you presurgery instructions, including feeding restrictions. Typically, you drop your dog off early in the morning. The vet does a health exam and sometimes a blood test. The pooch receives a sedative, a painkiller, and an intravenous anesthetic. A breathing tube provides oxygen and anesthetic gas.

After shaving and cleaning an area on the belly, the vet makes an incision. For spaying a female, the vet goes into the abdomen to remove the uterus, ovaries, and fallopian tubes. For neutering a male, the vet brings the testicles through the incision and removes them. Sutures on the incision might be internal and invisible or external and visible. The dog receives injections of an anti-inflammatory, a painkiller, and a long-acting antibiotic. For a few hours, while recovering from anesthesia, the patient remains in the vet hospital for observation and aftercare.

Your vet should give you detailed instructions for home aftercare, such as:

- Make sure the dog has peace, quiet, and warmth on the day of surgery and the day after. The dog will probably be sleepy. Don't let people or pets intrude on the patient's rest. For the first couple of hours offer only small amounts of food and water and watch for vomiting. If all goes well, offer a normal meal and plenty of fresh water.

- Restrict activity for seven to ten days— no running or rough play. You might need to administer sedatives from your vet.
- Don't let the dog disturb the wound or sutures. You might need to use a special restrictive collar recommended by your vet to help prevent licking and chewing.
- Call your vet if you see lethargy or decreased appetite beyond the first two days, missing stitches, excessive swelling or redness, oozing, pus, or bleeding.
- Follow the vet's instructions for postoperative checkups and suture removal.
- For females, rare side effects include urinary incontinence, which can be treated with medication or surgery. Some believe that spaying and neutering cause weight gain, but proper feeding and exercise make that easy to manage.

As with all major surgery, spay/neuter carries risks, but the vast majority of dogs sail right through and go home on the same day.

Dogs can be spayed or neutered as young as two months, though some vets feel it's best to wait until later. Your vet can help you determine if your dog has already been altered. If your female is in estrus, or heat, your vet might recommend waiting a few weeks before spaying her. Sometimes spaying can be done during pregnancy to prevent the births of unwanted puppies.

Affordable Spay/Neuter
For information on low-cost spay/neuter services across the country, go to www.neuterspay.org, or contact your local animal shelters.

Save a Life—Always Adopt

As the slogan goes, "Don't breed or buy while homeless pets die!" Adopt and save a life. Too many unwanted, homeless dogs need you *now*. Find a pooch of the breed, size, and age you like through shelters, other rescue organizations, individual rescuers, or right off the streets. Also take a look at Web sites such as Petfinder.com or contact breed rescue groups that offer specific breeds for adoption. See chapter 3, pp. 22–26 for more information on finding a pooch to adopt.

Try a Fruit Basket Instead—Don't Give a Pooch as a Present

Shelters report that one of their busiest periods is two to three months after December, when the cute little puppies given as holiday presents are growing and becoming difficult to manage. Droves of pet owners bring their animals in for surrender.

A study by the National Council on Pet Population Study and Policy (http://www.petpopulation.org/) found that 26 percent of people surrendering pets at shelters had received them from friends.

Dog ownership is a highly personal choice. A dog owner needs to be 1,000 percent on board and ready for the new responsibility. Receiving a pet as a surprise may or may not be right for the recipient at that particular time. Also, it's usually best that prospective dog owners select exactly which pooch they want. The sudden appearance of a canine with a bow around its neck—no matter how cute—deprives people of that highly individual choice.

If you give someone a dog, remember that your gift is a living being. That's very different from giving someone an inanimate object. Other presents are almost always a wiser idea than a dog. A box of chocolates doesn't need to be house-trained. A necklace doesn't need any vaccinations. A gift certificate doesn't need a securely fenced yard or several walks a day.

Although the recipient might seem thrilled at first, when reality sets in, things might not look so rosy. Unless your gift of a dog includes the additional gift of daily care and veterinary expenses for life, you'd do better to pick a lower-maintenance goodie.

There are times when giving someone a pooch might work. Maybe you're absolutely certain that the recipient wants and is ready for a dog, and you know this person well enough to make the selection. Perhaps you're a parent who wants to fulfill your child's fondest wish—a dog. In such rare cases, giving the gift of a dog might be the right thing to do, as long as you have completely thought out all the ramifications. The following section is a guide to the responsibilities involved in adopting a dog. The same guidelines apply to the responsibilities involved in giving a "gift" dog.

It's for Life

If you've decided to get a pooch from a shelter or rescue organization, congratulations! Without people like you, those groups could not function. Adopters are a critical—if not the most critical—part of the rescue process. At the end of that process, every dog needs a loving, permanent home. You are the one who puts the "happily" in the "happily ever after." Make sure, however, that you're doing it for the right reasons and that you can provide a loving home for the dog for its lifetime. Select carefully because returned dogs get a bad reputation. If you suspect it's not going to work, contact the original rescuer or group as soon as possible for help. If you do have to return, don't feel guilty. It's better for the dog to be in the right home.

Although you can't necessarily know everything about a dog before you adopt it, there is one thing you can evaluate with a relatively high degree of accuracy—*yourself*. The following section offers guidelines on how to decide whether you, your family, your home, and your future are prepared to make a lifetime commitment to a new best friend.

A dog is for life, not just for Christmas.
—slogan of the National Canine Defence League, in the United Kingdom

RIGHT REASONS AND WRONG REASONS FOR GETTING A DOG

Right Reasons

Want companionship for yourself and your family

Want to have dog-inclusive fun like walking, playing fetch, agility competitions, or volunteering for animal-assisted therapy

Want to save a life and nurture an animal in need

Have a lifestyle suited to adopting a new friend

Wrong Reasons

Want a home alarm system

Want the status symbol of owning a purebred

Want a dog to keep your current dog company because you're not home much

Want to teach your children responsibility

Want to give an animal as a gift

A Place for Us—My Residence

In the excitement of adopting a dog, it can be easy to forget that the two of you actually have to live somewhere safely and peacefully. According to the National Council on Pet Population Study and Policy, "moving" is the number-one reason pet owners surrender their dogs to animal shelters. The second most common reason is "landlord issues." The fifth most common reason is "inadequate facilities."

Ask yourself the following questions:

- Do the laws, codes, or rental agreements at my current residence allow dogs?
- Do I have a securely fenced yard? Or will I be able to walk my dog several times daily so that he can relieve himself and get proper exercise?
- Do I have reasonable neighbors who won't mind some amount of barking? What will I do if the neighbors complain?
- Will I be able to keep my dog if for any reason I have to move?

The Devil Is in the Details—My Dog's Daily Life

Before you acquire a dog, ask yourself about the nitty-gritty. The more decisions you can make in advance, the sooner you'll teach your dog and other household members to abide by them, and the smoother things will go.

Ask yourself the following questions:

- Where will my dog sleep and eat?
- Where will my dog hang out when no one is home? When I am home?
- Will my dog be allowed in all rooms or only certain rooms?
- Will my dog be allowed on the furniture, or will it have its own bed?
- Do I have enough space to store my dog's food and supplies? Do I have space for a crate?

Heart Smart—My Emotional Stability

Living with pets improves our emotional health. It can lower stress levels, help us feel needed and appreciated, and best of all, it's just plain fun. But because life has its ups and downs, we're not always in the best emotional spot to adopt a dog.

Ask yourself the following questions:

- Do I expect a dog to single-pawedly rescue me from loneliness or heartbreak?
- Do I have the patience to teach a dog how to fit into my household?
- Do I sincerely want to devote the time and attention required to love and care for an adopted dog, or am I indulging unrealistic rescue fantasies?
- Can I fulfill a dog's emotional needs for love and attention?
- Can I stomach the cruder aspects of dog ownership, such as cleaning up vomit or other accidents? How about picking up dog poop in the yard and on walks?

Money Matters—My Financial Stability

The happy-go-lucky, carefree nature of most dogs makes it easy to forget that it costs money to keep them that way. You don't need to plan for a pooch's college education, but you do need to budget comfortably for food, medical care, and other necessities. The third most common reason people surrender their pets to animal shelters is "cost of pet maintenance," according to figures from the National Council on Pet Population Study and Policy.

Ask yourself the following questions:

- Can I spend the *average* of $1,100 it costs annually to properly care for a dog?
- Can I pay high veterinary bills if my dog gets seriously ill or injured?
- Will I be able to meet possible higher vet expenses as my dog ages?
- Can I afford dog obedience classes or a private trainer?

SOME AVERAGE VETERINARY COSTS

Vet visits: $35–$45

Teeth cleaning and extractions: $350

Heartworm treatment: $300–$400

Fractured bone requiring cast only: $200–$500

Fractured bone requiring surgical repair: $1,000–up

Amputation: $800–$1,000

Ruptured umbilical hernia surgery: $2,300

A Dose of Reality—My State of Health

Living with pets can lower stress levels and prompt us to exercise, thus improving our health. But the flip side of the coin is that caring for a dog can demand extra physical stamina. Particularly in the initial stages of the adoption, you might have to deal with loss of sleep. In unfamiliar surroundings, many dogs feel stressed and thus need to urinate and defecate more often. They whine or bark at any new sight or sound, just when you've finally drifted off to dreamland. An ill dog might require nighttime medications and other care that could interfere with your sleep schedule.

If you're not a physically active person, ask yourself the following questions: Will I be able to:

- Take several walks every day?
- Bend over to scoop poop?
- Sit on the floor to trim nails?
- Give Bosco a boost to get into a car?
- Brush my dog, working arm muscles I didn't know were there?

How old will you be when your best friend is a senior? As your dog ages, his needs intensify. If your answers to these questions seem discouraging, keep in mind that somewhere out there is a pooch waiting to fit almost anyone's needs. Use your answers to the questions in this chapter to help you decide what age and type of dog to adopt. For example, a younger dog might have more years to spend with you, but an older, calmer one might be a better choice if your physical condition is less than prime. Each situation is different. Adoption counselors at a shelter or rescue organization might be able to help you make the right selection.

MOVE OVER, RICHARD SIMMONS!

Your pooch can boost your fitness. Brushing a large dog can provide a great upper-body workout. Throwing a ball or disk during a game of fetch can help tone arms. Sitting on the floor to clip nails or clean ears can provide a chance to stretch out your legs and increase flexibility. And—drum roll—a study at the University of Missouri-Columbia found that participants who walked dogs for just twenty minutes a day dropped an average of fourteen pounds in one year! Interestingly, the study also concluded that participants remained committed to their exercise program not so much because they knew it was good for them, but because they knew it was good for the dogs.

I think dogs are the most amazing creatures; they give unconditional love. For me they are the role model for being alive.

—Gilda Radner

THE POWER OF TOUCH

It's strange but true: just touching your hound is one of the most important elements of taking care of him—and yourself. When researchers studied canine pack behavior and human group interaction, they found that both species thrive on physical closeness. Dogs and humans alike use contact to create pack or family solidarity. They both crave touch for a sense of belonging and reassurance. Whether it's nuzzling and grooming or stroking and hugging, it's all saying, "We're in this together." When people and pooches live in a "pack," physical interaction reinforces bonds and builds an atmosphere of mutual assistance, cooperative comfort, and well-being.

It's About Time—My Commitments and Lifestyle

Every day people adopt dogs with the best of intentions, envisioning plenty of time for cuddling, games of fetch, and long walks at the park. Then life gets in the way, and sometimes the dog ends up alone in the backyard with little human contact.

Ask yourself the following questions:

- Do I have enough time in a typical day to provide for a dog's needs? Can I give him food, fresh water, exercise, playtime, grooming, love, and affection?
- Will I be able to keep my dog if I take a new job, get a divorce, or have a baby?
- Can I commit the extra time and attention to take care of my dog when he becomes sick or old, or both?
- Can I commit to this dog for his entire life span of up to fifteen and sometimes more years?

MULTITASKING WITH YOUR POOCH

Nail clipping, ear cleaning, and tooth brushing are easy to accomplish while you tune in to your favorite TV or radio show or listen to a book on tape. Learn Spanish or Chinese by popping in a language CD while you're grooming.

Family Matters—My Household Members' Level of Cooperation

If you share your home with family members or roommates, you'll need to evaluate them as well as yourself while you prepare to get a dog. Family dynamics, busy schedules, and chronic irresponsibility can be difficult hurdles to overcome in providing proper pooch care. The National Council on Pet Population Study and Policy cites "human lifestyle" as the reason for 25 percent of surrenders of pets to animal shelters.

Ask yourself the following questions:
- Will the other humans in my household approve of the presence of this dog?
- Will my family or roommates be kind to the dog or at least not behave cruelly?
- Will my fellow household members observe rules for the dog's safety?

HOUSEHOLD DOG SAFETY RULES

A dog-safe home is similar to a child-safe home. Think and rethink every possible kind of trouble your pooch might get into. Assume that Murphy's Law is in effect: if anything can go wrong, it will.

Make sure that all family members agree to the following rules. If desired, copy and post them. You might add more rules according to your own household's needs.
- Prevent escape! Keep exterior doors and yard gates locked at all times.
- If workers or delivery people have access to your home or yard, make sure they know they must keep all doors and gates shut and locked at all times, even while they're working. Preferably, schedule the work or delivery for a day when you'll be home so that you can prevent mistakes. Many dogs escape from their homes or yards and become lost—or worse—because a worker or delivery person forgot to shut a door or gate.

- Make sure window screens are securely fastened so that dogs can't slip through.
- If your dog is prone to chewing or other destructive or dangerous behaviors, confine him to a dog-safe room or crate to keep him out of trouble when you're not supervising.
- Tape or tie down—or preferably hide—all cables.
- Keep hazardous items, such as the following, out of the dog's reach: rope, twine, string, sewing pins, needles, tacks, nails, remote controls, wristwatches, cameras, and other small electronic components (they contain toxic batteries); fabric softener sheets, mothballs, antifreeze, ice melting products, liquid potpourri, rodent bait, and other pesticides and insecticides; chemicals of all kinds, including household cleaners, garden supplies, hair care and cosmetic products.
- On night walks, carry a flashlight and/or put flashing collar lights on your dog.

Who's on First?—My Household Members' Interest in Helping

If household members are willing to help, it's best to make a plan and a pact for the dog's daily care *before* you bring him home. It's a lot like caring for a child.

The stronger your plan, the smoother things will go.

Ask yourself the following questions:
- Who will be performing all the daily dog care chores?
- How and when will they be done?

Never assume that children—or adults, for that matter—will fulfill their excited promises to provide the care. Important chores will sometimes be left undone. Who will deal with that situation so that your dog always gets the excellent care he deserves?

HOUSEHOLD DOG CARE CHECKLIST

The following is a guide to the chores necessary for a dog's care. Your own dog's needs might require different tasks or scheduling. For example, maybe your dog needs to go outside to relieve himself six times a day instead of three, or maybe he needs to be bathed more than once a month. Think through the list, change as necessary, and copy and post if desired. (For more on pooch maintenance, see chapter 7.)

Daily

- Let the dogs out! Or take them for a walk so they can relieve themselves.
- Scoop backyard poop.
- Wash food and water bowls.
- Fill water bowls with fresh water.
- Morning feeding
- Medications
- Midday walk or backyard visit
- Afternoon obedience training session
- Afternoon walk or backyard visit
- Afternoon or evening exercise
- Evening feeding
- Medications
- Chew treats
- Brush coat. Check for fleas, ticks, thorns, foxtails, cuts, injuries.
- Brush teeth
- Cuddle
- Final walk or backyard visit
- Bedtime biscuit

Weekly

- Trim nails
- Clean ears

Monthly

- Baths
- Launder all doggie bedding and towels.
- Rinse out or wipe down crates and doghouses.
- Apply flea/tick prevention products (natural or otherwise) to dogs, home, yard.

ALL DOGS DESERVE THE BEST

Rescued dogs need the same high-quality care as any other dog. Some people feel that because they saved starving dogs from miserable lives on the streets, the dogs should be grateful for and content with any TLC that comes their way. But regardless of your dog's origins—prince or pauper—he always needs and deserves the very best.

More than One—My Other Pets

If you already have pets, consider the impact an additional dog might have on your life, on that of his new companions, and vice versa. (For more information on how to introduce and integrate a dog into a home with other pets, see chapter 5, pp. 68–71.)

Ask yourself the following questions:

- What will I do if they don't get along?
- Do my family and I really have time to meet the needs of multiple pets?

Oh, for a Crystal Ball!—My Plan for the Future

None of us has a crystal ball, but the more we can plan for what might lie ahead in life, the better off we and our dogs are likely to be.

Ask yourself the following questions:

- When I go on vacation, where will I leave my dog?

- If something dire happens to me—illness, injury, or death—who will care for my dog?

More Great Things You Can Do for Dogs Right Now

You don't have to adopt or rescue dogs to help them. Sometimes our lives and schedules don't allow for dog ownership or individual rescue efforts. But there are many other ways you can contribute to the well-being of dogkind.

Preach What You Practice

Spread the word about responsible dog ownership. You can use information in this book as a guide. Friendly conversation can be an effective way of improving attitudes toward dogs and the serious problems they face. Hearing trusted friends or relatives talk about their own experiences with dog rescue can really change ways of thinking. It might not happen overnight, but remember that you can gently plant seeds in other people's hearts and minds.

Encourage Spay/Neuter

One of the best things you can do for dogs right now is to encourage others to spay/ neuter their dogs. Below we describe some obstacles you might encounter in such conversations and provide some pointers on how to respond:

OBSTACLE: Some people get very emotional about spay/neuter. They feel that it's "mutilating" the dog, or that it deprives the dog of sexual experience.

POINTER: Dogs don't have any concept of sexual identity or ego. After being spayed or neutered, a dog does not suffer from any psychological trauma or feeling of deprivation.

OBSTACLE: Some men project those concerns onto themselves. They feel that if they castrate their male dog it's almost like castrating themselves. Some worry that their friends will ridicule them for having a neutered male dog.

POINTER: Some of the manliest men are the ones who are confident and secure in their own identities. They're strong enough to ignore teasing and do the right thing for their dog and for all dogs.

OBSTACLE: Some people want their children to experience the miracle of birth and the joys of a litter of puppies.

POINTER: If you breed your dog and she produces a healthy litter, you will need to find new and responsible homes for all her puppies. And each new home you find reduces the available homes for the many needy dogs already in shelters.

Why not go to a local shelter and adopt a pregnant female who is too late in her term to be spayed? Many shelters offer special services and benefits to such adopters, and will help place the puppies when they are ready for new homes.

OBSTACLE: Some people want to experience the thrill of "creation." Breeding gives them a feeling of power and mastery over the universe and its mysteries.

POINTER: The biggest thrill and the greatest power come when we save lives and end suffering.

OBSTACLE: Some people believe they can sell the puppies and make money.

POINTER: The cost of providing proper care and medical attention for a mother and her pups allows for little or no profit margin. Some breeders even lose money, especially if the mother or any of her young have health problems.

Also, of the three million to six million homeless dogs waiting in shelters, 25 percent of them are purebreds. Why should someone pay you hundreds of dollars instead of visiting the local humane society and adopting a purebred for a lot less money?

OBSTACLE: Some people think spay/neuter changes dogs' behaviors, perhaps rendering them unable to be protective.
POINTER: Spay/neuter does not change dogs' basic temperaments. They might become less combative with other dogs, but if they were protective before, they will remain protective.

OBSTACLE: Some people believe spay/neuter will make their dog fat or otherwise harm his health.
POINTER: Dogs typically won't get fat if they get adequate exercise and a wholesome diet in appropriate amounts.

It is healthier for dogs to avoid having any litters at all. Female dogs spayed before their first heat are typically healthier. Neutering a male dog prevents prostate cancer and other problems. Today, some veterinarians spay and neuter dogs as early as eight weeks of age, although others believe it should be performed later. Talk with your vet to help you decide.

OBSTACLE: Some people believe they cannot afford to spay/neuter their dog.
POINTER: Find low-cost spay/neuter services available in your community. Keep that info handy so that you can offer it when needed. Mention that having litters of puppies to care for can be far more expensive than spaying a female dog, and that the health risks to unaltered male and female dogs can add up to whopping veterinary bills.

Brighten a Dog's Day—Volunteer!

Volunteer work offers many benefits, and for dog lovers, it has the added attraction of putting us in the company of canines. We make new friends of both the four-pawed and two-footed varieties, learn new skills, and earn impressive credits to add to our job résumés or college applications.

Here are a few ways to improve dogs' lives through volunteering:

- Sign up at an animal shelter to pet and play with dogs waiting for adoption. Your attention and TLC can reduce their fear and insecurity and help them stay perky and healthy, thus making them more adoptable.
- Train with a rescue group to speak in schools about spay/neuter and dog care.
- Join a pet therapy program to take your dog into hospitals and nursing homes. It's some of the most gratifying volunteer work you'll ever do. Your dog does a lot of the work and loves it. Also it's a perfect opportunity to show off your rescued dog and advertise to others how great rescues can be.

To find out more about volunteering to improve dogs' lives, please see chapter 11, and contact your local shelter or rescue organization.

Rolling in the Grassroots—Politics and Community Action

Sometimes it's hard to imagine that we can make any kind of difference in our communities. It gets discouraging to hear about politicians' scandals and misconduct, and that can make us feel hopeless about changing the world. But we can make positive changes little by little, starting at the grassroots level. Government officials—especially the elected ones—are concerned about their constituents' opinions. Ultimately it's not money or influence that puts them in office—it's our votes.

Compassion and responsibility toward all of earth's creatures is slowly building. Evidence of this is the federal law covering pet evacuation procedures, enacted in 2006. This law came into existence for no other reason than the public outcry over the fate of beloved animals that evacuees had to leave behind during Hurricane Katrina in 2005. Many of us still remember the heartbreaking images in the television news story about the little boy forced to abandon his dog, Snowball. Citizens from all over the country flooded government offices with letters, faxes, e-mails, and phone calls pleading for a solution to this problem. Lawmakers responded with the Pets Evacuation and Transportation Standards Act (PETS). This is just one example of how individual voices can make a difference—and in this case, improve the future for dogs.

You, too, can work to improve the future for dogs by communicating your opinions and requests to government leaders. One way to do that is to write to them. Whether it's via letter, fax, or e-mail, your opinion counts. When enough people start expressing the belief that animals matter, our leaders have to sit up and take notice.

MAKING YOUR VOICE HEARD

If you live in a town or city, you could send your letters to the mayor and members of the town or city council. If you are in a county jurisdiction, you might write to the members of the county board of supervisors. Your governor and state legislators also have the power to enact laws that improve dogs' lives. Other entities to contact include your town, city, or county's animal control and services department. On a federal level, you can begin by contacting your state's senators through http://www.senate.gov, and your congress members at http://www.house.gov.

Sample Letter about Spay/Neuter

Use this sample (see page 20) as a general guide for how to write a letter in your own words to government officials. Personalized letters are taken more seriously than form letters. Shorter, to-the-point letters are easier to digest than longer ones. Focus on a specific issue or a particular action that you want them to take. If legislation is pending, let them know how you'd like for them to vote on it. If you believe that there should be a new law or policy on an issue, try to be specific about that too. Or you can turn your letter into a group effort by typing it in the form of a petition and gathering signatures.

Sign On, Join Up—The Organized Way

Rather than going it alone and reinventing the wheel, you can join and support any of the many organizations that promote animal welfare and protection. The Humane Society of the United States (HSUS) and the American Society for the Prevention of Cruelty to Animals (ASPCA) are among the larger and better-known groups. There are many others, such as Animal Place, the American Humane Association, the World Society for the Protection of Animals, In Defense of Animals, and Best Friends Animal Sanctuary. There are probably smaller local and regional ones serving your particular area as well.

An annual modest membership fee will

Your name and address
Government official's name and address
Date

Dear Mr./Ms. _____,

I am deeply concerned about the fact that three million to four million dogs and cats are impounded at shelters and many are euthanized at taxpayer expense in the United States every year. Countless more die horrific deaths from neglect, abuse, and abandonment.

One way to prevent the suffering and to make more efficient use of public money is to offer affordable spay/neuter options to all pet owners. Widespread spaying and neutering has been proven to dramatically decrease the numbers of unwanted pets.

The Montana Spay/Neuter Task Force reports that its Billings-area spay/neuter clinic events resulted in a 19 percent drop in animals being impounded in shelters and about a 24 percent drop in animals being destroyed. Dog bites decreased by 33 percent. In smaller rural areas, there were decreases of more than 50 percent in animals being impounded or destroyed. Subsequent clinics lowered the impound-and-destroy rate by as much as 75 percent.

I believe we can and should fund such a program in our community, as well as fund education and outreach about responsible pet ownership. The goals would be for all pet owners to understand the importance of spay/neuter for the health and well-being of our area's dogs and cats, as well as for our community, and to ensure that everyone can easily have their pets spayed/neutered. Please enact and fund measures to meet those goals.

Thanks for your time.
Sincerely,
Your Name

bring you the group's magazine or newsletter. These publications discuss pending legislation for animals and what you can do, and they offer specific step-by-step action plans on which government officials to contact, providing addresses and even sample letters. Your membership and your donations enable these organizations to lobby lawmakers and launch public education campaigns on animal welfare issues.

You're On Your Way!

This chapter has dealt with some of the ways you can help dogs right now. Just the fact that you're reading this book means that your heart and mind are in the right place; thus, you're already on your way toward making a difference in pooches' lives. Read on for information and inspiration about direct, hands-on ways to rescue individual dogs.

Happily Ever After True Story Number Two:

Frankie

• •

The sounds coming from the front yard were terrifying. Dogs barking, growling, and fighting. Someone screaming in pain. Police sirens and car tires screeching on pavement. People shouting. Then gunfire cracking, and more screaming. Only this time, the screams were those of dogs. Through it all, Frankie huddled in a closet, shaking. The arcs of blue and red police lights flashing in through the window were no comfort to this youngster. How could he know that the police were the good guys when he was a dog?

Frankie had been living in a "heroin house" in East Oakland, California, with three other dogs. He took the brunt of their unsocialized behavior. His ears still seeped blood from the last time they attacked him.

But now, all was quiet. People had stopped yelling. Frankie sensed that the dogs were gone. He crept through the garbage-strewn living room and then through the front door. What he saw outside was too confusing to understand. The pack of dogs that had tormented him now lay like heaps of fur in the weedy yard. Frankie could smell the blood that pooled under their bodies. Another body, that of a man who lived in the house, was being lifted onto a bed of some kind. They shoved it into a white van, and drove away.

Soon two men in green uniforms hoisted the bodies of the dogs into a truck, and they were gone too. Frankie noticed the younger man sitting against the house. It was the guy who sometimes fed him—the guy who, when he looked Frankie in the eye, seemed unable to focus. Frankie sat next to him, trying to get warm to stop the shaking. But the guy was shaking too.

"And that's how I found him," said Audrey, Frankie's adoptive mom. "It was my brother he was sitting next to. My brother, the heroin addict." Over the years, Audrey and her mother had tried many times to rescue her brother from his drug addiction, hustling him into rehab, but he would always return to the streets and to his love of the drug.

Audrey remembered, "That night, after the three dogs attacked a woman, the owner of the house had a heart attack and died on the spot." The city condemned the house. Audrey's brother and Frankie needed to vacate. That same week, Audrey was struggling with the grief of losing her old dog, Radar. "Radar was my best friend, but my vet told me it was time. Radar smiled at me as he died. It was such a heartbreaker."

Audrey took Frankie home and over the next year they mended each other. "I used to call him "my little heroin addict" because he was so skittish and would shake all the time." Audrey, herself a recovering alcoholic, was often visited by her sponsor from Alcoholics Anonymous. He would come in the door and go straight to Frankie. "You know, Audrey," he would say, "I love you, but I love coming here to visit your dog even more." Audrey acknowledges that Frankie reaches into people's hearts. She feels blessed that she stuck with him during his unfolding.

When Audrey rescued Schmooze, a small terrier that lived a lonely life in a deserted backyard, Frankie was ready to accept a new canine friend. And now, four years later, Audrey has rescued a third dog named Buster. "Here was this eight-month-old pit bull puppy, wandering the street outside where I work. He was skinny but so friendly and playful. I took him home and all three dogs just jelled."

After trembling in a dark closet hiding from the three dogs that terrorized him, Frankie now sleeps on a bed with two other dogs, his best friends.

3.
How to Find a Dog to Rescue
Adopting from Shelters, Private Rescue Groups, or Picking Up That Dog on the Street

---

Kellie: Spay Surgery

Once, my nose caught the scent of a thing that made my mouth drool and my legs weak. As I followed that smell, many other dogs began to follow me. They jumped on me. I twisted and turned and growled at them. Life on the streets is not always fun for a young girl like me.

Today, I am in a large room. There are strange smells. Nothing edible, that's for sure. The lady rubbed a noisy thing along my arm, and now the fur is gone. Next she poked me with something sharp. And suddenly I am sleepy.

When I wake up I feel pain, lots of pain coming from my belly. What happened to my energy? I am really sore and thirsty. I feel different. Am I different?

There are as many ways to find a dog to rescue as there are dogs in need of rescue. This chapter offers guidance on where to find and how to choose your own best friend in need.

First take a look at chapters 2 and 10 to determine whether you are really ready to add a pooch to your family. These chapters will also guide you in selecting a dog to fit the needs of your particular circumstances and household. In chapter 10, you'll find many of the nitty-gritty questions that rescue organizations will ask you as a prospective adopter. Answering those questions *before* you start your canine quest can smooth the way. Now the search begins.

> The soul is the same in all living creatures, although the body of each is different.
>
> —Hippocrates

Where to Find Dogs to Rescue

The bad news is that millions of dogs are in desperate need of homes. The good news is that those numbers give you plenty of choices. And because of you, one of them will soon become a lucky dog. But where to look? To help you hunt, here's an overview of different avenues for rescue.

Municipal Animal Shelters

Your local municipal shelter is a good first
stop. Most city- or county-run shelters are required to accept all animals brought through
their front doors. Yet their kennels and cages
can handle only a certain number of relinquished pets. Many of these facilities are unable to house animals indefinitely. This forces
them to euthanize in order to make room for
newcomers. By adopting at one of these shelters you save a life *immediately*.

Municipal shelters may only have limited
knowledge of a dog's past. The dog may have
been brought to the shelter as a stray, which
makes its history a mystery. If her previous
family surrendered the dog, they had the option of filling out a questionnaire, but the information on the questionnaire cannot be verified.

On the plus side, many municipal shelters
provide services to you and your new dog.
While there, the dog might have been spayed/
neutered, had a microchip implanted, been
vaccinated, and had its health checked. Municipal shelters may have a dog behaviorist on
staff or even a behavior hotline you can access
with your questions or concerns. They also
might offer obedience classes for you and your
new pooch.

Private Animal Shelters

Some private shelters that do not use taxpayer dollars have the freedom to carefully select the dogs they accept. If you want to know
serious details about a dog's past, visit a private shelter. Most of these agencies have
lengthy dossiers on each of their residents.

Be prepared for thorough screening before
you're allowed to adopt. Private shelters are
often very particular about who is qualified.
Most require you to sign a contract with a variety of stipulations such as those we describe
in chapter 10.

Because private shelters cannot accept
every dog, many have referral lists of dogs
awaiting adoption while remaining in their
current homes. Should you find a dog that interests you on a referral list, you can contact
the current owner directly for more information. The beauty of this method is that the
dogs are not uprooted, but are able to remain
in a familiar environment until a new family is
found. Not only is this less stressful, but it also
prevents them from being exposed to any
kennel illnesses.

times, clients who need to find their own dogs a new home often turn to their vets for help. Alert the staffs of your local vet hospitals that you'd like to adopt a dog. Finding your new dog through your vet might offer the advantage of knowing the animal's medical history.

Breed Rescue Groups

If you'd like to adopt a purebred, try a breed rescue group. They foster and rehome particular breeds. Most have active working relationships with local shelters so that when a purebred comes in, the rescue group is contacted and assumes responsibility for the dog.

Breed rescue groups tend to be knowledgeable and honest about the challenges presented by their specialty dogs.

Some people involved with breed rescue are also breeders themselves. Most are trying hard to help homeless dogs. But the occasional unscrupulous breeder might try to sidetrack potential adopters into buying instead of rescuing.

Pet Stores

Some pet stores allow rescue groups to set up weekend adoption booths. PetSmart and PETCO are both supportive of in-store pet adoption events in their stores and on their Web sites, http://www.petsmart.com and http://www.petco.com. Such rescue-friendly pet stores do not sell dogs and cats. Try not to patronize those that do.

Veterinary Hospitals

Animal abandonment is a common occurrence at veterinary hospitals. During the night, pets are sometimes left at hospital front doors. And clients who cannot afford to pay their vet bills might simply never claim their animals. Some-

WARNING: BAD DOG RESCUERS

Don't ever let anyone cajole or pressure you into adopting a certain dog. Although it's rare, there are pushy people doing rescue who might try to make you feel guilty for not adopting a dog.

They might say something like, "You're being too picky. At this rate you'll never find a dog," or, "If you don't adopt this dog today, it will have to be put to sleep." A statement like that is a strong indication that you should go elsewhere to find the right dog. Reputable rescuers know that a good, lasting match never needs to be forced.

Another problem is that some people do not tell the truth about dogs available for adoption. Common areas for truth bending and breaking include age, breed, temperament, and health. The first two, age and breed, might not seem all that important; however, a person's willingness to lie about these facts might indicate a willingness to lie about other things, including temperament and health, which are enormously important.

Before contacting any rescue groups, ask your local shelter for referrals. Even armed with those, be a careful, clear-eyed consumer. Go heavy on common sense and light on emotion in your search for a new best friend.

Specialty Rescue Groups

Small Dogs: Some groups focus on dogs forty pounds and smaller. They often work closely with shelters by taking their petite pooches, freeing up shelter space and giving larger dogs, which are harder to place, a better chance for adoption.

Puppies: Adult dogs are harder to rehome and thus are in direr straits, but puppies need homes too. Let's say you'd really like one, but (understandably) feel guilty about buying from a breeder or pet store. Banish the guilt, because there are people who specifically rescue and place puppies in need, and they are waiting for you.

Older Dogs: Seniors are some of the most overlooked yet eminently qualified available dogs. Many adopters shy away from taking in an older dog, so these animals tend to fall by the wayside. Fortunately, there are rescue groups that recognize the virtues of dogs with a little extra mileage, and they make these senior citizens their specialty.

International: Although there is no shortage of homeless dogs in our own country, the crisis of pet overpopulation extends all over the world. Some groups specifically target homeless dogs in other countries whose resources for animal protection are minimal at best. To locate a dog from abroad, do an online search focusing on a particular country or by typing "international dog rescue" in a search engine. When people hear about your "immigrant's" odyssey, your well-traveled pooch becomes an instant ambassador for homeless dogs around the globe.

The Price of Love
Adoption fees vary from one source to another. Adopting a dog from a private individual may be free of charge, whereas a private shelter might ask $100 to $300. These fees cover rescuers' expenses in caring for the pooch and sometimes additional costs like spay/neuter, vaccinations, other veterinary services, or implanting a microchip.

Internet Pet-Matching Services

Never before has dog adoption been so easy. From the comfort of your home you can access information on thousands of dogs in need. Yet this can also make your search more difficult. You might feel overwhelmed by the choices and by all those pleading brown eyes looking back at you from the photos. To stay focused, take a few minutes to create a profile of the type of dog you are looking for: breed(s), weight, coat type, male/female, and so on, using the guidance provided in this chapter.

For a well-rounded source of available dogs, visit http://www.petfinder.com. Hundreds of smaller animal rescue agencies use that Web site to list available dogs. Especially convenient are the online adoption applications that streamline the process.

Private Individuals

Whether they are friends, relatives, or strangers, many people have pooches they wish to re-home. Adopting from a private party comes with pluses and minuses. One advantage of adopting a dog directly from her current home is that you can get a thorough understanding of the dog's lifestyle, temperament, and state of health. Yet often, people needing to place dogs are under pressure to do so quickly (they are moving, a new baby has arrived, someone is suddenly allergic). They might oversell the dog, glowing over her love of children while forgetting to mention her penchant for chewing through doors.

If you decide to adopt privately, find out as much as you possibly can about the dog. Interview the owner thoroughly (see the sidebar "Questions to Ask during Your Search," pp. 32–36). Evaluate the dog's temperament (see guidelines in this chapter, pp. 33–35). Evaluate the dog's health (see chapters 6 and 7). The last thing you want is for the adoption to fail, forcing you to have to find this dog *another* new home.

Finding a Stray

Sometimes you don't have to go out looking. You see a dog wandering alone or one shows up on your doorstep and your choice is made for you. Street dogs can often be resourceful, adaptable, and quick learners because they have to be in order to survive. For a complete discussion of this option, see chapter 4.

You Witness Neglect or Abuse

Many of us first spotted our best friends under horrifying circumstances—chained up for endless days with no shelter or water or being beaten nearly to death by a vindictive owner. When you are able to save a canine victim from extreme neglect or abuse, it's enormously gratifying. You and your pooch share a dramatic history that can forge a bond like no other. However, keep this firmly in mind: *There are times when you can step into such situations and times when you absolutely must not.* See chapter 4, pp. 42–43, for important guidelines on this difficult issue.

SHOULD I EVER BUY A DOG TO SAVE IT?

A man in a parking lot is selling a litter of black Labrador puppies. There's no shade or water, plus they seem too young to be weaned. He shows off their parents' purebred registration papers. Or, your local pet shop offers purebred puppies for sale. Kept in unclean cages, the puppies look lethargic. Should you buy any of these animals in order to rescue them?

Buying a dog to save it may only increase the suffering of other dogs. The economic model of supply and demand also holds in the case of animal cruelty and profit. If you purchase a dog from someone who has little concern for the welfare of his product (the animals), you promote his success, putting more creatures in harm's way.

If you see any animal being mistreated, call your local animal control department, report the location, and ask that they perform a welfare check. If any city, county, or state laws require spaying and neutering of companion animals, or if any require dogs to be registered and licensed, report the violations.

Choosing the Right Dog for You

With so many wonderful dogs available for adoption, looking for Mr. or Ms. Right Rover can be a dizzying process. Before you start, give some thought to what kind of dog would be best for you and your family. That helps narrow it down. Here are a few parameters to consider.

Compatibility with Other Pets

If you already have pets, they should be one of your top concerns when choosing a new dog. The better your pets get along together, the less headache and heartache for you. For the sake of your current best friends, remember that you—not they—have chosen this addition to the family. Your pets won't have much control over the newbie. You owe it to these existing household members to give everybody the best shot at being one big, happy family. Here are some tips on how to do that.

If You Have a Cat or Cats

Shelters and rescuers sometimes have background information on whether their available dogs get along with kitties. Or they might allow you to take the dog into a get-acquainted room with one of their more mellow cats. Regardless of how that meeting goes, it's hard to predict what will happen at home with your own feline best friends. Ask to adopt on a trial basis. If things don't go well, consider a private trainer. But prepare yourself for the fact that you might have to return the dog. Many wonderful canines have a strong prey drive. Trying to shoehorn such a dog into a cat-friendly home might be doing a disservice to all concerned.

If You Have a Dog or Dogs

Keep the following general principles in mind. Dogs of opposite sex get along better than same-sex pairings. If your dog is submissive, look for one with a similar personality. Be careful about terriers, as they tend to bully mild-mannered medium to larger dogs, and can get killed by going after larger dogs that don't tolerate it. Dogs recognize other dogs that they resemble, so sometimes sticking to the same breed or breed mix can create a better pack partnership.

In most planned adoptions, you can take the time to introduce your current dogs to the adoption candidate before making the decision. Consider the following approach. Dogs use urine to access information: male/female, spayed/neutered, age, breed, friend or foe, dominant or submissive. Enlist a helper. Introduce the dogs through urination by taking them on leash, separately, to a neutral area—down the street, a local park, or outside the shelter. With *both* dogs still on leash, encourage the established dog to pee, then bring the new dog over, while the established dog observes from fifteen to twenty feet away. Do this several times. Caution: Never introduce dogs with one on leash and the other not. They must be on equal footing in that regard.

Take note of how the dogs urinated. Dominant behavior is generally when one pees on top of the other's urine. Submissive or non-threatening behavior is generally when, after sniffing urine, the dog pees away from it. Observe their body language: Is their overall appearance happy? Are their eyes wide open, ears perked forward or flat, and tails wagging? Are their bodies wiggling or prancing as they try physically to interact? Then let them meet and play on leash.

If you're unsure, get a partner dog walker and take the two dogs on lengthy daily walks for as many days as possible. Make sure your dog is always in front with you, never pulling. This shows both dogs that you are in charge. Your partner with the new dog walks eight to ten feet behind you and your dog. Allow both to sniff and pee and try walking together if both dogs are relaxed and happy. Next, allow interaction and play on leash. If the play is consistently respectful, they will probably be fine together. If one or both nip too hard, always pushing the other to the ground and never allowing the other dog to stand up or constantly mounting the submissive dog, it's time to carefully intercede. Can they live together? Probably, if you take the time they need to introduce them slowly for as many days—or months—as necessary.

Age

Puppy, young adult, middle-aged, or senior? Every dog is unique, but in general they follow some age-related patterns.

Puppy Pluses: (under seven months) Cute. Playful. Amusing. Affectionate. Triggers your nurturing instincts. Hasn't yet formed many bad habits.

Puppy Minuses: Vulnerable to viruses and other infectious canine diseases. Will have to go through puppy vaccination process. Usually not house-trained or leash trained. Needs more nighttime potty breaks, feedings, and comforting. Chews everything in sight. Dependent, needy. Cries when left alone. Mouthy—apt to chew on your hand, nose, and more. Requires *constant* supervision—much like a human child, because she can easily get into dangerous trouble. Requires lots of training. Basic temperament hard to judge.

Adolescent Pluses: (eight to twenty-four months)

Energetic, gung ho. Playful, goofy, clownish. Adorable in a gawky way, much like human adolescents. Bad habits not yet too entrenched. Basic temperament beginning to show.

Adolescent Minuses: *Too* energetic—needs a lot of exercise. Still chewing everything in sight—with bigger jaws. Still mouthy—with bigger jaws. Still requires supervision. Just like a human adolescent, can have attitude, half unsure of self yet half cocky. Tends to push the envelope and might sometimes deliberately disobey to see what you'll do. If basic temperament is bad, the dog's high energy and lack of focus can make for a volatile situation.

Young Adult to Middle-Aged Pluses: (two to eight years) The prime of life. Physically filled out and gorgeous. Still energetic, but not wild. Has grown out of many of the unwanted behaviors and round-the-clock needs of puppyhood. Has developed confidence. Often has had some training. Basic temperament, good or bad, will be more evident. Good resistance to infectious diseases.

Young Adult to Middle-Aged Minuses: Bad habits might be more entrenched and a little harder to change. Adult confidence, size, and strength can create a dangerous situation if basic temperament is bad.

Senior Pluses: (eight years and older). Calmer, wiser, less impulsive. Can be more mellow and easier to introduce to other dogs. Might better match the needs of a quiet, low-key household. Or might be a calming presence in an active household.

Senior Minuses: Might have more health problems than younger dogs. Might need more care and attention. Remaining time with you might be shorter. An elderly dog (ten and up) might not be able to keep up with your exercise routine.

YOUR WISE OLD BEST FRIEND

Senior or elderly dogs can be some of the very best friends you'll ever have. It's like having wise aunts or uncles you can turn to for a steady, relaxed, experienced view of life. They have been around the block and exude confidence and calm. "Hey," their demeanor tells you, "don't worry. Take a nap." There's nothing like the reassuring presence of a senior best friend to bring a sensible perspective into any hectic day.

My dear old dog, most constant of all friends.

—William Croswell Doane

Size

When it comes to dogs, size matters. Various factors in your life can affect your selection between small (under thirty pounds), medium (under sixty pounds), or large (over sixty pounds). Here are a few points to consider.

- If you rent, does your lease agreement limit the size of resident dogs?
- People who are petite, older, or have a physical disability might do best with small or medium dogs, unless the large dog in question is well trained.
- If you already have dogs, it might help if the new one is about the same size as the others, so that none of them feels intimidated or gets run over at playtime.
- Many folks are frightened by large dogs. If your heart's desire is a rottweiler or Irish wolfhound, you're likely to hear gasps or even shrieks when you're out in public. People will be much more likely to pet your friend's Maltese than your mastiff.

- In general, larger dogs tend to have more orthopedic problems and somewhat shorter life spans than smaller ones.
- Medium dogs do well in agility and flying-disk competitions.
- If you travel a lot, you can take smaller dogs into many hotels that allow pets under a certain weight and on board airplanes in carriers that fit under the seat.
- Smaller dogs can pose a higher escape risk, because, for example, they can fit through smaller holes under fences.
- Smaller dogs are more often the target of bullies or at least are more vulnerable if they're attacked. You need to be extra watchful when they're around other dogs.

IS MY BIG DOG HAPPY WITHOUT A BACKYARD?

A dog of any size that gets plenty of outdoor activity, sunshine, and time with you is just as happy in an apartment or condo as anywhere else. It's harder on you than on the dog because you have to take her out for several on-leash potty walks every day, rain or shine, and at least once a day for a longer exercise walk. Trips to a dog park give your pet the chance to run and be silly with pooch pals. Enjoying enough mental, emotional, and physical stimulation, your dog won't miss a backyard.

Coat Type

One of the most wondrous things about dogs is their fur. It makes petting them a delight. You can run your palm over a sleek, smooth pelt or bury your fingers into a thick, lush one. Coats can be short and velvety like a pointer's, long and silky like a spaniel's, or wiry and scruffy like a terrier's.

Beyond aesthetic considerations are the practical ones. Some dog breeds shed more than others. The less you like vacuuming, the more you might want a low-shed breed or mix. That said, there are those of us who think personality is a dog's most valuable asset. We'll blithely ignore the clouds of floor fur or clean house a little more often, just so that we can be with our best friend, the fuzz factory.

Coat type becomes a serious matter, however, for folks with allergies. Fortunately, there are breeds that are less likely to produce an allergic reaction, such as border terriers, basenjis, giant schnauzers, poodles, bearded collies, and many others. Another factor to keep in mind is that thick-fur dogs can be prone to more skin ailments, because the coat doesn't allow as much air to circulate as with shorthaired dogs. However, that as well as excessive shedding often can be managed with regular brushing, bathing, and perhaps nutritional supplements.

DON KING

When Nanette Hardin, a foster home volunteer for the Center for Animal Protection and Education (CAPE) was asked to care for a waddling, long-in-the-tooth, black cocker spaniel, she immediately began to observe him for any appealing qualities.

"Not easy," Nanette said. "He had a horrible skin condition that gave him an oily sheen. He had esophagus reflux, so much of what he ate came back up. And on the top of his head was this gray, greasy tuft of fur. That's how he got his name—Don King."

But Nanette knew she needed to uncover Don King's special attributes for use in appealing to adopters. "Don King was a mischief mastermind," said Nanette. "He was actually adopted twice and twice returned." One family, for example, found the dog's carpentry on moldings and doorways a distinct liability.

As time passed, Nanette realized Don King was already at home, so she officially adopted him. It was a relief knowing that she could retire from searching for Don King's buried treasure of greatness, and just embrace his nonchalant naughtiness and funny looks. "He was a dog with a will of iron—cool and confident. He never seemed bothered by how he was judged. Looking back on it, I see that was Don King's unique talent!"

Don King.

Male or Female

Both sexes make wonderful pets. A common misconception is that females are more tractable and males are rowdier. There aren't many significant differences.

Male: Neutering is easier, less invasive, and cheaper than spaying. Even when altered, a male dog can retain the urge to roam. He urine-marks his yard. On walks, he marks up the whole neighborhood. Most males get along with a female or submissive males.

Female: Spay surgery is more invasive and expensive than neutering. A female does not have as much of an urge to roam as a male. Typically she doesn't mark—just empties her bladder all at once. A female is more prone to bladder infections. She usually rules over other dogs in residence. She might have a longer fuse than a male, but when two females fight, it can often be more serious. Most females get along with males or submissive females.

Purebred or Mixed Breed

If there are specific traits you want in a dog, there might be a breed that fits the bill. On the other paw, maybe you love the uniqueness and serendipity of mixed breeds. No two are alike. It's really up to you. But there are a few differences to consider.

Purebred Pluses: They can fit the exact look and size you are seeking. They are bred to have certain tendencies and interests like guarding, retrieving, or rodent hunting.

Purebred Minuses: Because they have less genetic diversity, some can be predisposed to certain illnesses, deformities, and temperament problems, including aggression. Those from puppy mills, backyard breeders, and unscrupulous "professional" breeders can have deficient early nutrition, care, and socialization that linger for life.

Mixed-Breed Pluses: With broader genetic diversity, they might be less predisposed to some health and temperament issues. You have the fun of knowing that your dog is absolutely unique—it's not a cookie-cutter canine.

Mixed-Breed Minuses: Their tendencies and interests might not be as predictable as those of purebreds.

DOIN' WHAT COMES NATURALLY

Almost any pooch can perform any doggie task with proper training. Unquestionably, however, some breeds are more hardwired for certain aptitudes and interests than others. If there are any special activities you want to pursue with your dog, contact an organization that promotes that activity and ask what breeds tend to be most suited to it. Breed rescue organizations are ready to help you find the perfect partner.

Keep an open mind to mixed breeds too. Breed characteristics and drives can remain strong for several generations down from a purebred ancestor. And some tendencies are present in all dogs regardless of lineage. The talents of your pedigree-free best friend might meet or exceed those of the blueblood next door.

Personality and Temperament

Canine character varies about as much as that of humans. With so many dogs looking for homes, chances are you'll be able to find just the right personality to mesh with yours and with the needs of your household. The next section contains more information on how to detect a dog's true temperament.

MEASURING UP TO A PREVIOUS POOCH

You might expect your new dog to live up to standards set by a previous dog. If your beloved Bess loved to swim alongside you at the lake, but recently adopted Becky trembles at the sight of a full bathtub, it can be a disappointment.

If your last dog was a senior citizen when she passed away, it's a good bet that she was far better behaved than that nonstop wacky eight-month-old you just brought home. Variety is the spice of life!

AT THE SHELTER—WHEN TO KEEP WALKING

Your dog-savvy friend goes with you to the shelter. Walking past the kennels, you see dogs barking and lunging. Some dogs shivering at the very back of their runs eye you nervously, while a few others act like they couldn't care less, ignoring you and your family. They are busy trying to get the dogs in the next run to interact. Farther on, you see a dog that lifts its lip and lays its ears flat, growling, when you look it in the eyes.

You just saw two dozen dogs and your friend says not one was suitable. You agree to come back another day.

Questions to Ask During Your Search

When you're talking with the owners, rescuers, or caregivers of your possible new best friend, ask questions—lots of them. Here are a few for your list, the reasons you should ask them, and in some cases, pointers on verifying the answers.

QUESTION: What is the age of the dog?
WHY: Sometimes owners or rescuers will fudge, especially if the pooch is a senior. But for your sake, as well as for that of the dog, truth counts. For one reason, when you're dealing with any health issues that might come up in the future, knowing the dog's accurate age can help the vet with correct diagnosis and treatment.

VERIFYING: Here are typical indicators of a dog's age based on the teeth:

under four weeks—all gums, no teeth

four to six weeks—canines, incisors, premolars appearing

eight weeks—baby teeth have arrived

up to four months—molars starting to pop up

seven months—all permanent teeth are in

one year—teeth white and clean

two years—back teeth show some yellow

up to five years—all teeth show some tartar buildup, some tooth wear

five to ten years—most teeth show wear and some disease

ten to fifteen years—teeth are worn, heavy tartar, missing teeth

QUESTION: Has the dog undergone a behavior evaluation? By whom was it performed?
WHY: Temperament tests are administered by qualified trainers who understand canine body language. The tests measure emotional stability, friendliness, shyness, aggressiveness, protectiveness, prey instincts, play drive, self-defense instincts, and the dog's ability to differentiate between threatening and nonthreatening situations.

The tests aren't 100 percent reliable. Breeds vary so greatly that it's nearly impossible to devise a fair standard for acceptable temperament. And most homeless or shelter dogs are so stressed that they often don't demonstrate who they really are right away. Unfortunately, tests can lead to good dogs being destroyed because of a failing grade. But while a temperament test won't be the ultimate answer on which dog is the right one for you, it can give you an idea of the animal's basic psychological and emotional makeup.

A SAFE, QUICK, BEHAVIOR EVALUATION

A private rescuer has two dogs, Rocket and Sadie, available for adoption. They are contained in adjacent, secure kennels in the rescuer's backyard.

Stand back three to four feet from Rocket's gate. Stare directly into her eyes. If she advances with a snarl or makes you feel like she will, drop your gaze and move on to Sadie. When you stare into Sadie's eyes, if she's an emotionally stable dog, she'll either drop her gaze or look at you with friendly interest, wagging her tail as she approaches the gate to say hello. She does the latter.

Pull a treat from your pocket and feed Sadie a small piece through the gate. Was she gentle taking the food from your hand? Now squat down and try to lure her into a sit as you say, "Sadie, want a treat? Sit." She has no idea what you're talking about, but she's trying to figure it out, focused on the treat and on you.

Inquire about Sadie's history and temperament tests and ask to meet her.

QUESTION: Is there any known history on the dog? Where and how was she rescued? Who was the previous owner?

WHY: The more background you can get about your prospective pooch, the better you'll be able to understand her in the future.

QUESTION: Has this dog displayed any aggression toward humans?

WHY: It is *imperative* that the dog's owner, rescuer, or shelter personnel be honest with you on this issue. Unless you are a highly experienced, professional dog trainer, you should *never* adopt a dog with unusually aggressive behavior.

VERIFYING: Signs of normal aggression toward humans:

- Protective and territorial aggression— barking to protect territory
- Possessive aggression—silly-sounding pretend growling, barking, or even snapping, when playing with toys or with a human or when overexcited for a treat or meal

Please note: Although the signs above are listed as normal, be aware that you will need to guide and control these habits so that they don't escalate.

Signs of more problematic aggression toward humans:

- Dominance aggression—growls or snaps when human disturbs the dog in an area that she feels is her own. Perceives her rank in the hierarchy to be higher than a human's.
- Fear-motivated aggression—dog perceives she is in danger of being harmed as human reaches out to pet her.
- Redirected or displaced aggression—a dog is barking at someone unfamiliar walking by. Frustrated that she can't reach that person, she turns and bites the human standing next to her because that human is accessible, and in the heat of the moment the dog doesn't think about whom she's biting.

QUESTION: Has this dog displayed any aggression toward other dogs or pets?

WHY: Again, honesty is the *only* policy. Many dogs are animal-aggressive to some degree. This is not an automatic disqualification, as described next.

VERIFYING: Signs of normal aggression toward other dogs:

- Barking at dogs on other side of fence or window, to protect territory
- Face and body play biting, not breaking skin or causing pain (bite inhibition)
- Two dogs, nose to nose, go around in a circle to play, or one collapses to a prone position; may expose underside, inviting inspection
- Lady gets her paw caught in the car door as it is being closed and begins screaming. Shandy and Tara begin attacking the shrieking Lady. Awful as it sounds, it is normal pack behavior to attack the weak, yelping one. Nevertheless, you need to prevent its occurrence and stop it when it happens.
- In another example, six dogs are loose at an off-leash area. Your own two are walking by your side off leash. The pack of six spots your dogs and charges them. Yours take off running. The loose dogs chase them like mad, but eventually calm down and disband.

VERIFYING: Signs of abnormal aggression toward other dogs:

- Ripping with teeth and nails at a fence, gate, door, or window to get at another dog.
- Face, body, and neck biting, using extreme force, breaking the skin. (Lacks bite inhibition. Can cause serious injury, even death.)
- Two dogs nose to nose. Ralph starts to attack Kona aggressively on the neck, face, back, or maybe the tail. Victim

Kona is now yelping in terror, which intensifies Ralph's aggression.

- During the paw-caught-in-door incident, Shandy and Tara seriously injure Lady.
- During the loose-dogs-in-park incident, the roving pack relentlessly pursues and severely injures your dogs.

QUESTION: What are the dog's behavioral quirks or problems?

WHY: Don't accept "none" for an answer. All dogs, like all people, have behavioral eccentricities. Some might just be quirks that need some work. Others might be problems that need serious training. The more you know, the better.

VERIFYING: Quirks that need work:

- A shy cockapoo lowers her head as you pet her. She pees in submissive urination.
- The confident collie mix grabs your purse and takes off at warp speed around the room, spilling the contents everywhere. She stops, letting you catch up. You almost reach her when the dog's off again.
- Walking the beautiful, six-month-old Irish setter on leash is impossible. She drops to the ground and rolls over, whining.
- Walking the husky/dalmatian mix seems easy until you get outside, where she almost drags you off your feet.

VERIFYING: Problems for serious training:

- As you walk a German shepherd mix you notice her reluctance to pass near people. She reacts to anyone making eye contact by staring back and stiffening her body.
- The tiny Yorkshire terrier snuggles happily in your arms, until your teenage son reaches out to touch her and the dog snaps at his hand.
- The pit bull mix hides behind your wife to get away when you try to touch her.

- The ninety-pound Anatolian shepherd puppy knocks your toddler over to get her peanut butter sandwich, and then stands on top of the child while sniffing around for more.

AT THE SHELTER—RUBY

In the get-acquainted room, you, your family, and your dog-savvy friend meet six-year-old Ruby. She makes her rounds, greeting each one of you with a big grin, never jumping, tail wagging slowly. You all are in love.

Your dog-savvy friend asks you all to sit on the floor. Ruby crawls into one lap at a time, licking faces. Next your friend has you all stand up and talk to Ruby. She starts to jump on you, but when your hand reaches to her, she stops and nuzzles it. Then she makes the rounds again, without jumping. Obviously Ruby is very aware of body language—to her, your hand moving toward her was enough of a message.

Your friend asks you all to speak in high, squeaky voices. Ruby drops her front end, with her rear up in a play bow, tail wagging. She spins around, eager to see what you're all going to do next. Your friend gets a squeaky toy and moves it all around. Ruby tracks it with her eyes. Your friend drops the toy. Ruby picks it up and gives it back.

Your friend picks up Ruby's leash and asks your kids to make noise and run back and forth on the other side of the room. Ruby watches curiously, wagging her tail. Ruby is clearly in heaven. She pushes her body into their caresses. Ruby never pulls on the leash.

Your friend leans over the top of Ruby's back, then touches all over the dog's body, followed by staring straight into her eyes. Ruby's response is to wag her tail and lick your friend's face. Your friend recommends highly that you adopt this wonderful girl.

Caution: *Never* evaluate a dog yourself if she is exhibiting agitation, snapping, snarling, lunging, a stiff stance, or if she is excessively hyperactive, trembling, urinating often, or cringing in the corner. The dog could be dangerous.

Question: Is the dog house-trained?
WHY: This is no big deal either way. Most dogs are fairly easy to house-train. Naturally inclined to keep their "dens" clean, they prefer to accomplish their business outdoors. But it can help you plan better for the coming weeks if you have this answer.

Please note: A dog who is perfectly house-trained in a shelter or foster home might lose that skill in the transition to your home. You might need to retrain her.

QUESTION: Does the dog have any health problems?
WHY: Once again, it is vitally important that the dog's owner, rescuer, or shelter staff personnel level with you on this question. Proper care of the dog depends on your knowing as much as possible about her health status. And if she has any medical issues that would surpass your resources to care for the dog, it would be a mistake to adopt her.
VERIFYING: For tips on how to spot health problems, see chapters 6 and 7.

QUESTION: What is the shelter's policy on spay/neuter?
WHY: Many organizations and even individual rescuers require that the dog you adopt be

spayed or neutered. Some might even want to have the surgery done before you take the dog home. Some pay for it themselves. Others might give you a time frame for having the surgery done after the adoption. This might be required at your expense, or you might be asked to pay a deposit that will be refunded when you provide a vet's certificate as evidence of the surgery. Ask about the policy before you adopt.

QUESTION: If I adopt this dog but it doesn't work out, what do I do?

WHY: Shelters, rescue groups, and reputable private rescuers all require you to return the dog to them if you decide you cannot or do not wish to keep it. This is not the case for all private rescuers or individuals seeking a new home for their dog. Indeed, many of them will *absolutely* not accept the dog back from you. Determine the answer to this question in advance. If there is a return policy and you're counting on being able to take advantage of it should the need arise, make sure it's in writing.

QUESTION: What postadoption services are offered?

WHY: Some organizations and individuals offer free, vouchered, or discounted spay/neuter, vet exams, training, or even boarding. These are by no means required or common, but if you ask you might be pleasantly surprised.

Caution: This Substance Can Be Habit Forming

Some of us are dog addicts. Dogs bring such happiness that just one of them is never enough. When it comes to rescues, and your heart is breaking for all the dogs who need help, it's hard to resist the temptation to bring home yet another stray or shelter death-row

inmate. You might feel guilty or inadequate for not being able to do more.

The hard fact is that each of us can only do so much. If we overextend ourselves, doing rescue can wreak havoc on our lives and relationships. And we can't forget our responsibilities toward the pet or pets we already have at home. Sometimes, less is more.

> Old age means realizing you will never own all the dogs you wanted to.
> —mystery writer Joe Gores

Sad and Alarming Facts about Animal Hoarders

Animal hoarders are those who collect large numbers of animals, usually dogs and cats, for whom they cannot provide even the most basic care. It is a psychological disease tied to obsessive-compulsive disorder (OCD) or the early stages of dementia.

Hoarders profess a strong love of animals and believe they are rescuing animals from death. They do not comprehend the magnitude of the problem they've created; therefore, they seem blind to the suffering of the animals in their care. Despite the hideous or even fatal conditions, hoarders will not release any of their animals for adoption, humane euthanasia, or to animal control.

Each year, close to two thousand cases of hoarding are reported in the United States. Seventy-two percent of hoarders are women, most of them older and living alone. Hoarders tend to have few social outlets and little or no family. They are usually unemployed, on disability, or retired. The dwellings of animal hoarders are often uninhabitable, filled with animal feces, urine, decaying bodies, trash, and foul air. Animals held by a hoarder are often malnourished, disease ridden, terrified, and reproduce unchecked. Seizing hoarded animals can overwhelm an animal shelter's resources, straining personnel, consuming valuable shelter space, and depleting finances.

Most hoarders are charged with minor violations, such as failure to provide proper sanitation or veterinary care. Animal cruelty ordinances often don't go far enough to stop a hoarder. Repeat offenses occur at a rate of almost 100 percent. Strengthening and enforcing the laws could help, along with psychological counseling for offenders.

Bachelor.

Happily Ever After True Story Number Three:
Bachelor

• •

Bachelor, a Labrador retriever, is sprawled out in the tall, green grass that sprouts beneath a quiet ski lift. He has just finished fetching a tennis ball for the thirty-seventh time. Two children and several adults are his companions for the moment. They had "checked out" Bachelor from the hotel concierge, and since their time with him was almost up, the family was taking pictures so their hour together would never be forgotten.

For Bachelor, playing beneath the brilliant blue sky and loping along sweet-smelling trails was a life he was still getting used to. Because it was only a few months before that this young dog was lost and alone, wandering the streets of Denver.

A few days before the Fourth of July, around 10:00 p.m., Gina Biernat was wiped out. It had been a busy and frustrating day at Nikeno's Second Chances, the animal shelter she had founded a few years earlier. Fireworks were being shot off in the surrounding streets. Gina spent hours trying to settle the dogs down. She climbed into her truck and began the drive home—until something yellow darted past her headlights.

She thought, "Oh shoot! I did *not* see that," and told herself to just keep driving. Gina was drop-dead tired, but that didn't stop her from pulling over and coming to a stop. "I actually thought something was wrong with the truck—it wasn't responding to me the way I wanted it to." Of course, Gina was never going to let a stray dog remain stray, so she grabbed the leash she always had on hand, got out of the truck, and approached the dog. "I remember sticking my fingers under his collar and thinking, 'It's late, I'm pooped, so please, just don't bite me.' " Gina got the dog into her truck, made a U-turn back to the shelter, found an empty kennel, and told him, "You're safe; I'll see you tomorrow."

During the next month, Gina tacked up "Found" signs all over the area. She placed ads in the newspaper and reported the dog to the city animal shelter. Not one person inquired about him.

Because he had the look of a purebred Lab, with luscious brown eyes and a gleaming honey-colored coat, Gina had thought he'd be adopted quickly. Then she began to realize that his behavior might be discouraging potential adopters.

"He was like a rubber ball in a rubber room." In her eighteen years of training and rescuing dogs, Gina recognized that this fellow was a classic case of the typical dog euthanized in America's animal shelters: a young, nonneutered male with zero training. "In my book, every dog is salvageable. All they need is time and training. I knew even though this guy was a little nutty, he was destined for greatness."

A few weeks later, Steven Holt, the public relations director at the Ritz-Carlton Hotel near Vail, Colorado, was online looking for a dog to adopt. The resort had a program called Loan-A-Lab, where hotel guests could reserve a Labrador for walks. But their resident Lab had to resign from his position because his dad, a Ritz-Carlton employee, had received a promotion within the company. Since Steven was ready to welcome a dog into his life, his future dog could become the hotel's new Loan-A-Lab.

"I knew the dog I was about to adopt was going to be given a great life," said Steven. "He could come to work with me every day, play with kids, spend lots of time outdoors—but he had to be the right dog." The Ritz's Loan-a-Lab program was the envy of other Ritz properties around the globe. Steven wanted to ensure that the program lived on with as few glitches as possible.

"So as I scrolled through pictures of available dogs, I suddenly saw this face looking straight into the camera. He had these amazing soulful brown eyes, and I thought, this guy looks like he might fit in." Little did Steven realize that Gina laughingly described those same eyes as "buzzing like he'd just had a shot of espresso!"

Steven and the general manager of the hotel drove to meet Gina and the Lab. Of that first meeting Steven said, "I pretty much knew right away he was the right dog."

"You could just tell that Steven was like a little boy at Christmas time, trying to hold in his exuberance," said Gina. Of course, when the dog rubbed up against the general manager, the deal was done.

During the next eight weeks, Gina and Steven worked hard to prepare Batch for his new position. They brought him to the resort for several trial runs, introducing him to his new fellow employees, his own bed by the concierge desk, and the most beautiful backyard any Labrador could wish for—mountains, valleys, trails, meadows. The grimy streets of his days as a stray must have seemed like a world away.

Now, Monday through Friday at 9:30 a.m. sharp, Batch is picked up by the fortunate resort guest who has reserved him for a morning hike. Before snapping on his leash, the guest is shown the "Bachelor Basics Card." Steven said, "It just asks three things: Only feed him the healthy snacks we have for him at the concierge desk, always keep him on a leash, and don't take him into the restaurants or out the front door."

Besides fresh air and a fun workout, what do the hotel guests gain from the time spent with Batch? Steven summed it up: "Having a dog in the hotel makes people have that at-home, comfortable feeling. We tell people they are welcome to bring their dog, but if you don't, we'll loan you ours."

The night she rescued Batch, Gina was so tired that she almost didn't stop the truck. But this rescue confirmed for her that all dogs come into our lives usually because we need to learn something. "Here was this crazy, wild child who needed some guidance. And training a dog is not just about saving him. We can learn from him, too—how to have a relationship, how to have compassion."

That is, in essence, what Batch does each day as he mingles with the guests at the hotel. At the end of the outing, the guest is invited to make a donation to the Eagle Valley Humane Society. To date, Batch has raised $2,300. He found his place in the world and now he's helping other dogs like him find theirs too.

4.
What to Do If You Find a Dog in Need: The First Few Hours

How to Evaluate Yourself, the Dog, and the Situation:
The Immediate Basics

Kellie: Getting Adopted

I feel hot and sick. I am inside a car that rumbles, bumps, twists, and turns. I can't even think about my favorite garbage can without feeling sick all over again. Hey, we stopped moving. Ahh, fresh air.

Jumping out is hard when you're stiff and sick. What is this? A lady and a boy are all over me! Oh, hello. A very shaggy dog. Who are you? Well let's see, you're a girl like me. You have a nice smell. You're not growling at me, and you seem very calm. I like you. I hope you like me.

It's an all too common scene. You see a dog alone on the street or in the park, one shows up on your doorstep, or a neighbor moves away and leaves Beanie behind. Many people would just look the other way, but you can't. That means you have a bigger spirit than most. It also means you have some hassles ahead of you. We'd like to help smooth them out. So what do you do in the first few hours?

> I could not have slept to-night if I had left that helpless little creature to perish on the ground.
>
> (Reply to friends who chided him for delaying them by stopping to return a fledgling to its nest.)
>
> —Abraham Lincoln

Your Immediate Choices

Once you decide to get involved, you have three main choices. The first two are relatively easy—contact your local animal services agencies or take the dog to a shelter. The third choice, helping the dog yourself, is anything but easy and thus merits much of the space in this chapter.

Choice Number One: Contact the Authorities

Let your fingers do the walking, and as quickly as they can. Whip out your cell phone and dial your local city services. The sooner you report the lost or abandoned pooch, the faster someone can come to rescue it. If possible, let the dispatcher know that you will try to stay near the dog to track its whereabouts.

This might not work—roaming dogs don't always stay in one place for very long. For a dog that's stationary, such as the one in your absent neighbor's backyard, make sure to give the authorities the exact address and everything you know about the situation.

If you choose this option, don't feel that you're copping out. Contacting a public agency for help is sensible, responsible, and enormously helpful to the dog. He will be taken to a municipal shelter where he'll have food, shelter, and safety while waiting for his owners to find him or for a family to adopt him. Yes, many overburdened shelters euthanize dogs they can't rehome. As horrific as that is, it's often better than the excruciating illnesses, crippling injuries, and cruel deaths faced by dogs out on their own.

Choice Number Two: Take the Dog to a Shelter

Easier said than done. Some dogs won't let you approach. Some dogs you shouldn't even *attempt* to approach. Let's say that after following the guidelines in this chapter on how—and whether—to approach and collect a stray dog, you get him to the nearest animal shelter. The staff will ask you to fill out some paperwork.

After business hours, some shelters have drop-off kennels where you can leave the pooch in safe confinement. If all the shelters are closed and have no drop-off spot, *and* if public animal control services don't respond to your SOS, you're in a bit of a pickle. Read on for tips on helping the dog yourself. Or perhaps you know a dog-friendly someone who could safely host the dog for the night until the shelter reopens.

It might be hard for you to leave your rescue at a shelter. You might feel you're abandoning him. For some of us, it takes about two

seconds to bond with a dog, so after the trip to the shelter we already feel like his long lost soul mate. But if you can't keep the pooch, remember that some of the folks who love dogs the best are the ones who *don't* have any, because they honor the heavy responsibility involved. You are doing this dog a big favor by taking him to a place where he'll be safe from hunger, cars, poisoning, abuse, and the many other horrors that can befall a dog all alone in the world.

Think you might want to adopt this rescue later? Make that crystal clear to the shelter staff and ask them to put a hold on the dog's paperwork for you. Then be sure to check back frequently until the owner claim period is over (up to seven days).

Please Note: See chapter 6, pp. 76–96, for guidance on emergency rescue situations, including those in which the dog is ill or injured.

IS IT SAFE TO APPROACH A DOG IN NEED?

Getting yourself hurt while trying to help a dog in need won't do anybody any good. Assess the situation thoroughly before you approach. Look for car traffic and other hazards. Observe the dog's behavior. You could get bitten—or worse. Here are some tips on how to decipher a dog's demeanor, but there are no guarantees.

Approaches You

Dogs that come up to you in a friendly manner are the easiest to help. They know they need you.

Approachable

The dog's overall appearance is happy to see you—eyes wide open, ears forward and perked or flat, showing respect, tail wagging and generally held up. The mouth may be open slightly or wider. His body may be wiggling, even prancing. He gives you a feeling of warmth and happiness.

Skittish but Approachable

The dog doesn't run far away. She is standoffish and may shy away but repeatedly comes back. Avoids direct eye contact. The eyes are open, showing the whites, or they are slits. Her tail is lowered or tucked under the body. Her body is tense and lowered or crouching, and she may expose her belly when physical contact is made.

Skittish, and Unapproachable

If cornered, the dog becomes defensive. Most likely he would bite out of fear. He is growling or whining, with ears back, wrinkled nose, corners of mouth back, and may expose his teeth in a snarl. The body is lowered and tail is tucked.

Aggressive/Dominant Offensive, Growling

A dog is ready to attack if her ears are forward or back, eyes are narrowed or staring in a challenge, nose is wrinkled, lips open and drawn back to expose teeth, teeth are bared in a snarl, the corners of the mouth are forward. She stands tall and forward with her hackles up over the neck and hindquarters, her tail fluffed and held straight out from her body.

Choice Number Three: Help the Dog Yourself

Think about this choice long and hard. Consider the following points.

Possible Heartaches

Evaluate yourself emotionally. Rescuing a dog can be painful and draining. It can also be joyous and rewarding. Either way, it is sure to be intense. If you'd rather not get on that roller coaster, choose one of the options above.

Possible Headaches

Evaluate yourself pragmatically. See chapter 2 for questions to ask yourself before adopting a dog. Many of the same questions apply to this case. To rescue a dog, the following are important:

- A schedule that allows for such things as walks, dog park visits, vet visits, obedience training classes, TLC moments, and the ever-popular picking up poop
- A budget to cover food, treats, bowls, collar, leash, ID tag, bedding, veterinary care, obedience classes, training, and more. Just the basic supplies and equipment *for the first week* can cost around $100 to $200, not counting veterinary or training expenses.
- The ability either to keep the dog or to foster him in your home indefinitely
- A cooperative family
- Cooperative other pets, if you have any
- Cooperative neighbors who won't complain about occasional barking
- Limitless patience and love
- Low attachment to possessions and landscaping that might get chewed on, shredded, and/or dug up
- Friends/family who can help, for example, if you get sick

Risks

In most cases, you have never seen this pooch before in your life. You know zero about his temperament or health. The dog could be aggressive or ill. You or your loved ones could get hurt. Your pets could catch a contagious disease (although it's unlikely if they're vaccinated).

Examine your risks from all angles. As much as you'd like to help this dog, you must *never* put yourself or members of your household in danger.

For more information on how to read a dog's demeanor and assess his temperament, see chapter 8, p. 142, as well as the sidebars in this chapter. To get an idea of the dog's state of health, see chapter 6, p. 75, and chapter 7, pp. 110–113.

If You Witness Neglect or Abuse

Those terms can mean different things to different people. Your standards of care for a dog can be light years away from those of your neighbors. Owners who provide basic needs such as adequate shelter, water, and a daily bowl of food are probably not breaking any laws. However, some states and local jurisdictions have more specific laws, such as those prohibiting pet abandonment, and others regulating the amount of time a dog can be chained or tethered.

Should you suspect that laws are being violated—especially if you see incidents of blatant mistreatment, such as a dog being beaten or slowly starving to death in a backyard—think twice before stepping in yourself. Be especially careful in a case of violence. People who hurt animals are capable of hurting humans too. It's almost always best to contact local animal control services. They are equipped to handle the problem better than you can. You may remain anonymous, but without your testimony it is more difficult to prose-cute offenders. Note and report important facts about the perpetrators: license plate numbers, addresses, name of the offender, description of the animal(s), specific type of cruelty/neglect, whether or not the situation is an emergency. Also, leave your contact information in case the officers have additional questions for you.

What about less severe cases, when you see troubling lapses in care for a dog but nothing that breaks the law? That's where it gets sticky. How good are your interpersonal skills? And how receptive is the owner? Assuming that there's no danger of violence toward you, you might try planting seeds of change. Let's say your cousin's Skippy spends his whole life in the backyard with little or no human company. You could offer to walk the pooch a couple of times a week. Or, you might simply teach by example. Invite Skippy's humans over for lemonade and let them see first-hand how you care for your dog and how great it works for both of you. This approach is a subtle but often effective way to change minds. Whatever you do, avoid hurling accusations, which can create a wall of defense and close down communication—which won't help Skippy at all.

> If you have men who will exclude any of God's creatures from the shelter of compassion and pity, you will have men who will deal likewise with their fellow men.
>
> —St. Francis of Assisi

Keep the Dog or Rehome Him?

Before you take the plunge, give some thought to whether you will keep your rescue as your own or try to rehome him.

Keeping a pooch is a lifetime commitment. Are you really ready for a dog (or an additional one) right now? Please see chapter 2, pp. 11–17, and chapter 10, pp. 182–184, for questions to consider.

Rehoming dogs is no piece of cake either. It can take a lot of time, work, and energy. Some are easier to place than others because of their size, appearance, or temperament, but count on fostering your new friend for no less than four weeks before you are able to find a permanent home for him. Then, it can be emotionally wrenching to rescue, care for, and bond with a dog only to place him with someone else.

See chapter 10 for what you'll need to do to find a new home for your rescue.

Your Legal Responsibility

Research ordinances in your area regarding what to do when you find a homeless dog. For example, some municipalities may require that you notify the local shelter with a description of the pooch, in case her owners come looking for her.

To Help the Dog Yourself

You've decided that it's safe to approach the dog. Then what?

Taking the Dog into Your Care

If you're driving and it's safe to stop, do so at some distance from the dog. Speak calmly to him as you walk slowly in his direction. He might rejoice when he sees you, then follow you back to the car and hop right in. If not, drop some food—whatever you have available—to see if you can lure the dog to the car by making him follow a trail.

Now you have this strange dog in your car. Any number of things could go wrong. For one thing, some dogs feel trapped or cornered in cars. You cannot be 100 percent sure that the dog won't become aggressive or just agitated or playful to the point where you can't drive safely. You might want to reconsider your decision to help this pooch yourself. Having the dog contained in your car makes it relatively easy for animal control services to come get him. That might be the best option.

If instead you decide to continue helping the dog personally, try to protect yourself while driving. With a leash, rope, or even a necktie, you might tie your rescue securely to some stationary part of the car interior so that he can't reach you while you're driving. Caution: *Never* leave a tied-up dog unattended. He can strangle and die.

If you're close enough to walk the dog to your home, consider doing that rather than driving. Or call a friend or family member for help.

A FEW WORDS OF CAUTION

Never attempt to rescue a dog when you have a child with you.

Never reach over the top of the body of an unfamiliar dog. This is a threatening movement that might elicit a fearful or dominant response.

Rather than pet the dog's head, which can also seem threatening, you might try rubbing his chest and sides in slow, continuous, circular motions, which can be calming.

All too often, stray dogs are not wearing collars. Depending on the situation, you might need to get a collar and leash on the dog in order to get him to safety. If that's the case, but the dog is shy, fearful, or resistant to those attempts, *do not* force the issue. In such cases it's usually best to call local animal control agencies for help.

I FOUND A PUPPY!

Puppies without mothers face many dangers, including death. If you find one and wish to care for him yourself as opposed to taking him to an animal shelter, be aware that pups need intense care—including, in some cases, round-the-clock feedings.

First off, you'll need to get him to a veterinarian for a checkup and any necessary vaccinations. This is especially important if the puppy displays any of the following symptoms: listlessness, crying, weakness, low temperature, diarrhea, vomiting, sneezing, or coughing. Ask the vet for detailed instructions on puppy care. Here are a few pointers:

To make sure the puppy is well hydrated, gently pull up the skin on the back of the neck. If the pinched skin does not release back to normal, the puppy might be dehydrated and possibly need IV fluids from your veterinarian. If the pinched skin moves right back into place, its hydration levels are probably fine.

Puppies up to ten days old have their eyes closed. These infants must be kept warm. A dog crate lined with soft towels can be a nursery. Drape a blanket over the crate to block chilling drafts. Use a warm water bottle to keep him warm.

Nonweaned puppies—under four weeks of age—can be fed replacement formula using nursing bottles found in pet stores or through your vet. Pups under ten days need to be stimulated to release urine and feces. After feedings, use a warm, moist washcloth to gently wipe the genital area until they release urine or have a bowel movement.

Puppies over four weeks can be introduced to small servings of canned puppy food warmed with formula. Puppies at this age can also regulate their body temperature better, so additional heat in their nursery is probably no longer needed. At six to eight weeks, pups should be weaned and eating puppy food without formula.

SUPPLIES YOU'LL NEED AS SOON AS POSSIBLE

- High-quality dog food (see chapter 7, pp. 117–118, for guidance on selection)
- Large(ish)-sized biscuits for bedtime
- Small treats to give as rewards during the day
- Collar for everyday use, safe to be left on unsupervised, such as a nylon or leather buckle or clip collar
- ID tags
- Training collar (see chapter 8, pp. 157–158)
- Leash (see chapter 8, pp. 158–159)
- Food bowl deep enough so that food doesn't fall out while the dog is eating; stainless steel preferable to plastic, which is hard to sanitize and can irritate dogs' muzzles
- Water bowl, preferably stainless steel, of a size to contain enough fresh, clean water so that you only have to change it twice a day
- Crate (see chapter 8, pp. 153–156)
- Dog bed (see chapter 5, pp. 58–59)
- Dog toys (see chapter 7, p. 134)
- Chews (see chapter 7, pp. 133–134)
- Grooming brush
- Dog shampoo

- Flea/tick prevention (see chapter 8, pp. 104–106)
- Poop bags or other poop collection tools (see chapter 5, pp. 53–54)

Food and Water

When you find a homeless dog, one of your first impulses is to quench his hunger and thirst. Although your urge is understandable, restrain yourself. You can do more harm than good by giving a malnourished or dehydrated dog too much food or water at once, as detailed in chapter 6, p. 84, and chapter 7, pp. 115–116.

During the first few hours, offer small amounts of water every hour. For feeding, give a small dog (under twenty-five pounds) about a quarter of a cup of kibble; a medium dog (twenty-five to sixty pounds) about a half cup, and a large dog (sixty pounds and up) about one cup. You can also give very small treats in between.

Unless the dog seems ill, do feed your rescue, albeit sparingly, as soon as possible. Aside from the physical comfort, food can also help establish the dog's trust in you, and a feeling of well-being. That can help prevent a lot of behavioral headaches.

Veterinary Care

If possible, go straight to the vet. Have the vet scan for a microchip. If the dog has one, it might help you find his owners. Either before or after a good-faith effort at finding the owners, visit the vet for vaccinations, a thorough exam, any necessary treatment, and information about caring for your rescue.

Microchipping
Microchips save lives. Dogs are good at getting lost. During the confusing and stressful initial period after rescue, your rescue might

be especially prone to escape. Despite your best efforts, he might succeed. The dog's ID tags can get lost, too. Whether you find the dog's owners, keep him, or place him in a new home, a microchip can be a lifeline. Millions of dogs and their families have found security in this device that's as small as a grain of rice.

For a modest fee of $25 to $40, your vet or local shelter can microchip your dog. The chip is quickly injected under the skin at the back of your dog's neck. The ID number on the chip is entered into a computer database, along with your contact information.

Most veterinary hospitals and animal control agencies have the equipment to detect the microchip, should they receive your lost dog. A scanner waved over your dog's shoulders detects the chip and displays your contact information on a computer. If ever you need to change your contact information, simply call the microchipping company listed in your paperwork.

Plan for Spay/Neuter

If the vet approves, and if the dog is not too emotionally traumatized, make an appointment for spay/neuter. If your rescue is nervous or frightened, consider waiting a few days until he has become more accustomed to his new surroundings. During this time, however, it is imperative to keep the dog under close watch and completely separate him from other unaltered dogs so that there's no chance the dog could mate. The last thing you want to do when you rescue a dog is to create even more puppies to add to the millions already seeking homes.

HOW YOUNG TO SPAY/NEUTER?

Some veterinary experts believe that healthy animals as young as six weeks can undergo the surgery safely. Others maintain that six months is an ideal age. Still others argue that the dog should be eight to sixteen months old when the procedure is performed.

For the sake of preventing unwanted births and the dreadful results of pet overpopulation, the earlier spay/neuter is done on every dog, the better. If you wish to wait until later, you need to take great precautions to make sure your dog does not reproduce—or get hurt trying to do so. A female in estrus can attract males from a several-mile radius, and females come into season about twice a year—sometimes when you least expect it. A male in search of a receptive female is determined to surmount any obstacle in his way. Doors, windows, gates, and fences mean little. Both males and females will go under, over, around, or through anything to get to each other. Talk with your vet, research the medical facts involved, and weigh all the risks and benefits to decide when to spay/neuter your dog.

HOW TO TELL AND WHAT TO DO IF A RESCUE IS PREGNANT

If you rescue a female, she might be either in season or pregnant. Even if she looks slender or starved, she might be carrying pups. On the other paw, an enlarged abdomen is not a reliable clue for pregnancy. It can be a symptom of several ailments.

During the initial exam, ask your vet to determine whether your rescue is pregnant. If she is, ask if it's still early enough in her term to spay her. Typically spaying can be done safely up to a month into the term. Yes, this is a sad option, as it involves removal of developing puppies. But you may request that your vet humanely euthanize the fetuses. Otherwise, you must ask yourself if you are prepared emotionally and financially to care for this dog and her puppies through pregnancy, labor, delivery, nursing, weaning, and all the havoc that a litter of puppies wreak on a household. Then, will you be able to find safe, loving homes for as many as fourteen puppies?

If your rescue is too far along in her term for spaying, you will face these questions head-on. Some rescuers welcome the chance to be in on the miracle of birth and enjoy the puppy chaos. Others don't have the time, money, or lifestyle to commit to a pregnant pooch and her brood-to-be. In that case, put the word out to shelters, rescue organizations, friends, family, and anyone who will listen that you and your especially needy rescue could use help. You might receive donations of money or volunteers' time to help you care for the little family, or offers from responsible foster homes to take them in.

When Worse Comes to Worst
Sadly, there might be cases where the dog you're trying to rescue is so ill, irreparably injured, or emotionally unstable that she needs to be euthanized. See chapter 7, pp. 135–137, for guidance on this difficult decision.

Collar and ID

If the dog does not already have a collar and identification, get those on him as quickly as possible. The collar helps you handle the dog more easily and the ID helps in his return to you in case he gets lost. A quick ID collar can be made by using a bright-colored nylon collar and clearly writing your telephone number on it with an indelible ink marker. Some pet stores have vending machines that make instant ID tags.

Once You Get Home

At home, keep things low key. Give your rescue as much peace and quiet as your household can muster. Think about how new everything seems to the dog and how you would feel under the same circumstances. Try to throw as few new experiences at him as possible. Don't bring in friends and neighbors to meet the dog just yet. Keep family interaction with him to a minimum too.

Avoid introducing the dog to existing pets for now. Keep them confined and away from the new dog. (See chapter 6, pp. 97–102, and chapter 7, on possible infectious illnesses.) Even if you're positive all your pets will all get along, they might very well surprise you. And in any case, it's best to give your rescue time to decompress and acclimate before making her go through a possibly stressful encounter with the household's pets. Right now your rescue needs some serious down time.

If you can get a crate, do so. Follow the guidelines in chapter 8, pp. 153–156, on how to use and accustom the dog to it. Or you might opt to keep him tied securely to a stationary object near you, on a comfortable, soft surface with lots of toys and small treats. Try to pick a spot that can be "the dog's," where he will never be left unattended.

For the first few hours—even the first few weeks—most rescues are either hyper and agitated or quiet and subdued. Their sleep can be restless, almost with one eye open. Or they might sleep heavily for hours on end as a way of coping with stress.

Keeping the dog's environment calm and nonstimulating will help increase his sense of security and let him relax. This, in turn, helps you. The more relaxed the dog is, the more you and other household members can rest on this eventful day.

See chapter 5, p. 53, for information on how to handle housetraining and potty breaks and ways to tuck your rescue in for a bark-free bedtime. In chapter 6, p. 75, and chapter 7, pp. 110–113, find tips on how to spot symptoms of illness in these important first few hours. Chapter 8 offers information about flower essences like Rescue Remedy that might help your dog cope with all the changes in his early postrescue life.

Don't Forget a Potty Break

Before you take your rescue into your home, make sure he's had a chance to pee and poop. Otherwise the stress and excitement could cause even the best-trained pooch to have an indoor accident. See chapter 5, p. 53, for tips on housetraining and a potty routine that you can start right away.

SAFE, COMFORTABLE CONFINEMENT

Even when you're home, you can't devote 100 percent of your time and attention to a new dog. In those moments when you're nearby but can't have your eyes glued to him every second, confine him in a safe, comfortable way. Consider the following:

Crates—you might have one that you move from room to room, or have several in different rooms (see chapter 8, pp. 153–156, for description and guidance).

"Puppy pen" or "exercise pen"—you can set one up in various configurations and easily move it around from room to room. It should be tall enough so that the dog can't jump over it.

Leash or line—use one to tie the dog to a stationary piece of furniture, a stairway banister, or a sturdy ring you've installed in the wall. Use a chewproof leash or line made of chain or metal. *Do not* leave your dog unattended while he is tied.

Regardless of the method you choose, the confinement option should be made comfortable and familiar with nice, soft blankets or cushions, safe toys your pooch enjoys, and treats now and then.

Looking for the Dog's Owners

In the best of worlds distraught owners would be searching frantically for all the homeless dogs we see out there. That rarely happens. But just in case, make an effort to determine if anyone's looking for your rescue.

Check for tags or other ID. Call any telephone numbers provided. A veterinarian or your local shelter can scan the dog for a microchip ID. If those methods of identification don't pan out, call local shelters and give a description of the dog in case anyone comes in looking for him.

You can put up "Found" flyers around the area. Use big lettering, and state only the dog's general color and size (small, medium, large), the date you found him, and your phone number. Don't give a lot of information, because you want to be able to verify the dog's true owner if calls come in.

Many newspapers and Web sites allow free postings of Found notices where you can provide general—not too specific—information about your rescue.

If calls come in, make sure you hand over the dog to the right person. Unfortunately, there are crazy people out there, as well as people called "bunchers" who collect lost pets then sell them to research labs for medical experimentation.

Speak with possible owners on the telephone, *not* in person. *Do not* answer any questions about the description of the dog. Have the caller give *you* a detailed description. Offer open-ended statements such as, "Describe your dog's markings." If answers ring true, for safety, arrange to meet in a populated public place and take another adult with you.

You might ask how the dog escaped the owner's care and how future escapes will be prevented. If the owner wishes to reward you for finding the lost dog, you might just say thanks and ask instead that the money be used to fix that loose gate, to buy a crate, or for some training classes to avoid other near misses like this one.

Clues about the Past

Chances are that a thin, sickly, or unusually scared dog either came from a neglectful and/or abusive home or has been on her own for a long time.

What If I Don't Like the Owner?

If you find the dog's owner and suspect that the person is irresponsible (or worse), giving the dog back can be troubling. You might offer to take the dog off the owner's hands. In some cases, the owner will be greatly relieved. But keep in mind that in most states the rightful owner has "superior ownership interest" over the finder of a lost dog. Nevertheless, you can contact your local animal control service, which is required to investigate and possibly confiscate any mistreated dog.

A Bath and Parasite Control

If the vet approves, give your rescue a bath as soon as you can. You might need to apply a flea/tick control product too (see chapter 6, pp. 104–106, and chapter 7, pp. 127–129).

Taking Care of You

Congratulations! You have performed a miracle—saved a life! Whether you alerted the authorities to this dog in need, took him to a shelter, decided to keep him yourself, or plan to rehome him, you're probably exhausted now, and deservedly so. Today you exercised your compassion. Rescuing a dog gives those kinds of muscles quite a workout. And, tomorrow, if the pooch is still in your care, you'll need to roll up your sleeves, because today was only the beginning.

Tonight, try to pamper yourself. Although your rescued pooch will require quite a bit of your evening, don't feel you have to spend every minute with him. Set a few moments aside for a relaxing bath or a good book. The stress of a day like today can really catch up with you. Ward it off with a good night's sleep. Devote some time to preserving your own health and well-being so that you can continue to safeguard those of your dog.

THINGS WE HATE AND LOVE ABOUT RESCUING DOGS

Things We Hate: When people assume we do rescue for fun and that we're just itching for more dogs to save. When people assume we are making money from it. When people can't believe that the beautiful purebred we found dying in a ditch was really abandoned, saying, "Anybody who pays good money for a purebred will take care of him." When people don't lift a pinky for a dog in need, yet criticize the care we provide when *we* rescue him.

Things We Love: When the shy, unsure dog we rescued months ago finally believes he's home, and barks at a passer–by for the first time. When the feisty, hyper pooch we rescued months ago finally foregoes barking at the passerby, and opts to remain in his spot on the sofa, snuggling with us. When the adopter of a dog you rehomed sends you a postcard from the family vacation with Fido. When rescuing a new canine best friend leads you to a new human best friend.

I tell my friends they don't let themselves see them, because then they would have to do something, too. People ignore stray dogs the same way they ignore stray people, the way your friends in the city insist that they have never seen any homeless people or, when pressed, offer the opinion that these people choose to be on the street and wouldn't want a home if they had one.

—Ken Foster, from *The Dogs Who Found Me*

Shelley Frost

Gabrielle and Boomer.

Happily Ever After True Story Number Four:

Boomer

. . . .

If you throw a tennis ball across a grassy lawn, and a golden retriever is nearby, it's a good bet you'll get that tennis ball back. In the case of one particular golden retriever, her rescue was like a bouncing ball. No matter how many times she was rescued and brought to the shelter, she always found a way back—to the LaMond home.

Gabrielle LaMond, and her two daughters, Sarah, twelve, and Alysse, six, were busy packing their home in Ann Arbor, Michigan, for a cross-country move to Burlingame, California. Gabrielle's husband, Stephen, was already in their new home and working at his new job. Three weeks before Gabrielle and the girls were to board the airplane, a "funny"-looking golden retriever arrived on their front doorstep. The dog had been running alongside a groundskeeper at the local golf course for most of the day. Seeing Gabrielle, the groundskeeper told her he needed to head home and could not take the dog with him. The dog's coat was dull and matted. Her chest and belly were distended, making her look chubby but without the glow of good health.

That night, Gabrielle and her daughters bathed the dog and brushed out her coat. The dog was proving to be so affectionate that her lack of house-training, as evidenced by the puddle someone left on the kitchen floor, was quickly forgiven. The next day Gabrielle reluctantly left the dog at the local animal shelter, hoping that the owners would find her and enjoy a happy reunion.

A few days later Gabrielle learned that the owners had in fact picked up their dog. "We were so proud of ourselves for doing the right thing," Gabrielle recalled. At this time, their two-year-old pet rabbit, Toki, died. She was "a rabbit with a huge personality," Gabrielle said. She and the girls were devastated.

Two weeks before they were to board the airplane to California, they got the news from a neighbor. The golden retriever was back. The neighbor knew that Gabrielle had rescued her once before, so he assumed she would want to rescue her again.

Taking a deep breath, Gabrielle opened the front door and the dog bounded in as if she had just been away for a moment. Both dog and daughters were delighted to see each other.

When Gabrielle called the shelter, the staff refused to take the dog back. She had been in and out of the shelter many times and the owners never did what they promised, such as spay, vaccinate, or put an ID tag on her. Gabrielle said the shelter hoped her family would adopt her.

In between packing boxes, Gabrielle took the dog to the veterinarian. The dog was suffering from tapeworms, ear infections, a yeast infection, and she was nine pounds overweight. Plus she needed to be spayed and vaccinated.

Back at home Gabrielle's daughters were thrilled that this dog seemed to be coming with them. They begged and pleaded. Even Stephen agreed that the dog was incredibly affectionate, despite the charges to the family credit card.

So that's when "the dog" became "Boomerang"—"Boomer" for short. Two weeks later, Boomer arrived safely at the airport in San Francisco and is now living the life of a California dog.

Sarah said, "When she showed up at our house after Toki died, I knew it was meant to be. Boomer has helped me make new friends, and I really love her."

The feeling is mutual so far as Boomer is concerned. She follows the two girls everywhere through the house. She sleeps with them and looks after them. Boomer is often off leash in dog-safe areas yet never runs too far from her family.

Looking back, Gabrielle said, "It just amazes me that her previous owners neglected her so badly. Boomer has no bad habits; she is smart, loving, and so well behaved. I can't imagine why they did not notice what a wonderful dog she is."

Then the girls clattered through the front door and Boomer rushed out to meet them. They ran off to the backyard, laughing, on a day full of bright California sunshine.

5.
Your New Friend in Need Comes Home: The First Forty-Eight Hours

Safety, Health, and Behavior Tips to Help Those Challenging First Couple of Days Go More Smoothly

Kellie: I Could Live Here!

Hmmm, this grass would be a good place to relieve myself. Wow! The lady is so excited! She is petting me and making really nice noises. I guess my deposit was properly deposited!

Inside the house the floor is nice and cool, and . . . whoa! There's a cat! Stay calm. He's sniffing me. Doesn't he know I'm a dog? Suddenly I need to release the water. I drop my bottom and let it go. Yikes! The lady pulled me outside. At least she's petting me and speaking softly.

The shaggy dog, whose name is Abby, is running into a yummy-smelling room. I know there's a garbage can in here somewhere! The lady put a bowl full of food under Abby's nose. And wonder of wonders—she gave me one too!

The first forty-eight hours of any rescue typically are the most chaotic, and also the most critical. Whether you are just fostering, or adopting for keeps, it's a time to pay special attention to the dog's needs, as well as to your own. This chapter offers guidance on how to manage, at least to some degree, the inevitable madness of having a new pooch in your home, and how to begin building a framework for the weeks or years to come.

Dogs are not our whole lives, but they make our lives whole.

—Roger Caras

Establishing a Basic Routine

See chapter 4, pp. 43–49, for the initial steps to take after finding or adopting a new dog and bringing her home, as well as a list of useful supplies. After those first few hours, you can begin easing the dog, your family, and yourself into a new life together, whether it's for a short-term fostering period or a long-term, happily ever after.

Try to establish a routine, giving meals, exercise, and bedtime at more or less the same times every day. This isn't always possible, especially in busy households, but the steadier you can keep the daily schedule, the sooner the dog will feel secure, and the fewer health and behavior hassles you'll encounter. Dogs aren't much different from humans in this regard. Though we all enjoy excitement, most of us are creatures of habit and we function best when we can count on some structure from day to day. (See the Household Dog Care Checklist in chapter 2, p. 160.)

House-training and Potty Breaks

Just as with humans, canine elimination habits are affected by stress. During the first few days in your home, your pooch's potty habits might go haywire. Even the most fastidious dog might have accidents. The two keys to success are (1) establishing a routine, and (2) prevention.

When you arrive home with your newly adopted or rescued dog, the very first thing you should do is take her on leash to the yard, or if you don't have a yard, take the dog to the area where she will be doing her business. This introduces the dog to her "bathroom." Males will probably urinate right away to leave their mark. Females aren't as eager to mark, so it might take a while for a female to urinate. But be patient and keep walking around, letting her sniff. Eventually she'll probably "go." As soon as the male or female does so, say, "Chumley, potty." Then praise the dog, saying, "Chumley, good potty!"

Inside, keep that leash attached, creating a physical connection. Observe body language. Most dogs will "tell" you when they need to go. Signs include circling, whining, sniffing, or squatting. If you see these, calmly walk the dog outside and encourage her in a soft voice with the words, "Chumley, potty," and praise the dog when she goes.

Dogs typically defecate after meals, either right away or fifteen to twenty minutes later. Accompany your dog outside in that time frame, using the command and praise.

Never leave your new best friend unsupervised in the house or accidents *will* happen. Always make sure the dog is on "empty" while you're away.

Pay attention to the dog's signals and take her right out when she asks. If you get distracted on the phone, she might wander off and leave you a little present somewhere in the house. An hour later you step in it. Don't chastise the dog—it was your fault for not listening to her. Right now the dog needs your constant guidance and instruction.

Eventually, you'll get to know your dog's potty-time rhythm, and you can plan on taking her out at more or less certain times every day.

On "Rubbing the Dog's Nose in It"

Never rub your dog's nose in potty mistakes. This used to be a popular house-training technique. It is cruel, ineffective, and counterproductive, teaching the dog nothing except that you are mean and weird.

Nothing cruel is useful or expedient.

—Cicero

Cleanup Stations

Keep cleaning supplies handy in two or three spots around the house to make it easier on yourself while house-training your new pooch. For each cleanup station have a roll of paper towels, an enzymatic odor and stain remover such as Nature's Miracle, a spray bottle of disinfectant cleaning liquid, plastic bags, and whatever else you use to deal with those inevitable oopsies.

Chowtime

Give the dog her own food and water bowls, and keep them in the same spot. This establishes dependability and familiarity. Feed the dog at set times every day. With meals at certain hours, she'll develop a pattern for potty breaks, and you can plan accordingly.

Although smaller breeds can be fed once per day, dividing it up into two meals, morning and evening, can help curb behavior problems. Dogs love to eat, so feeding them twice gives them more to look forward to, and provides a greater sense of well-being. Eating also releases relaxing hormones. Getting the benefit of a more relaxed dog twice a day, instead of just once, is much in your favor. For larger breeds, two daily feedings are necessary for health reasons, to lower the risk of stomach torsion, or "bloat" (see chapter 6, pp. 89-90).

Don't leave food out for free feeding. It attracts bugs, can cause fights if you have more than one pet, and encourages the dog to become a food guarder.

Talk with your vet about what and how much to feed (see chapter 7, p. 116).

Exercise Time

You might be exhausted in this early phase of rescue or adoption, but you still have to exercise the dog every day. It's super important for your sake and your dog's. Tired dogs find it hard to be naughty. Much bad behavior is just working off excess energy. Plus exercise contributes to your mutual bond. Your pooch sees that you're her safe, reliable ticket to the wide, wonderful world, and together you share the fun of new experiences.

Sufficient exercise might consist of a romp around the backyard or a brisk walk through the neighborhood. The length and intensity depend on your dog's fitness level (see chapter 11, p. 208). In general, let your dog guide you on what's too much or too little. She'll let you know, perhaps by lying down when tuckered out, or by leaping around excitedly when she's up for more. See chapter 8, pp. 157–159, for information on collars and leashes for those outings.

WHAT IF YOUR RESCUE HAS NEVER BEEN ON LEASH?

Some rescued dogs have never seen a leash before in their lives. We know of at least one who started out terrified of leashes because they looked too much like the rope an abuser once tried to hang the dog with. Fear of being on leash makes outings almost impossible. There aren't many places you can go without one. If you don't have a fenced backyard where the dog can pee, poop, and exercise, you might need to reconsider keeping a leash-fearing rescue. It might be best to take her to a shelter or rescue organization.

If you do have a backyard, you might use a trainer's help in habituating your dog to the leash. If you go it alone, remember to proceed slowly, gently, and cautiously. Never try to force a fearful dog, which is more prone to bite. Refer to the guidance in chapter 7, p. 114, on how to get dogs accustomed to grooming equipment, and use the same general strategy to overcome this rescue's apprehensions about the leash.

LEASHED IS LOVED

You and your on-leash, well-trained dog are enjoying a stroll through the park. An off-leash dog comes galloping up to you. If you're lucky, the dog is friendly, there's some mutual sniffing, the visitor dashes off and safely returns to her human at the picnic table across the field. Unfortunately, however, off-leash dogs often pose great danger to others and to themselves.

As an off-leash dog approaches, it's impossible to know whether she will attack you or your dog. In case she does, make sure to carry your self-defense gear with you (see the sidebar below on "Self-Defense on Dog Walks"), and don't hesitate to use it.

Dog owners who let their dogs wander off leash are not only violating the law in most jurisdictions, they are also putting their own dog at terrible risk. When that dog runs up to you, your dog might attack her as a preemptive strike to defend herself and you.

Many dog owners think it's OK to let their dog off leash anywhere they please if they stay nearby, and if they believe their dog is friendly. But unless the dog is under total voice control, always responding to their commands, the owners are being irresponsible toward you and your pet, as well as toward their own. Even the friendliest of dogs can sometimes attack or be attacked.

Don't join the ranks of such ninnies. Always obey the leash law, and be considerate of other folks, other dogs, and your own. Everyone has the right to enjoy public spaces safely and worry-free.

SELF-DEFENSE ON DOG WALKS—A WALKING KIT

After having been attacked several times by dogs off leash while out walking, some of us now never leave the house "unarmed." We use a fanny pack or pockets to carry plenty of poop bags, moist hand wipes, and at least one of the "weapons" described below. In addition, you can use your voice to bellow commands like "*Hey*!" and "*Beat it*!" in deep, loud, sharp tones. Sound authoritative and in control, not panicked and scared (even if you are). Please note: Our suggestions are homemade and relatively harmless. Some people are more hard-core, toting things like pepper sprays.

Emergency or sports whistle: If you're cornered by hostile dogs in a remote or unpopulated spot, blow it to summon help. It also helps to distract the dogs and break up the action for a few seconds to buy you time.

Shake can: An empty soda can, sealed up and with a few pennies in it (see chapter 8, p. 157, for details) can be rattled to frighten off hostile dogs and to get the attention of your own pooch. It can be annoying to carry with you because it rattles constantly, especially if you're a brisk walker, but it's highly effective.

Squirter: Rinse out a small (three- to six-ounce) plastic travel shampoo bottle with a squirt top. Fill it with water and a few teaspoons of vinegar or lemon juice. If a dog is attacking you or your dog, aim for her face and mouth.

Chain throws: Get some short (four- to five-inch) lengths of large-link metal chain from the hardware store, and keep a couple in your walking kit to throw at attacking dogs. At home while watching TV, practice your aim on a piece of furniture across the room.

The disadvantage is that these are bulky, and you can only throw each of them once. By the same token, if you don't have any of these "weapons" with you, you can use your keys, rocks, or even trash you find on the ground.

The goal is to intimidate hostile dogs into backing off, and to show your dog that you will protect her. *Do not* under any circumstances assume that your dog can or should fight the dogs, and try not to let her intervene. If a fight does happen, *do not* put yourself in the middle of it. You will be no good to your dog if you get hurt too. Use your weapons and your voice. (See the sidebar in chapter 9, p. 177, "How to Break Up a Dogfight.")

THE CARSICK DOG

Ninety-five percent of motion-sick dogs are reacting not to motion but to stress. Your dog could associate car rides with previous bad experiences. Common stress signs are panting, drooling, yawning, and shaking. To reduce the dog's anxiety when the car door slams shut, here are a few tips that can make every ride a joy ride.

Driveway ride: You won't need the car keys for this drive, because you and your dog are going to sit in the parked car enjoying treats and toys. During the "drive," in a soothing tone of voice, praise your dog for riding in the car. Do a one- to five-minute driveway ride a few days a week until you notice your dog's stress level dropping.

Test drive: Take your dog to a nearby park, no farther than a ten-minute drive. While there, play her favorite games. On the ride home, to keep stress at bay, talk in happy tones, reliving all the fun the two of you just enjoyed together. Once at home, give your dog treats and praise. Repeat several times until you feel ready for the next step.

Road trip: Plan to visit a destination that is at least thirty minutes away from your home. Bring along toys and a familiar dog bed or blanket that can keep your dog company inside the car. While driving, speak to your dog, praising and encouraging.

For the 5 percent of dogs that continue to become sick in the car, consult your veterinarian, who might recommend helpful medications.

Playtime

Remember how much you loved recess in grade school? All dogs need time every day to play, be goofy, abandon their cares, and just have fun.

Chew Time

Every day at a certain time, provide safe chews under supervision for at least fifteen minutes. The act of chewing causes a dog's system to release calming substances into the bloodstream. (See chapter 7, p. 134, for guidance on safe chews.)

Comfort Toys

Give your pooch a couple of toys she really likes. Many dogs turn to familiar items, such as a favorite toy, to comfort themselves when they're feeling stressed. Some dogs rip them apart. Others keep a plush toy their whole lives. Hard, rubbery ones like the Kong toys are nearly indestructible, but you have to spark some dogs' interest in them by stuffing them with treats, such as cookies, peanut butter, or a spray-in filling. Regardless of what the favorites are, rotate them out now and then to maintain your dog's interest. Give your dog two or three toys at a time, then put those away every week or so, bringing out fresh ones.

Cuddling

You might be so busy fulfilling immediate needs that you don't have time to just relax, pet, and snuggle with your new pooch. Try to find some moments here and there. Some dogs lap it up, while others are less receptive. Most pooches will accept your overtures gladly and start making some themselves.

Training

You don't have to set aside a formal training time quite yet. Your dog has an awful lot to absorb, and so do you. But in the ordinary course of the day you can begin sneaking in "teaching moments." For example, praise the dog when she waits for you to go through a doorway first, or if she stands calmly while you put on her leash, or if, for once, she refrains from ear-piercing shrieks of excitement at meal time. After a few days, you can begin obedience classes and ten-minute training sessions two or three times a day.

Bedtime

The first few days or even weeks after rescue can be so stressful for a dog that she might sleep for hours on end. On the other paw, the dog might be so anxious that she barely gets a wink. This can cause the whole family to stay awake too if your new dog is a noisy insomniac. There is no way around the fact that you might lose some sleep in the initial days. To get the most quiet nights possible for one and all, try these tips.

For about an hour before you plan to go to bed, don't let your pooch drink a lot of water. Take her out to potty just before bedtime and make sure she does so.

Make a ritual out of bedtime. Lead the dog to the place where she'll sleep—whether it's a crate, a dog bed in your room, or in your bed—and say, "Daisy, bedtime." As she settles into her sleep spot, say, "Daisy, good bedtime," and give her a big dog biscuit. If she gets up after finishing the biscuit, gently lead her back to her spot and repeat, "Daisy, bedtime." Most dogs will only get up a few times before they realize that's where they should be. They're especially contented if they're in the same room with you, and can see you settle down on your bed. This signals that it's sleep time.

Unless your new pooch is extremely mellow, you might need to confine her in a crate for bedtime (details in chapter 8, pp. 153–156), or in a puppy pen enclosure (details in chapter 4, p. 48). Keep a shake can handy (described in chapter 8, pp. 157), so that if she does bark or cry during the night, you can rattle it and say, "Quiet!" Some dogs get the picture right away. Others need several repeats of this throughout the night.

An alternative is to put the dog in a crate in a remote room of your home, if you have one, where you, your family, and the neighbors can't hear her ruckus. Don't feel guilty about "abandoning" the dog. We all need our sleep, and this might be the best temporary alternative until things settle down. (See chapter 8, pp. 153–156, and chapter 9, pp. 171–172 for details on proper crating and ideas on how to calm an anxious dog.)

FROM STREET STRESS TO SWEET DREAMS

Dogs sleep ten to sixteen hours per day. With that much time spent off their paws, all pooches need a comfy place to lay their bodies down. Older dogs and those who cannot stand or walk for long periods especially need a soft place to rest their bones.

For a pooch whose past included living alone on the streets, sleeping on concrete, enduring cold, heat, rain, or snow, having a cozy place to curl up is a dream come true. Finding a safe, comfortable place to rest is a big problem for homeless dogs. In areas with several strays, you'll often see them jockeying for position or even bickering over the slightest bit of shelter, like the doorway of a shop or a shady patch under a tree. Providing a special, snuggly spot for your new best friend can boost her sense of security, and help her feel that she really belongs.

Your dog's snooze space doesn't need to be fancy. If it's large enough for the dog to stretch out on fully with a few inches left over, and has a yielding yet supportive surface, it will be just right. If you do want to go all out, the sky's the limit. Doughnut beds, snuggle balls, sofa beds, and many more styles come in a vast selection of colors and fabrics.

Dogs with orthopedic problems should sleep on beds made of thick foam that molds to the body. These can be custom-ordered to size and weight. An online search of soft dog beds or orthopedic dog beds should turn up several products.

BED CHEWING

A frustrating fact of life is that many dogs chew on their beds, or even shred them to bits. You might spring for a magnificent mattress that costs about as much as your own, only to find it grotesquely mangled by the next morning. This does not mean that the dog does not like the bed. It just means the dog needs to chew, and the bed was there. It doesn't matter that there are toys and chews nearby. The bed, at that moment, was more intriguing.

There are some companies that make chew-resistant—notably not chewproof—dog bed covers. These discourage many chewers but not all. You might also try making a tight-fitting cover out of a smooth, stretchy, slippery fabric. That makes it harder (but not impossible) for the dog to get a satisfying grip on the fabric with her teeth.

You might also try training. When you see Muffy chewing on her bed or even just licking it—often a prelude to chewing—tell her to "leave it," then immediately give her a toy, urge her to chew it instead, and praise her for doing so. The problem is that usually you're not watching when Muffy decides to dismantle her bed. Refer to chapter 8, p. 145, and chapter 9, p. 168, for more on how to deal with destructive chewing.

JUMPING ON THE FURNITURE

Don't want Heidi on your recliner? One quick solution is to use products such as "Sofa Scram" or "Scat Mat" that emit a loud, startling beep when Heidi jumps on the bed, or that deliver a mild electric shock about like the static electricity zingers you get in dry weather. These devices are typically battery-operated, and in the form of mats or strips. They are available online or in pet stores.

WHY YOUR DOG SHOULD LIVE INDOORS

Outdoor dogs:

- love you and miss you.
- suffer stress and anxiety when deprived of companionship.
- can develop unwanted behaviors out of boredom and loneliness, such as escaping, digging, inappropriate chewing, barking, howling, whining, obsessive tail chasing, and self-mutilation.
- can only guard the yard, not the interior of the house.
- are at risk of being stolen and poisoned.
- can suffer from severe weather effects such as heatstroke and frostbite.
- are susceptible to fly bites on their ears, maggots on open wounds, and insect-borne diseases such as heartworm.
- are more difficult to train since they aren't with you enough to learn to read your personality and body language.
- are more likely to be abandoned or euthanized than indoor dogs because they and their owners don't have much time together to form a bond.

Health

The stress of unfamiliar circumstances during the first forty-eight hours—or longer—can trigger health problems. Most are temporary and easy to treat. If you haven't yet gotten your dog to the vet for an initial exam, do so as soon as possible.

Check chapters 6 and 7 for symptoms and possible treatment of many health issues. Here are some common ailments that you might find in your adoptee or rescue: diarrhea; lack of appetite; excessive thirst; ear infection; eye inflammation or infection; intestinal parasites; heartworms; skin parasites, such as fleas, ticks, and mites; skin inflammations; fly-bitten ear tips, embedded foxtails; overgrown nails.

VETERINARY EXPENSES

Your rescued dog might have many health issues that require treatment. Ear mites, heartworm, broken bones—the list can go on and the out-of-pocket expenses can shoot up. Ideally, you'll fix all of your dog's health problems. But maybe you simply can't afford to address every need right away. Don't give up. If you shop around a bit, you might find a vet who will discount fees when he hears that you have rescued this pooch, especially if you are fostering her for future placement. The hardier souls among us might pull on a pair of knee pads and beg family and friends to pitch in. Even the media might help. Once in a while, television news shows run dog rescue stories with public appeals for donations toward the ailing pooch's medical expenses. You might also ask local shelters and rescue organizations if they have charitable funds available for foster cases.

SAMPLE DOGGIE DOSSIER

When you catch your breath, try to start keeping notes on your rescued or adopted pooch in a Doggie Dossier. This helps you remember useful details and keep them all in one place. It becomes especially important if you plan to re-home the dog, so that you can give a full picture of her to prospective adopters. Here's a sample to get you started.

General Information

Dog's Name: Breed: Age: Sex:
Altered: Yes_ No_ If not altered, this is the reason:

Physical Description, including color, size and weight:

Licensed: Yes_ No_ Microchip Number:

Feeding Times:

Food portions/brands:

Treats/when given:

Health Information

Veterinarian and contact info:

Flea/parasite program:

Vaccinations:

Health certificate information:

Detailed health issues and treatments:

Behavior Information

Training experience (see attached obedience class results):

Exercise schedule:

Experience with and response to dogs, cats, kids, adults:

Favorite activities:

Least-favorite activities:

Positive behavior:

Not-so-positive behavior:

Behavior

The chaos, neglect, or abuse in a dog's previous life might have ill equipped her for life in a normal household with you. Even a dog that was always well cared for will need time to adjust to the kaleidoscope of change. Stress can cause dogs to act out when they're in unfamiliar surroundings with unfamiliar people. You might see behaviors you wouldn't see if the dog was feeling more secure.

Another cause of naughtiness during this time is the simple fact that the dog doesn't yet know what's expected, or what to expect. A dog takes her measure of you and of the situation early on. Start setting some ground rules right away. Allowing the dog to jump on you or tear up a pillow today isn't doing her any favors. It's just reinforcing an unwanted behavior that she'll have to unlearn quite soon.

Mistakes are bound to happen. This is the time for superhuman patience and understanding. But everyone will be happier in the long run if you start, gently, showing your pooch what you expect from day one. Don't worry. It will get better with time as your dog settles in.

Bribery Works Wonders

Some dogs are not the least bit food motivated. You could dangle filet mignon in front of them to no avail. But the vast majority of canines respond instantly to the offer of the tiniest treat. You, of course, will exploit that fortunate fact to your full advantage. Now and then, dispense small bits of treats to reward good behavior. (Keep the treats small, about the size of a peanut so as not to cause weight gain.) This helps your dog begin to see you as not only a fun, friendly type, but also as a reliable food source. Don't you appreciate friends and family who are reliable? So does your pooch.

Some people feel that using food is cheating—that you're bribing your dog to like you. If that is cheating, your dog doesn't care. She's perfectly happy to be manipulated in such a delightful way. She feels right and normal, because it's part of wild canine behavior. The pack leader is a food provider, often bringing home a kill to share with the family.

And of course the treats are accompanied and bolstered by a deep, strong relationship that you'll build in a thousand other ways. It's a win-win situation.

On Best Behavior

It might be months before you really "meet" your new dog. Sometimes it takes that long for her true personality to surface. At first, dogs in an unfamiliar environment might be on their best behavior. As they grow more comfortable they might start testing you and the rest of the family, including other pets, to see where the boundaries lie. Don't be surprised if, after your pooch has had a few good meals and some time to relax, she starts to let down her hair and get feistier. Prepare for this with fair rules that you enforce gently and consistently from the start.

Professional Training, the Sooner the Better

Right away, a good professional trainer can help you evaluate the dog's temperament and guide you through effective training. See chapter 8, pp. 145–146, for tips on finding a qualified trainer. You might have to stretch your budget to pay for group classes or private lessons, but in the long run, it's worth it, saving you heartaches and headaches.

Vets Are Doctors, Not Trainers

Don't assume a veterinarian can correctly diagnose a dog's temperament. Most are not behaviorists, and they must focus more on the dog's physical needs and condition than on her behavior. Also, many dogs behave quite differently in the vet's office than they do elsewhere, because they feel intimidated.

The Wacky Attack

When a dog needs to pee or poop, but doesn't know how to tell you, she might get hyper, noisy, and destructive. If your pooch suddenly seems to go berserk, take her outside for a potty break, even if you just took her out half an hour ago. You might be surprised at how fast her wacky attack disappears.

THEY KNOW WHEN YOU'RE ON THE PHONE

It's uncanny but true that your dog knows when you're on the phone. She either wants you to get off, and does everything she can think of to get your attention—including pulling the covers off your bed or gnawing on your ankle—or she takes the opportunity of your distraction to sneak off to another room and devour that houseplant she's been eyeing. To avoid wrecking your phone life, set up controlled training situations. When you have a few free moments, pretend to talk on the phone, and correct your dog for the misbehavior while you continue talking. That way the dog knows that your being on the phone does not mean that you won't correct her.

Safety

Perhaps the single most important thing you can do for your new friend in need is to pooch-proof your house and yard. Dogproofing and childproofing have a lot in common. Dogs, like children, are very good at getting themselves injured by doing things you would never imagine. Your job is to imagine and prepare.

As soon as you possibly can, evaluate your property and lifestyle for hazards. See chapter 2, p. 15, and chapter 10, pp. 198–199, for safety checklists. Even in those first couple of days (or in the case of a planned adoption, *before* you bring the dog home), you can start ensuring your dog's long-term safety in the following ways.

Preventing Escapes

The common canine penchant for roaming is a top hazard. Just like people, many dogs like to get out and see the world. This is no reflection on your dog's love for you; it's just a dog thing. Most will try to get out if they can. Some are regular Houdinis. All face severe threats to life and limb when they are out on their own.

Your first couple of days together could be the time when your dog is most likely to try to leave. It's strange but true that no matter how bad her life was before she met you, the dog might try to go back to it, just because it was more familiar. Even if you're giving the dog heaven on earth, she might be too confused to appreciate it right now.

Your job is to be her benevolent jailer, for the dog's own good. Roaming dogs very often and very quickly become dead dogs.

Securing the Yard
Fences
A surprising number of dogs are able to climb or jump to the top of a fence. They hold on with their paws, and use upper-body strength to actually vault to the other side—and they are out.

Make sure your fence is at least six feet tall. If your dog is particularly large or motivated, you should have an even taller fence. Some dogs can easily climb a wire or chain-link fence. A board fence is slick and discourages them.

To prevent your dog from jumping over a board fence, cut two-by-fours into one-foot lengths—enough to space one every few feet along the whole top of the fence. Nail one end of each into the top rail. Using thin, flexible wire or plastic cable ties, attach chicken wire (or other small-gauge link fence material) to the two-by-fours and the top rail to create a barrier that your dog will hit if she tries to jump out.

On a chain-link or wire fence, you can install the type of angled posts that are normally used for barbed wire at the top of a fence. They slip over the existing posts of a chain-link fence. Instead of barbed wire, however, use chicken wire (or similar material). If you want a ninety degree angle on the posts, you might opt to get smaller fence posts, bend them yourself, and attach them with wire or screws to the existing posts.

"Invisible" electric fences work well only if you have an existing physical fence and a large one-half-acre (minimum) yard. Without a physical fence there is nothing to stop stray dogs, children, delivery people, and letter carriers from entering your property. Your dog is at their mercy, and she might bite to protect her territory. Or, if the yard is too small, such as a yard in a standard fifty-foot-by-one-hundred-foot lot (the house and garage take up most of the area), the dog might panic, thinking the yard itself is zapping her. The dog could then become destructive to the outside of the house, trying to "escape" inside.

Digging Out
Many dogs love to escape and love to dig. Bad combination. But there are preventive methods.

Ideally, if you are putting up a new fence, first pour concrete two to four feet below ground, and four feet into the yard, all the way around the perimeter. This can be quite pricey. A cheaper method is to sink prefab cement board vertically to those depths. Even less expensive is to install chicken wire or another stiff wire fence material (with one-half-inch to one-inch holes so that your dog can't get a claw stuck in it) all along the perimeter, attached to the fence with pieces of wire. You can either dig and bury it vertically to a two-foot or four-foot depth, or lay it on the surface horizontally at those widths and cover it with dirt, bark material, or landscaping. Yet another option is to use composite rolled roofing that comes in a three-foot width, and slip it under the fence, laying it horizontally on the ground. You may cover this, too, with dirt, bark, or landscaping. Its sandpapery, abrasive surface discourages digging paws or ripping mouths.

Securing the House
Make sure all doors and gates shut and lock securely.

Fix broken screens and windowpanes.

Do not leave windows open if a dog can jump or climb out of them.

CONSIDER THE CRATE

One quick and easy way to keep a dog safe is by using a crate to confine her when you can't supervise. While the dog's in her crate, not much harm can come to her. See chapter 8, pp. 153–156, for guidance on crate use and training.

DOGGIE DAY CARE

At these places, your pooch is a pampered guest enjoying playtimes, cuddles, and treats until you finish with work or errands. Though not cheap, doggie day-care facilities have become a popular option for owners who are away from home for long hours.

Dogproofing Your Home

Dogs have been severely hurt, even killed, because new adopters or rescuers didn't realize they needed to dogproof their homes as they would childproof for a youngster. Here are some tips to help:

Make electrical cords impossible for the dog to reach.

Keep the toilet seat down. Water dogs love to drink it and play splash all over the place—highly unsanitary. Little dogs can even drown.

Lock your cupboards with childproof latches.

Store vitamins and medications in secure, out-of-reach cupboards. The sound of pills when you take yours might make your pooch think it can have "candy" too.

Keep all garbage including plastic bags, aluminum foil, food wrappers, all recyclables, and food waste in a secure bin with a latch, in an area inaccessible to your pooch. Ingesting trash can kill a dog.

Remove candy and nuts from the coffee table and all accessible spots—they can be toxic. At trick-or-treat time, your dog might find your child's stash, consuming the entire six pounds . . . wrappers and all. Put it where your dog can't get to it.

Keep plants out of your dog's reach. Learn which are poisonous, and give them to someone who does not have pets.

Mothballs are poisonous. Dogs eat them. Use cedar instead. They hate the smell.

Make all chemical substances inaccessible—cleaning products, disinfectants, antifreeze, fertilizers, perfumes, hair gels, and more.

Household and hobby glues, paints, needles, and even thread are highly dangerous, often causing pain and death. Keep all these things locked up.

Secure heavy items, such as televisions and pottery, that can fall on your dog.

Things We've Seen Dogs Chew and/or Eat

Knives, rocks, glass, dentures, priceless antiques, carpeting, sanitary napkins, pens and pencils, combs and brushes, books, flashlights, cell phones, bars of soap, each other's collars and tags, children's favorite toys, doorframes, doors, pull knobs on dressers, car upholstery, car dashboard, car rearview mirror, lawn irrigation pipes, sprinkler heads, wrought-iron patio furniture, barbed wire.

Safety No-No's

- Never leave a choke collar, prong (pinch) collar, or leash on a dog unattended—anywhere, anytime. These devices can strangle and kill.
- Never tie out a dog in a public place. She can be stolen, abused, or she can bite someone.
- Never allow a stranger to touch your dog without your permission.
- Never allow anyone to do harm to your dog. That includes friends, relatives, groomers, veterinarians, trainers, pet sitters, and everyone else.
- Never trust repair workers, pool maintenance staff, gardeners, house cleaners, meter readers, or any other visitors to shut and lock doors and gates. Be there to monitor the situation yourself, or arrange for a trusted family member, friend, or neighbor to do so. Or confine the dog to a crate if the time period is short enough, or board her.
- Never allow a dog walker or trainer to take your dog out until the person demonstrates his or her expertise, and until you confirm the individual's background and experience.
- Never allow a child to walk your dog unless the child is old enough, strong enough, and experienced enough to handle her.
- Never allow your dog unsupervised freedom around a swimming pool, empty or full.
- Never remove the leash in off-leash areas unless your dog is under voice control.
- Never allow your dog to eat garbage, pieces of food, or anything encountered in public without your express permission.
- Never feed your dog spoiled food thinking that dogs' systems can handle it. They can't.
- Never leave a dog in a car without adequate ventilation, water, and plenty of shade. Be aware that open windows might allow your dog to escape, or strangers to harm her. It's better to leave the dog at home.
- Never leave two dogs alone together if they don't get along 1,000 percent. Confine separately in comfortable quarters (use crates, gates, and closed doors).
- Never leave a nonneutered male and nonspayed female alone and unsupervised by a knowledgeable person—you'll soon have one to fourteen new pups!

FOODS YOUR DOG MUST AVOID

Most real animal bones are not recommended for dogs.

Chocolate contains theobromine, which is toxic to dogs. Especially dangerous is dark or unsweetened baking chocolate.

Corncobs can be deadly to dogs, as they are not digestible and can cause intestinal blockages.

Raisins, onions, and alcohol are toxic.

Antifreeze is not a food, but many dogs think it is because of its sweet taste. The problem is that even in small amounts spilled on the garage floor, it can be lethal.

If Your Dog Is Lost

As a precaution, take photos of your dog as soon as possible after her rescue or adoption.

Make up a "Lost" flyer to have on hand so that you can post copies quickly in case the dog escapes. If your dog is missing, use these guidelines.

Call friends and family to help with a two-mile-radius search.

Ask neighbors and local postal workers and delivery drivers to be on the lookout.

Go to all local animal shelters and rescue facilities to search their kennels personally. Phoning them is not enough.

File a lost dog report with all animal agencies in your area.

If your local animal facility provides blank lost dog posters, get a copy. Posters increase your chances of finding your dog by 200 percent. Place them at high-visibility areas—grocery stores, gas stations, dog parks—but always get permission to post first.

To make your own poster, include the following information (use large, black letters):

- clear, recent photo of your dog
- dog's name
- breed or mix of breeds and description of colors and markings
- description of collars, harnesses, scars, injuries
- location or cross streets, date, and time the dog was discovered to be missing
- your phone numbers in prominent lettering

When you and your dog are reunited, remove all the posters you put up.

HOLIDAY HAZARDS YOUR DOG THINKS IT LIKES

Aluminum foil, electric cords and wires, plastic food wrap, turkey leg baking twine, tinsel and ornaments, Christmas tree needles and tree water, holly and mistletoe berries, Halloween candy (especially chocolate), poinsettias

Please note: Swallowing twine, string, or thread of *any* kind can kill a dog. It can get wound up and choke off the intestines.

HOLIDAY PET SAFETY TIPS

Christmas trees should be anchored to walls with fishing line.

Burning candles should be inaccessible to dogs.

Fourth of July and New Year's Eve fireworks can be frightening, and many dogs try to escape from their homes. Keep dogs under close supervision on those nights.

Halloween means ringing doorbells and trick-or-treaters. Isolate dogs from the front door and the scary costumes. Keep track of where your trick-or-treater leaves that bag of candy. Your dog could die from eating it. Also be aware that the Halloween season is a time when wackos are especially prone to stealing and using animals in torture rituals, so keep pets indoors or under close supervision for a month surrounding that date.

For as long as man continues to be the ruthless destroyer of lower living beings, he will never know health or peace. For as long as men massacre animals, they will kill each other. Indeed, he who sows the seeds of murder and pain cannot reap joy and love.

—Pythagoras

Emergency and Disaster Planning

Prepare now to ensure that your dog is safe during a large-scale disaster. Whether it's a fire, earthquake, hurricane, flood, or tornado, planning ahead is the most important thing you can do to save lives in case the worst happens.

- Your dog must wear her ID at all times.
- Arrange a buddy system with a neighbor, so that you will assist each other's animals in case one of you is not home during an emergency.
- Check with your city or county about a public disaster program. It might include a pet evacuation plan in conjunction with local animal control authorities.
- Put a sticker on your front window or door telling how many pets are inside.
- Home Escape Route: Make sure your four-legged family members are capable of exiting your house from whichever door or window is in your plan.
- Never leave your dog behind. Dogs can become trapped, or escape into dangerous situations.
- Research the following: friends, relatives, motels, or hotels outside your area that allow dogs, as well as shelters, veterinary hospitals, and boarding kennels that might accept dogs during a disaster evacuation.
- At the first sign of a pending disaster (storms, flooding), bring your dog indoors.

In Case of Emergency: Dog Supply Kit

Dog first-aid kit (see chapter 6, pp. 77–78)

Unbreakable food and water bowls

Enough bottled water to last seven days (renewed periodically for freshness)

Enough dry food to last seven days (renewed every two or three months for freshness)

Medications that your dog requires (also renewed to maintain freshness)

Extra collars, leashes, harnesses, ID tags

Blankets

Plastic garbage bags and paper towels for cleanup

Crate or carrier

Dog bed or soft sleeping surface

Chews and toys

Proof of vaccination and other important medical records

Photos of your dog for identification purposes

Creating a Happy Family

You've given the dog some time and space to decompress. Now you can start building good relationships between the dog and other family members, including other pets.

Building Relationships with Human Family Members

Gradually let human family members interact more with the new addition. Avoid mob situations where the pooch can feel overwhelmed. Try introducing just a couple of family members at a time. For the first few days, limit visits to household members so that the dog can understand who her family actually is. Ask all to be calm, quiet, and patient.

Take things at the dog's pace. If she's shy and reticent, don't push. Have people sit down and read a book or watch TV. When the dog shows interest in interaction, use a soft voice and a light touch. If, on the other paw, the dog is spunky and wants to play, go right ahead—but use a toy to focus her energy, and don't wrestle or roughhouse.

Take special care to instruct children on all the ground rules. (See sidebar below.)

GROUND RULES FOR GETTING TO KNOW A NEW DOG

Do not hurt the dog in any way, shout, stare at her in the eyes, bend over the top of her body, put your face near her face, play roughly, try to take things away from her, bother the dog while she's sleeping, bother her in her crate, bother her while she's eating or enjoying a chew or a toy. When you get to know the dog better, you might be able to ease up on these restrictions, but for now it's best to err on the side of caution.

Do treat the dog with kindness, respect, fairness, and consistency; respond happily when she seeks you out; remember that she is a dog, with doggie needs and motivations.

Toddlers and small children move and squeal and grab and even bite—just like prey. They can be extremely mean to a dog without realizing it. I have worked in the vet field long enough to find pencils pushed into a dog's ear canal so deeply that they went undetected until autopsy after the bite! So, if you have children it is your job to educate and constantly supervise when they are with the dog. Dogs cannot run to Mom and tattle. They try to get away, but their only final defense is a growl or bite. Don't ever forget this. Many dogs destroyed every year were innocent victims of uneducated child abuse.
—Rita Martinez, CPDT, Rescues Are Special

Building Relationships with Canine Family Members

If this was a planned adoption, your dogs met before you brought the newbie home (see pp. 27–28). In an unplanned rescue, perhaps you haven't yet made the introduction. In either case, the parties in question don't know each other very well.

Think of the introduction as a long-term process. In most cases, dogs won't immediately and forever get along perfectly. A healthy relationship needs time to grow, and requires give and take on both sides.

Unplanned Rescue:
Toward the end of the first forty-eight hours, you might go ahead and make the initial introduction, following the guidelines in chapter 3, pp. 27–28. Then proceed as described below for a planned adoption.

Planned Adoption:
Although your dogs met before you adopted the newcomer, you've since allowed her some quiet downtime in your home.

Continue to keep them separate. You can use the confinement methods described in chapter 4, p. 48.

Take lots of leashed walks together, if possible with one adult per dog. While on walks, dogs are a lot more interested in what's around them than in each other. It's a way to get them accustomed to just being together and sharing a fun experience, without the pressure of having to figure out one another's intentions and motivations.

After a few walks, go into the house together, and spend a few supervised minutes letting the dogs interact, still on leash. Focus their attention on you by playing games (see the sidebar "Pack Order Games—Taking Turns," p. 70).

When you have time to supervise, stage more interactions at home. Don't attempt this at high-excitement times of the day, like just before meals, exercise, or when household members are departing or arriving. One of the best times is after exercise, when both dogs are tired. Try to recruit an adult helper to have both dogs on leash, one person per dog. If you don't have a helper, tie one dog to a stationary object, and keep the other on leash. Play games as before.

The longer you keep up this gradual introduction process, the better. It builds trust between your dogs. If things go well, you can begin to drop (but don't remove) the leashes during supervised interactions. Next step, remove the leashes, still supervising.

When both dogs seem completely relaxed around each other, you can bring them together for longer and longer periods of time, with or without leashes. But for a very long time, you should follow these precautions:

- *Do not* leave the dogs alone together, not even for a few minutes in the living room while you go to the kitchen.

- Feed them in separate areas, at least ten feet apart, and supervise. Pick up food bowls as soon as they finish. Don't leave them alone with valuable items such as chews and toys that inspire disagreements.
- Be especially watchful of any "real estate" that either dog considers especially valuable—perhaps the kitchen, your bedroom, the dining table, a window with a view of the street, or even just a sunny patch on the floor. One dog might have no clue that she has "trespassed" when the other dog suddenly attacks her.

Most important, show your dogs that you are a strong and reliable leader. You set fair rules and enforce them. You will not let anyone in your pack get bullied or hurt. Your original dog will see that her new friend is not a threat to her, to her territory, or to you. Your new dog will see that she has a secure, valued place in your family, and that you will help the dog maintain it.

PACK ORDER: GET STARTED ON THE RIGHT PAW

Wild canine families are not democratic, but they are remarkably well organized and fair. Each member has a rank and a role in the social hierarchy. As long as everyone acknowledges and respects the ranking, the group can function smoothly to obtain food, raise young, and take care of all its members.

To create harmony, you can set up this logical pack order among your dogs too. You are the pack leader. Next below you is the dog that was there first, then the dog that came second, and so on.

Please note: Different trainers have different opinions and some no longer use pack order in their training techniques. Your best approach is to research a variety of training methods and find what works for your dog and household.

Demonstrate the ranking by *always* giving the top dog everything first—meals, treats, toys, walks, potty breaks, playing, affection—everything. Then the second dog gets things second, and the third gets things third, and so on if (heaven help you) you have more dogs.

Humans might feel this is unfair or even cruel to the lower-ranking pooches, but to the dogs it's not. They want to know where they stand. Guessing causes anxiety and conflict. Pack members who don't know their relative positions in the hierarchy often have to duke it out to decide. Save them the trouble, and create a strong, confident group.

Family and friends might ask, "Why don't you just let them work it out for themselves?" That's a splendid idea if you enjoy watching your dogs fight and paying the vet to patch them up.

Pack Order Games—Taking Turns

Take Turns for Treats: With your dogs assembled, hold a bag of treats and give a command such as "sit," "down," or "stand." As soon as the pooches comply, give each praise and a treat, but in specific pack order, starting with the highest-ranking member, going down to the lowest. This game clearly illustrates ranking to your dogs, so that they can see just where they stand. It's also a shared, fun activity. And it shows them that they can enjoy treats side by side.

Take Turns for Toys: Assemble your dogs at an equal distance away from you—just a few feet. Toss a toy to the top-ranking dog. Say her name and, "Catch." Praise the dog if she catches the toy, then take it from the dog (using the "drop it" command, if she knows it), toss it to the next ranking dog, and go through the same procedure. Repeat several times over days or weeks. This game again clearly illustrates ranking to your pooch, and it gets them used to the idea of sharing toys and other "valuable" objects.

TIPS FOR A MULTIDOG HOUSEHOLD

Now and then give your established dog special outings, just the two of you. It provides a break from the newcomer and reinforces the first dog's bond with you. Take her to her favorite places, such as the dog park or pet store.

Do the same for the new dog to give her a chance to bond more closely with you, while not having to worry about displeasing the established dog.

Once in a while, when the established dog will not notice, sneak extra treats and attention to the newbie to build and maintain her confidence.

Make sure the established dog sees that you value the newbie. Although you give attention, treats, and everything else to the established dog first, never skimp on anything for the new dog. Let the established dog see you pet the new dog, praise her, and give her treats.

Don't let either dog horn in roughly when you're giving attention to the other. Gently but firmly instruct the other dog to sit and stay at a polite distance until her turn comes.

Building Relationships with Feline Family Members

Introducing your new dog safely and successfully to your established cat depends on the dog's level of prey drive. This instinct allows canines to survive in the wild and can be hard to shake. In the case of a planned adoption, you screened your new pooch for cat interaction before you brought it home. In the case of an unplanned rescue, you didn't have that luxury. In either case, you might try the following procedure. Stop if you begin to sense that your rescue is highly aggressive toward the cat. And *never* leave them alone together until you're certain it's safe.

Place Kitty in her carrier, high on a table. Put Fido on leash, give him treats, and walk him around the room where Kitty can see that you control him. Do a few simple training exercises, such as teaching him to sit or lie down, to further demonstrate to Kitty that you're in complete control of this big, hairy monster.

An adult helper holds Fido's leash, or you tie him to a stationary object fifteen to twenty feet away from Kitty. Feed Kitty her favorite treat and chat about nice Fido. Go to Fido and do the same, chatting about nice Kitty. Repeat several times over days or weeks.

An adult helper wraps Kitty in a thick towel, while she has access to something she loves such as tuna or shrimp. You enter with Fido on leash. Have him sit about fifteen to twenty feet away from Kitty, and feed him something he loves. Chat calmly with your helper while the animals eat. Repeat several times.

Slide your fingers inside Fido's mouth over his gums and let Kitty smell your fingers. Do the same with Kitty. Run your hand over each of their bodies, then let them each smell your hand in turn. Repeat several times.

Let Kitty loose in the room, lured and entertained by food. Keep Fido on leash. Always keep yourself or another human between the two animals. Repeat several times.

With this seemingly odd and time-consuming set of exercises, you can accustom each pet to the other's presence from a safe distance, where neither gets too excited. It also gives them positive experiences together. Eventually, still using these controlled situations, you can bring the animals closer and closer to each other, until their mutual comfort level rises high enough for safety.

Ultimately, however, success will depend on the dog's prey drive. We have to accept that some pooches just aren't cut out to be friendly to felines.

Caution: Kitty might object strenuously to being wrapped in a towel. You might have to eliminate that step and keep her in her carrier until she seems comfortable enough to be allowed loose in the room without being either fearful of or aggressive toward Fido.

BEWARE OF KITTY CLAWS

When canine meets feline, it's not always the dog that attacks. Some cats, because of fear or past experiences, really have it in for dogs. The results can be tragic. With one swipe of a cat claw to a dog eye, the dog can be blinded for life. For both animals' sakes, make sure their relationship is harmonious before you allow free interaction.

Protect yourself during their encounters too. If Kitty scratches or bites, you can develop a life-threatening infection. Consult a doctor *immediately*.

Ralphie.

Happily Ever After True Story Number Five:

Ralphie

Sylwia Luttrell was driving to the park with her dog, Ralphie, who was lying in the backseat of the car. The day was warm so all the windows were rolled down. Up ahead, the light turned red, so Sylwia slowed to a stop. Out of nowhere a strange man ran up to her car and grabbed the door handle as if to climb inside. Sylwia was paralyzed with fear. In that moment, she couldn't even muster a scream. Then Ralphie leaped up from behind her, lunging and barking at the

man. The man ran off and Ralphie settled down. But Sylwia was so unnerved that she turned the car around and headed home. Once there, she hugged Ralphie with all her strength. "Poor guy," Sylwia remembered. "He would have preferred the park to being squeezed by me."

When Sylwia told her husband, Dan, about the incident, he was thrilled. Dan is an airline pilot, which keeps him away for up to six days at a time. Knowing that Ralphie is at home and has made it his job to protect Sylwia, Dan finds much-needed peace of mind.

"And to think we were not even supposed to adopt him," said Sylwia. After immigrating to the United States from Poland, Sylwia met Dan in New York City. Although he was based in New York and loved living in Manhattan, Dan also owned a home in Palm Springs, California. So, once Dan and Sylwia were married, they made a point of spending a few weeks each year in the desert. Even in Palm Springs, Dan still had to work, so instead of sitting around missing Dan or the excitement of the city, Sylwia began volunteering for the local animal shelter, walking and socializing the dogs.

One day she was assigned to visit with a dog that had been brought in the previous day. The border collie/Bernese mountain dog mix was found in a parking lot of a grocery store belonging to the Ralph's supermarket chain. "The shelter staff named him 'Ralphie,'" said Sylwia. "He was in pretty bad shape. They kept him in the front offices because he was so shy and scared, and his rear leg seemed lame. That day I could not walk him because all he wanted to do was sleep." Sylwia sat with Ralphie, just petting and talking to him.

After a few days, Sylwia agreed to foster Ralphie for two weeks, so he could regain his strength and his confidence, which would make him an adoptable dog. But he was so weak and so fearful, he could not even walk to Sylwia's car.

A kennel attendant carried him and laid him down on the backseat.

"The first three days, all Ralphie did was sleep. When I was able to put a leash on him, it was clear he had no idea what it was. And he was so scared of everything—fast movements, brooms, golf clubs—anything that looked like a stick."

At the vet's, Sylwia learned that Ralphie was suffering from an old injury to his rear leg, and that it might never heal properly. But after having watched Ralphie begin to "blossom," as Sylwia said, she knew this dog would never be happy unless he could run and play. So each day she and Dan massaged Ralphie's hind leg, gently drawing out the pain and replacing it with their belief that this dog could be whole again.

Two weeks later, the Luttrells were scheduled to return to New York, and neither of them was ready to let Ralphie go. They considered every option they could imagine: fly Ralphie back east so he could live with Sylwia's mother in New Jersey, smuggle him into their five-hundred-square-foot apartment in Manhattan, or sell their apartment and move to a bigger one. Then came an unexpected turn of events.

Sylwia, a lawyer in Poland, had to get a law degree in the United States before she could practice in this country. She had applied to universities in New York City, as well as to one in Southern California. That week, there in the mailbox, was an acceptance letter from University of California, San Diego. "It's true," Sylwia said with a smile, "we left New York City for Ralphie."

Looking at Ralphie, whose black coat glistens with health and who now runs like an athlete, Sylwia wishes that she could find the people who abandoned Ralphie and show them what a wonderful dog he is. "Ralphie is a treasure. I don't understand how someone hurts a dog to the point where he is so scared and sick. I look at him now, and see how smart and handsome he is." Once a tired, frightened animal in the backseat of a stranger's car, now Ralphie is a sleek, highly trained, and confident dog who proudly owns that backseat. The dangerous man who tried to hurt Sylwia while she was stopped at a traffic light might never forget the magnificent canine that Ralphie has become.

6.
Urgent Health Needs of Rescued Dogs

Everything You Always Needed to Know but Were Too Panicked to Ask: How to Spot and Handle Health Emergencies

Kellie: So, This Is My Veterinarian

Mom (the lady who takes care of me) wants me to get into the car. But what about my breakfast? If I get in, my breakfast will come out. The car starts moving, and I feel sick. Now I'm inside a room that smells like a million dogs . . . and cats! Just show me the kitties! A man wearing a white coat looks down at me. Now he feels my chest. He presses on my tummy. What's that? Is something being inserted into . . . yikes! Remain calm. I am a calm dog. Now Mom is wrapping her arms around me and speaking very gently. This can't be good. The man has something in his hand. It's behind my head. Hey, what just stung me? And now everyone is smiling and telling me how wonderful I am. Not the car again! When the car finally stops and Mom opens the door, I can't hold it down anymore. If the car wanted my breakfast that bad, he can have it!

Rescued dogs have no more or fewer health issues than purchased dogs, but there can be differences because of their previous experiences and care. It's vitally important that all dogs receive a veterinary exam, vaccinations, and any necessary treatment as soon as possible after rescue.

In this chapter you'll find information on some life-threatening situations and conditions, including tips on prevention. In chapter 7, you'll find advice for dealing with some of the more common, longer-term maladies. If your dog has a set of symptoms you don't find in this chapter, make sure to read on to the next.

Please note: The symptoms listed are just possibilities. Your dog might exhibit none of the symptoms discussed or might have different ones. Almost all of the ailments discussed below are extremely dangerous and *require urgent veterinary care*. First aid should be given only as a temporary measure, if necessary, while you arrange to get to the vet. This chapter is an initial guide to help you prepare for emergencies. It is not intended as a diagnostic reference or treatment plan or as a substitute for immediate veterinary attention.

> One of the reasons we rescue things is to feel a sense of control that we may not really have in our own lives. If we can save something, maybe then we can do anything.
>
> —Ken Foster, from *The Dogs Who Found Me*

HEALTH WARNING CLUES

Unfortunately, dogs can't tell us where they hurt—at least, not in words. But they do sometimes give us clues, and it's our job to watch for them. If possible, do a hands-on, nose-to-tail check of your rescued pooch, and relay anything you find to your veterinarian. Be alert for the following health warning signs.

Physical Clues

Eyes—discharge, film, cloudiness, redness, inflammation, excessive blinking, shying away from light, pawing at eyes, rubbing eyes on the floor or furniture

Ears—swollen or red ear interior, insect bites on flaps, shaking head, scratching or pawing at ears, rubbing them on the ground or furniture, unusual odor

Nose—discharge, swelling, difficulty breathing, change in pigment or color

Mouth—redness or swelling of gums or lips, bad breath

Teeth—yellow, brown, or black; cracked, broken, or missing

Skin—redness, rawness, inflammation, itching, insect bites, growths, bald spots

Coat—dull, lackluster, greasy, sparse patches or bald spots, dandruff

Weight—unusual loss or gain

Stomach/intestinal—bloated abdomen, passing gas, vomiting, arched back or tight, pulled-in abdomen (indicating pain); change in frequency, amount, or consistency of bowel movement, including diarrhea or constipation; blood in stool

Urinary—change in frequency, amount, or duration of urination; blood in urine

Skeletal/muscular—limping, weakness of legs or back

Respiratory—coughing, sneezing, gagging, labored breathing, discharge

Neurological—tics, twitching, unusual eye movements, head tilt, walking in circles, difficulty walking, passing out

General—growths or lumps; change in breathing rate, pulse, or temperature

Behavioral Clues

Change in appetite—increase or decrease

Lethargy, low energy level, or exercise intolerance

Restlessness, agitation

Excessive scratching, munching, or licking of skin

Excessive licking of lips

Excessive panting

Yelps or whimpers of distress or pain

Unusual aggression

Unusual fearfulness

PUREBREDS VERSUS MIXED BREEDS

A *purebred* dog is one whose ancestors for many generations have been of the same breed. A *mixed breed* dog is one whose parents are from different breeds or who are themselves from mixed breeds.

Buying a purebred from a breeder by no means ensures you will have a healthy pet. Time after time, people pay hundreds or even thousands of dollars for a puppy, only to get him home and realize that he is ill, or to find later that he has congenital defects such as hip dysplasia or corneal dystrophy of the eye.

Some veterinarians believe that mixed-breed dogs are generally healthier than purebreds because their gene pool is more varied. Others argue that, statistically, there is no appreciable difference.

For certain, we know that mixed-breed dogs carry broader genetic diversity than purebreds. A richer gene pool can prevent inheritance of defective genes and thus allow for better health. Purebred dogs might be at higher risk for inheriting defective genes. These can include bone, joint, bleeding, and neurological disorders; cancers and tumors; and diseases of the eye, heart, skin, and immune system.

Further, the harsh body characteristics often found in purebreds are softened in mixed breeds. Such characteristics can be the cause of health issues. For example, the foreshortened snouts of boxers, Pekingese, and Shih Tzus

impede proper breathing. The exaggerated body length of dachshunds can cause ruptured spinal discs. The dwarf legs of basset hounds can mean limited mobility.

Ultimately, however, it's the luck of the draw. Adopting a mixed breed is no guarantee against health issues. The important question is whether you are prepared to commit to your dog emotionally and financially and to address all of his health needs in a caring, responsible way.

Dealing with Emergencies— Get Prepared

When rescuing a dog, you are sometimes faced right away with an emergency. Perhaps you see a pooch hit by a car or one that is bleeding heavily or one that is lying listlessly on the pavement on a scorchingly hot day. Even if you have rescued a dog under calmer circumstances—for example, if you have adopted from a shelter—at some point during the dog's lifetime you will probably encounter an urgent health situation.

Your best bet for dealing with emergencies is a well-stocked first-aid kit and some basic knowledge about dealing with a variety of situations. For example, do you know how to staunch a wound that won't stop bleeding? Move a dog who is severely injured? Save him from poisoning or heat stroke?

The information that follows can help you be a better-prepared dog rescuer and owner, one who knows how to assess urgent situations, ascertain what action must be taken, administer first aid, and understand when to seek immediate professional help.

Create a First-Aid Kit

To deal with emergencies, a first-aid kit is essential. Gather tools and supplies in an easily portable, water-resistant bag or box. Keep it in a spot in your home that is cool, dark, and inaccessible to pets and children, yet easy for you to grab in a matter of seconds. Check quantities and expiration dates on a regular basis to keep the kit fully stocked and fresh. A basic kit should include the following items:

Tools

Muzzle—one that comfortably and reliably fits your dog. If you think you might be muzzling dogs other than your own, perhaps in emergency rescue situations, consider keeping on hand extra gauze or a couple of pantyhose legs that you have cut from the pantyhose, to use on a one-size-fits-all basis (see the sidebars on muzzling, pp. 79-80.)

Latex gloves

Scissors with rounded tips

Splints in a variety of sizes

Ace bandages

Ear aspirator

Eye dropper

Rectal thermometer (preferably digital and plastic)

Tweezers

Tick remover

Supplies

Nonstick sterile gauze pads

Sterile stretch gauze

Cloth tape

Roll of sterile cotton or Dacron

Porous adhesive or elastic tape such as Elastikon

Telfa pads or similar product

Vet wrap (self-adhering stabilizing wrap for injured limbs)

Alcohol wipes

Emergency cold packs and warm packs

Blanket

Plastic bags

Medications and Substances

Isopropyl alcohol

Povidone-iodine product such as Betadine Scrub and Solution

Hydrogen peroxide, 3 percent

Bicarbonate of soda (baking soda)

K-Y Jelly or petroleum jelly such as Vaseline (to insert thermometer)

Antibiotic ointment

Eye wash such as Opticlear

Normal saline—one to two liters or quarts (for wounds and burns)

Sterile water (available at pharmacies)—one or two liters or quarts

Ascriptin (for pain)

Activated charcoal tablets (in case of poisoning)

Benadryl (to alleviate allergic reaction)

Antidiarrhea medication such as Kaopectate or Immodium

Hydrocortisone cream, 0.5 percent or 1 percent strength (to relieve skin irritation and itching)

Biocaine Lotion (to treat wounds, abrasions, minor burns)

Styptic product such as Kwik Stop (to stop bleeding while nail clipping)

Know Your Dog

Get to know your dog's vital signs *before* an emergency strikes. Learn what's normal for your particular pooch so that you will be able to recognize what's abnormal. During the veterinary exam, ask your vet to show you how to check your dog's heart rate (pulse), respiratory rate, an estimate of blood pressure called capillary refill time, temperature, gum color, and whether the dog is dehydrated.

Keep medical records current with up-to-date documentation of all vaccinations, health conditions, treatment, medications, and weight.

Post the phone number of your veterinarian and the nearest emergency vet clinic in an easily spotted place in your home.

Give your dog daily exercise, plenty of water, and a wholesome diet. Just like humans, physically robust dogs deal best with health crises, healing better and faster.

Know What to Do

Most homeless dogs encounter a wide range of dangers. They must navigate car traffic, cope with extremes in weather, and try to avoid hostile humans, aggressive dogs, wildlife, and poison. Sometimes, even owned dogs meet with mishap.

Arming yourself with basic first-aid knowledge for a variety of situations can empower you to remain calm and focused. Here are some of the most important things you need to know about helping a pooch in crisis.

Caution: *Never* try to administer first aid to a dog until you protect yourself against biting (see the sidebars "Beware of Injured Dogs," below, and "To Muzzle or Not to Muzzle," p. 79).

BEWARE OF INJURED DOGS

Even the sweetest dog in the world might bite when in pain or distress. And an injured dog might be in a dangerous environment that threatens you too. Before attempting to help, protect yourself. You will be of no use to the dog if you get hurt.

If it's your own dog in severe pain or distress, consider muzzling him as described in the sidebar "An Emergency Muzzle," pp. 79–80. If you're dealing with an unfamiliar dog, try to contact local animal services or the police or fire departments. When no such help is available, remember that you are taking a risk by approaching an injured dog. Even a seemingly immobile dog can bite and do a lot of damage when stressed and panicked.

For an unfamiliar dog, again, proceed with extreme caution. If the dog seems relaxed, friendly, and not fearful, you might be able to safely administer basic first aid. You might also opt to muzzle him. But remember that you could get bitten just in the process of muzzling. Also there might be other dangers. Whatever has hurt the dog might hurt you; for example, car traffic, fire, or bad weather. Put your own safety first.

If you feel that the dog might bite or that there's some other risk to yourself, you might decide not to intervene. *Do not feel guilty!* Again, getting yourself hurt will not help the dog or anyone else. In a situation that seems too risky, it's best to err on the side of caution and keep trying to enlist the help of public emergency services. If possible, stay as near to the dog as you can to monitor his condition and follow him if he moves to another location so that you can report it accurately to emergency workers.

Finally, remember that in some cases, sadly, we have to just walk away. This is extremely difficult for kind-hearted people, but sometimes it is the right thing to do.

TO MUZZLE OR NOT TO MUZZLE?

Muzzle a dog if:

- the procedure might be uncomfortable.
- the dog is already unsure and fearful.
- you think there is the slightest chance it will bite.

You might not need to muzzle if:

- you know your relationship is rock solid with mutual trust *and* if the procedure is 100 percent pain-free and if the dog has no anxiety.

Caution: *Do not* muzzle if the dog is coughing, vomiting, experiencing difficulty breathing, or is unconscious.

An emergency muzzle.

AN EMERGENCY MUZZLE

No one likes muzzling, least of all dogs. But sometimes it's a good idea. It won't help either you or the injured dog if it bites you while you're trying to help him.

Try to muzzle early, before you begin any procedures and before the dog figures out what's coming. If you don't have a commercial muzzle, use other materials such as strips of cloth, lengths of gauze bandage, shoelaces, a scarf, a necktie, a leash, or pantyhose. Make a large loop with a single slip or half knot, with the knot at the top of the loop. The loop should be several times wider than the dog's snout, so that you can swiftly slip it into place over its nose and snout. Quickly tighten the knot, so that the dog is immediately unable to open its mouth to bite. Wrap each end of the material around the snout again, firmly, one and a half times, so that the ends are underneath the chin. From there, cross the ends over each other once, and take them back behind the dog's head to just under the ears. Pull tight so that the material can't slip off over the ears. Tie a bow. The dog should be able to breathe freely through his nose but not be able to open his mouth.

Caution: *Do not* muzzle a dog for more than ten minutes at a time. Muzzles inhibit breathing and panting. *Never* leave a muzzled dog unattended. He might frantically try to work off the muzzle and injure himself further. *Do not* muzzle a dog who is coughing, vomiting, experiencing difficulty breathing, or is unconscious.

IF YOU GET BITTEN

Dog bites hurt. The teeth can puncture and rip and the jaws can bruise and crush. It can be emotionally traumatic too. Do everything you can to avoid it. If it happens, though, here's some guidance.

Get yourself and all other humans and pets safely away from the dog.

Attend to your injuries immediately. Get assistance, including first aid and professional medical care. Bites need disinfecting and possibly bandaging or stitches. You might also need antibiotics, other medications, or rabies treatment.

Depending on the severity of the wounds and other factors, recognize that you might go into shock, even though at the moment you feel fine. The adrenaline that your body produced in response to the crisis might be numbing pain and other symptoms. *Do not* assume that you're all right. Seek help and professional medical attention.

If the dog that bit you was a homeless dog in need, summon local authorities to rescue him instead of continuing the effort yourself. Reporting the fact that the dog bit you means that the dog will henceforth be labeled as a biter, perhaps making his future grim, but it also means that you are protecting rescue personnel, shelter workers, and the general public from being bitten themselves—or worse.

Be aware that if he was your own dog that bit you and you report that fact to medical personnel, they are usually required by law to report the bite to local authorities, who might in turn be required to quarantine and/or confiscate your dog.

Chest compression for CPR.

Craig Burleigh Photography

Rescue Breathing and Cardiopulmonary Resuscitation (CPR)

These procedures might be necessary in many emergencies, such as poisoning, shock, head injury, long-lasting seizure, electric shock, or choking, among others.

To determine if rescue breathing or CPR is needed, see if the dog is breathing. Does the chest rise and fall? Hold your cheek near the dog's nose. Can you feel air?

If the dog *is* breathing, pull out the tongue so that the airway is clear.

If the dog is *not* breathing, check for a pulse. Feel for it on the inside of the hind leg, at about the spot where the leg meets the abdomen.

If there is a pulse, perform rescue breathing (see below).

If there is no pulse, perform CPR (see below).

Rescue Breathing
For Dogs under Thirty Pounds and Puppies
First, see if the dog is choking on something. Sweep your fingers side to side in the back of his mouth. If you find an object, grasp and remove it. Also, wipe out any mucus or fluids with a cloth or tissue. Continue with the rescue breathing steps below.

If the object does not come out easily, *do not* try to pry it out or wrap your fingers around behind it. That could make it slide farther down into the throat. Instead, perform the Heimlich maneuver described in this chapter's section on "Choking," p. 82. If breathing does not resume, continue with rescue breathing as follows:

Pull tongue out so that it meets the canine (longest) teeth, then close the mouth.

Put your mouth over as much of the snout as possible, covering the nose and lips. If your mouth can't cover the lips, seal them with your hand around the muzzle to prevent air from leaking out. Gently blow in. Chest should expand.

Remove your mouth to let air come out— important to avoid internal damage.

If the chest does not begin rising and falling, blow harder and make sure you've tightly sealed the lips.

Give twenty to thirty breaths per minute until the dog breathes independently, or for as long as there's a heartbeat.
Large or Medium Dogs
Follow same procedure as above.

Continue giving twenty breaths per minute until breathing is independent, or for as long as there's a heartbeat.

CPR
For Dogs under Thirty Pounds and Puppies
Check for and remove airway obstructions as described above.

Lay dog on a flat surface with the right side of the body downward.

Cup your hands on each side of the rib cage over the heart, just behind the elbow. You'll have to slip one hand underneath the dog to accomplish this. (For puppies, put your thumb on one side and your remaining fingers on the other.)

Squeeze or compress the chest inward to about 25 percent or 30 percent of its width. The compressions should be firm and quick. Do about sixty per minute.

Breathe into the dog's mouth after every eight to ten compressions. (Give the breaths in the manner described in the "Rescue Breathing" section above.) If you have a helper, one of you can do the compressions while the other gives a breath.
For Large and Medium Dogs
Lay the dog on a flat surface with the right side of the body downward.

Kneel close behind the dog's back.

Put the heel of your hand over the widest part of the rib cage. Put your other hand on top of the first. Caution: *Do not put your hands over the heart.*

Keeping your arms and elbows straight, compress or squeeze the rib cage. Push downward to about 25 percent or 30 percent of the chest's width. Compressions should be firm and quick. Do about sixty per minute.

Breathe into the dog's mouth after every eight to ten compressions. (Give the breaths in the manner described in the "Rescue Breathing" section above.) If you have a helper, one of you can do the compressions while the other gives a breath.

For all dog sizes, continue performing CPR until breathing is independent and the pulse is steady. If neither occurs after ten minutes, there is little hope that continuing will be successful.

Caution: Performing CPR can cause internal injuries. But in some cases the benefits outweigh the risks. Also, *never* use a healthy dog to practice CPR.

Heimlich maneuver.

Choking

This occurs when something is caught in the dog's airway.

Symptoms: Pawing at mouth, coughing, or breathing difficulty or distress.

First-aid steps: If the dog is still able to breathe, get him quickly to a vet.

If the dog is unable to breathe and collapses, lay him on his side. Pull his tongue out forward. Sweep your fingers side to side in the back of the mouth till you find the object. Grasp and remove it.

If it does not come out easily, *do not* try to pry it out or wrap your fingers around behind it. That could make it slide farther down into the throat. To get it out, perform the Heimlich maneuver as follows:

Position yourself behind the dog. Extend your arms and hands below his ribs, around the belly. Make a fist with one hand and grasp it with the other. Position them near the middle of the dog's abdomen, just below the breastbone, where the rib cage makes a V shape. Compress inward and upward four times by squeezing quickly, sharply, and forcefully. Sweep the fingers at the back of the mouth to try to remove the object.

If the object is still there, do some rescue breathing. Give five mouth-to-nose breaths. This might dislodge the object by forcing air outward from the throat. Again, sweep the fingers at the back of the mouth to try to remove the object.

If the object remains, try clapping a cupped hand over each side of the dog's chest, or striking a sharp blow between the shoulder blades. Then again, sweep the back of the mouth with your fingers.

If the object has not been removed, perform all the steps above again, until the object comes out.

After it comes out, check the dog's breathing and pulse, and give rescue breathing or CPR, if needed.

Swallowed Foreign Body

Dogs can ingest a variety of foreign bodies that might lodge in the gastrointestinal (digestive) tract, blocking or even perforating it. A blockage can cause vomiting that can lead to aspiration pneumonia, or it can bring abrasion that can lead to irritation, scarring and

YOUR ADOPTED DOG

narrowing of the tract, or eventual perforation. Perforation can quickly bring on infection or death.

Symptoms: Gagging, retching, vomiting, loss of appetite, constipation, cough, fever, shock, weight loss, or possibly no symptoms at all.

Prevention: Keep dog's environment clear of objects that could be swallowed.

First-aid steps: *Do not* give anything by mouth. Record the amount of time between vomiting episodes to report to the vet. Get to a vet immediately.

WHEN A CAR HITS A DOG

Dogs—especially homeless ones—are frequently hit by cars. There can be multiple and severe injuries, such as wounds, broken bones, bleeding, and organ damage.

If you decide to help a dog who has been struck by a car, first remember to keep yourself out of danger. The same car traffic that hit the dog could also hit you. Even being on the shoulder of the road is dangerous. (See chapter 4, pp. 40–41, for more guidance on deciding to help a dog in crisis.)

Prepare yourself emotionally. The scene might not be a pleasant one. There can be grotesque injuries to the dog, and he might be writhing, twitching, or screaming in agony. Or he might jump back on his feet, appearing normal, even while suffering from severe internal damage.

If you decide to help, you must focus on quickly assessing and planning what needs to be done. This is especially difficult if the injured dog is your own.

Here are some questions to guide you:

Do you know where the nearest vet is? If not, how can you find one? As soon as possible, call a veterinarian. Describe the injuries: Is the dog breathing? Losing blood? Is he conscious? This information will help the vet prepare for the dog's arrival.

Is there first-aid care that you can give? Or are the injuries of a type that only the vet can address?

Do you have the proper equipment available to administer the necessary first aid (including a muzzle for the dog)? If not, what other items can you use instead?

Is there anyone available to assist you in helping the dog in need?

Before you act, try to make a basic plan for the situation, thinking through what you'll do. It might have to change as you discover more information, but making a preliminary assessment and plan can reduce and manage the chaos.

Shock

This is a condition in which the body is not receiving adequate blood flow or oxygen. Causes include loss of blood, heart failure, anaphylactic (allergic) reactions, poisoning, and dehydration, among others.

Symptoms: Early signs of shock can be panting, increased heart rate, bright red lips, gums, and tongue. Signs of more advanced shock include slow breathing; weak or no pulse; pale or grayish skin, lips, gums, and tongue; extremities that are cold to your touch; shivering; listlessness; decline in mental alertness; unconsciousness.

First-aid steps: If there is no breathing or heartbeat, perform rescue breathing or CPR as described above.

If the dog is not conscious, check the airway. Clear mucus or other secretions from the mouth using your fingers and cloth or tissue. Gently pull out the tongue so that it goes beyond the front teeth. This makes breathing easier.

Address any underlying causes, such as excessive bleeding, by using appropriate first-aid measures.

Until you get the dog to the vet, keep him warm with a blanket or other covering. Keep the head lower than the body, perhaps by placing a folded blanket or article of clothing under his rear half. Allow the dog to get into his most comfortable position. Keep the dog calm. Reassure him with your voice and touch.

DEHYDRATION AND STARVATION

Dogs trying to fend for themselves can have a hard time finding water and food. They are likely to suffer from dehydration, malnutrition, or both. Owned but neglected dogs can also fall victim to these deprivations.

For more information on malnutrition, please see chapter 7, p. 115.

Dehydration is life threatening. It occurs when a dog does not get enough water or when it loses too much body fluid. It can be caused by vomiting, diarrhea, heat stroke, and other illnesses. In a dehydrated dog the skin loses elasticity. If you gently pull up the skin along the back and it doesn't return quickly into place, that's a warning sign. Others include dry and sticky gums and tongue, thick saliva, sunken-looking eyes, signs of shock, and collapse.

Most dehydrated dogs need immediate veterinary care and intravenous fluids. If you are some distance away from a vet, you might offer multiple, very small drinks of water, spaced out over time. Be cautious about the amount. The dog can vomit, and it can do more harm than good all around for him to ingest water too soon and too fast. *Only* offer water if it's going to take you a while to get to a vet.

Bleeding:
A wound that bleeds more than just a trickle, or excessively and nonstop for more than three minutes, requires urgent care. Rapid bleeding (such as from an artery) could quickly cause death and needs immediate veterinary attention.

First-aid steps: The main goals are to stop bleeding and prevent infection.

Remove any foreign objects, such as slivers of glass, from the wound.

Use a gauze pad or the cleanest cloth available to apply pressure to the wound until the bleeding stops, generally five to ten minutes.

Do not keep checking on the bleeding by lifting the pad, as it might dislodge the clot that is forming. If the first pad becomes saturated, place a new one on top of it.

If there is swelling beneath the pad, loosen the pressure.

Move the animal so that his wound is higher than its heart (reduces blood flow).

If the wound is on a limb or the tail, and *only* if the pressure method doesn't work, apply a tourniquet, which can be made from a strip of cloth, gauze, a necktie, or belt. Loop it around the affected limb or tail and slowly tighten until the bleeding stops.

Caution: Be very careful not to leave the tourniquet on for very long. Release it every few minutes to allow blood flow to return to the limb.

When bleeding slows significantly, reapply a pressure pad as described above.

When bleeding stops, keep the pressure pad on for another ten minutes, then start with wound care as described in this chapter on pp. 86–87. If bleeding resumes, reapply the pressure pad. Apply the tourniquet *only* when the pressure pad does not work.

Moving an injured dog.

MOVING AN INJURED DOG

To get a severely injured or immobile dog out of danger, and to transport him to the vet, you have to move him. The two top rules: *Do not* hurt yourself and *do not* make the dog's injuries worse.

Speak calmly and reassuringly. Try not to telegraph your own anxiety.

A dog of any size is best transported on a flat board. If you don't have a board, you can move the dog by slipping him onto a blanket or towel. Place the board or spread the blanket next to the dog. Gently slip it under the dog. Avoid touching any injury sites. Avoid pulling the dog by the legs.

For a smaller dog, if you're using a blanket or towel, mold the fabric into a sort of a clamshell shape to enfold and support the patient.

A larger dog is best transported on a flat board by at least two people. If that is not available, or if you are alone, you can try to carry him hammock-style on a large blanket. That is, *if* you are strong enough and *if* the effort won't cause you to injure yourself. Even the blanket method is best done with at least one helper.

For either a smaller or larger dog, if you don't have a blanket or towel, and you have no choice but to lift the dog, put one arm around his chest, or slip it between his front legs. Wrap your other arm around the rump. Or, if you think there might be an injury in his back legs, put that arm between the back legs. Lift slowly, bending your knees. Some dogs will go limp and can thus slip out; others will wiggle and can make you drop them.

Be cautious as you're lifting, carrying, and moving the dog, paying special attention to protect any injured body areas by having the dog's injury toward your body. Hold the dog snugly to your chest, gently but firmly supporting his body. Watch your step. Walk carefully and don't rush, but get the dog to the desired location as quickly as you can.

Caution: Carrying an injured dog in your arms makes your face, neck, and head prime targets for biting. It's almost always best to muzzle any injured dog before attempting to care for him. (See the sidebars in this chapter on muzzling, pp. 79–80, and p. 160.) And again, only lift a dog *if* you are strong enough and *if* the effort won't cause you to injure yourself.

Whenever the dog is not in your arms or on the transporting board or blanket, allow him to find his most comfortable position. He might be standing instead of lying. *Do not* force his body into any position that you think would make him more comfortable or conform to what you think is normal. You could cause further damage.

Wounds

Cuts, lacerations, punctures, and scrapes of every type and degree are very much a part of the life of a dog in need. Whether homeless or neglectfully owned, it's all too easy for dogs to encounter sharp objects. Sometimes humans purposely wield such objects to do the dog harm.

Symptoms: Visible gaps or openings in the skin, bleeding, oozing, redness, swelling, excessive licking (matted fur might hide a wound).

First-aid steps: For superficial wounds (no deeper than the first layer of skin), first stop the bleeding. (See the section "Bleeding," pp. 84–85.) Then clean the wound by washing with water and mild soap.

For deeper wounds, such as lacerations or cuts or punctures, because they penetrate more deeply into the layers of skin and underlying tissue, contact a veterinarian as soon as possible for instructions. If necessary, stop the bleeding and provide shock care as discussed on pp. 83–84. Keep the dog as quiet as you can to avoid further injury. While transporting the dog, try to keep the wound facing upward.

If you are not able to get to a vet or to phone one immediately, and if you do not have sterile first-aid supplies available, it is better to leave the wound alone than to attempt to clean or bandage it with nonsterile materials.

If the veterinarian recommends that you clean the wound, you might follow this procedure: Flush the wound with normal saline to remove debris, dirt, and clotted blood. If normal saline is not available, use generous amounts of flowing water (tap water or hose water are OK).

If the veterinarian recommends that you bandage the wound, and if you have first-aid supplies available, you might follow the procedure below for a three-layer bandage that consists of a contact layer, an absorbent layer, and an outer layer.

First, wash your hands. With a pair of rounded-tip safety scissors—for example, kindergarten craft scissors—clip away any adjacent hair to keep it from entering the wound. Gently pat the area dry with sterile gauze pads.

The contact layer should lie directly against the skin but should not stick to it. The material used should be sterile, flexible, free of threads or particles that might enter the wound, and absorbent enough to allow drainage to pass through to the second layer. A useful product for the contact layer is a Telfa pad, sold at many pharmacies. If possible, spread an antibiotic ointment on the pad before applying.

Caution: A layer of this type could make the wound too moist if left on too long. The bandage should be a temporary measure until you can get the dog to the vet.

The absorbent layer should cover the contact layer to accept drainage and help cushion the wound against further injury. It will wrap around the limb or body, thus helping hold the underlying contact layer snugly against the skin. The best material to use is a roll of sterile cotton or Dacron made for this purpose, available at pharmacies. Use a one-inch-wide roll if the wound is on a small limb. Use the three- or four-inch rolls if the wound is on a larger limb or the body. Wrap the material around the wound and the limb or the body part where the wound is located. If the wound is on the tail or a limb, begin wrapping from the tip of the tail, or the toes if the wound is on the leg, toward the body. This will allow freer blood flow and help prevent swelling. Continue wrapping until there are several layers of the material around the wound.

Caution: Make sure to use the appropriate-width roll for the absorbent layer. Material that's too thin can cut off circulation and cause swelling; too wide and the material can bunch up into ridges and wrinkles that make your dog uncomfortable, and the uneven pressure can lead to death of the underlying tissues.

The outer layer should hold the bandage in place. Use a porous adhesive or elastic tape such as vet wrap or Coban, available at many pharmacies. To prevent slipping, apply the tape so that it is in contact with the skin or hair at the margins of the bandage. To maintain proper blood circulation, begin wrapping the tape from the point near the wound that is closest to the toes or the tip of the tail. Try to make it snug but not tight. Try to keep it smooth and free of wrinkles.

The bandage should be changed whenever you notice saturation of the material, swelling, discoloration, odor, unusual coolness of the skin, or if it seems to be making the dog uncomfortable. Usually it should be changed daily. Check with the vet on how long the bandage should be kept on.

Broken Limbs

Limb breaks are not uncommon in either homeless or owned dogs. Causes can be from a wide range of traumas—being hit by a car, falling from a height, or being kicked or beaten. They can bring distress, pain, and permanent disability.

Symptoms: Not using a leg; limping; leaning when standing; limb at an unusual angle; atrophied, withered look; swelling.

First-aid steps: Contact a vet immediately for instructions. Many vets recommend the following:

If the bone is sticking out through the skin (open fracture), *do not* splint. *Do not* try to push the protruding bone back in place. *Do not* try to clean the wound unless it is grossly dirty. *Do not* try to bandage it. Instead, until you can get to the vet, keep the dog as quiet as possible and off his feet, perhaps by confining him in a transport kennel or by tying him to a strong and stable object. Try to keep the wound from getting dirty or from getting hit or jostled by movement.

If it will be a long time before you can get to a vet, you might flush the wound with normal saline, if it's available, or tap water or hose water. Caution: Flushing this type of wound can be quite painful for the dog.

If there is no bone sticking out through the skin (closed fracture), try to keep the dog as quiet as possible, as suggested above. If you cannot get to a vet soon, you might immobilize the leg by gently applying a splint as described next.

Use stiff material like folded newspapers, magazines, coat hangers, or even tree branches. For small dogs use tongue depressors, wooden craft sticks, Popsicle sticks, or tree twigs. Fasten these with string, tape, a necktie, or strips of gauze or cloth. The splint should be long enough to extend beyond at least one joint above and one joint below the suspected injury site.

Do not twist, contort, or try to straighten the limb—you want to splint it in the same position you found it. Place the splint against the limb as instructed above.

Gently wrap the fastening material (tape or gauze, etc.) around both the limb and the splint. It should be snug enough to keep the splint on securely without slipping. *Do not* wrap too tightly, which can reduce blood flow to the injury. The goal is to stabilize the injured limb to prevent further damage while transporting the dog to the vet.

Caution: *Never* try to realign or reset a bone. *Do not* splint if the dog objects. Some vets do not recommend splints as first-aid measures. They find that splints pose too many dangers, such as impairing circulation, causing nerve damage, or puncturing a blood vessel with a bone fragment, and that these risks outweigh the benefits. Others maintain that splinting can be helpful. This is a question to ask your vet.

BROKEN RIBS OR PELVIS

A frothy mixture of air and blood coming from the mouth and nose is an indication that a lung might be punctured. This is extremely life threatening and requires urgent veterinary care. *Do not* try to bandage the ribs, as that will restrict breathing and can bring on pneumonia.

The pelvis might be broken if the dog is down or dragging its rear end, cannot use one or both rear legs, if there is a grating sensation in the hips, or if

every movement seems painful. *Do not* let the dog try to walk.

For both situations, keep the dog as still as possible while you get to a vet.

Joint Sprains, Muscle Strains, and Dislocations

These can mimic breaks and it can be difficult to tell the difference. The dog might limp severely or even be unable to stand. Until you can get to the vet, err on the side of caution and treat the injury as a break.

Joint Sprains

These involve partial tearing or stretching of ligaments or tendons in the vicinity of a joint. Limping comes on suddenly. Usually the dog bears some weight on the limb. There is possible swelling or bruising. The vet will typically recommend resting the limb, applying cold packs during the first twenty-four hours, and restricting activity for at least three weeks.

Muscle Strains

Strains involve tearing or stretching of muscle fibers resulting in sudden limping. The treatment is the same as for joint sprains.

Dislocations

Dislocations occur when the bone at the joint is skewed out of position because of injury to the connective tissues by a powerful force, such as being hit by a car or falling from a height. This produces sudden limping, and the dog cannot bear weight on the limb. Tissues are swollen and discolored, and the limb or body part might look deformed or twisted. The vet will likely need to put the dog under anesthesia to reposition the bones and then immobilize the site in a splint or sling. Aftercare usually includes restricted activity and physical therapy.

Please note: Limping can also be caused by many other ailments, such as osteoarthritis, genetic orthopedic diseases, spinal cord and nerve damage, and tumors. For more information on such longer-term ailments, see chapter 7.

FINDING THE SOURCE OF A LIMP

A variety of injuries and illnesses can cause limping and lameness. The following steps can help you take a rough guess on the source and cause, but always seek veterinary care for any dog that is either favoring or not using a leg.

To determine which leg is hurt, notice that the dog will take shorter steps on the hurt one. Also his body will rise upward to some degree when he steps on the painful limb.

Check the paw. Sometimes the problem is a thorn, foxtail, splinter, or wound.

Check the leg for external wounds, swelling, or unusual masses. Then use gentle, massaging pressure to find any internal tender areas.

Gently and slowly flex and extend the joints, all the way from the shoulder down to each toe. Do they move freely and easily? Does the dog try to pull away?

HEAD AND SPINE INJURIES

Head and spine injuries might not be immediately apparent. Look for decreased mental alertness and odd behavior such as a head tilt, abnormal eye movement, one pupil larger than the other, circling when walking, loss of limb function, or labored breathing. Loss of consciousness and seizures are more obvious signs. There might be damage to the brain and nerves. This is a life-threatening condition that must receive immediate veterinary care.

Until you can get to a vet, keep the dog as quiet as possible.

INTERNAL DAMAGE

Signs and symptoms of internal injuries are often difficult to perceive but deadly nonetheless. The dog could have shortness of breath, increased respiratory and heart rates, and a decrease in blood pressure. An unusually full or distended abdomen might be a sign of bleeding into that region. Bleeding into the lungs might be evidenced by pink, frothy mucus from the nose and mouth. The dog will most likely be in pain. In some cases the dog cannot move. Keep him as quiet and still as possible. Seek immediate professional veterinary care.

> **Learn to Recognize Bloat**
> Bloat is the second-leading cause of canine death, after cancer!

Bloat: A Fast, Silent Killer

Bloat kills quickly and painfully. Your dog can be dead in less than an hour. Many dog owners have never heard of it and don't recognize the symptoms.

Also called gastric dilatation-volvulus (GDV) and stomach torsion, it is a condition in which the stomach fills with gas and fluid and then twists, preventing the fluid and air from escaping. Large, deep-chested dogs and older dogs are more susceptible, as well as certain breeds such as Dobermans, German shepherds, and Great Danes. But it can strike any dog, at any age, at any time.

Symptoms: In the early stages there might be minor symptoms like lethargy, a stiff-legged walk, and hanging of the head. As it progresses (sometimes within minutes or hours), there might be restlessness, pacing, whining, discomfort trying to sit or stand, a sprawling stance with legs spread, rapid pulse, pale gums and tongue, change in lip color, cold mouth, drooling or gagging, foamy saliva, repeated and unproductive vomiting attempts, weakness, or collapse. Overt signs such as a big, tight belly may be absent.

Prevention: Feed the dog two or more smaller meals per day instead of one big one (bloat can be triggered by eating too much, too fast).

Restrict the dog's water intake during the hour before or after exercise.

No strenuous exercise for at least an hour or two before or following a meal.

Elevate the food bowl.

Add acidophilus or yogurt to the diet to promote good intestinal health.

First-aid steps: Get the dog to the vet *immediately*.

Poison

Dogs often eat things that can sicken or kill them. Below we describe some of the most common poisons ingested by dogs. Each type has its own set of symptoms and first-aid steps. In every case, contact a vet or poison control center for instructions. Many vets will recommend the first-aid steps described below:

Chocolate

Symptoms: Vomiting, hyperactivity or nervousness, frequent urination, nausea, diarrhea.

First-aid steps: Induce vomiting with 3 percent hydrogen peroxide. (See the sidebar "How to Induce Vomiting," p. 91.)

Snail and Slug Bait

Dogs can be poisoned by eating the bait pellets directly or by eating creatures that have eaten the bait, such as slugs, snails, or rodents. Liquid or powder baits can poison a dog if it gets on the dog's fur or paws and he licks it off. Even small amounts can cause poisoning. Symptoms appear soon after ingestion.

Symptoms: Twitching, restlessness, anxiety, sensitivity to noise, lack of coordination, racing heartbeat, rapid breathing, diarrhea, vomiting, fever, muscle tremors, seizures, body goes rigid, respiratory failure. Can bring on liver failure.

First-aid steps: If less than an hour has gone by since ingestion, induce vomiting (see the sidebar "How to Induce Vomiting," p. 91), then give the dog activated charcoal—one five-gram tablet for every ten pounds of weight—and get the dog to the vet. However, if the dog is twitching quite a bit or showing many other symptoms, vomiting could do more harm than good, and an immediate trip to the vet is necessary.

Caution: To prevent further poisoning, hose down the yard to dissolve the bait and keep the dog out of the area for two weeks. If you have bait in your yard now, but your dog has never yet shown interest, don't assume he never will. The bait smells and tastes terrific. Ask a gardening store about pet-safe pest control methods.

Rodent Bait

Symptoms: Weakness, pale gums and tongue, bruises on skin, bleeding gums, nosebleeds, vomiting blood, rectal bleeding. (Symptoms do not usually appear until days after ingestion.)

First-aid steps: Induce vomiting (see the sidebar, p. 91). Get to a vet immediately. Knowing what product the dog ingested can help the vet determine the correct treatment. Take the product package with you, and/or save the dog's vomit, and take them to the vet so that they can be analyzed to identify the poison.

Please note: Most problems with rodent bait poisonings arise either after massive ingestion or repeated ingestion. By the time you see a symptom like bleeding, the poison has already been in the dog's system for a while, and vomiting won't help. However, if you suspect your dog just ate the poison, induce vomiting (see the sidebar below) and consult a vet immediately.

Antifreeze
Symptoms: Vomiting, lethargy, disorientation, "drunken" walk, seizures.

First-aid steps: Induce vomiting (see the sidebar below). If you cannot get to the vet right away, give the dog activated charcoal as described above, immediately after vomiting occurs.

Acids, Alkalis (Such as Detergent or Paint Removers), Petroleum Distillates, or Stinging Nettles

Symptoms: Burning to lips, gums, tongue, pawing at mouth, rubbing mouth, vomiting, retching, severe diarrhea.

First-aid steps: *Do not* induce vomiting, as these substances are considered corrosives and can be injurious to the animal when coming out. Instead, use water to rinse the mouth and all areas that came into contact with the poison, and then give the dog, by mouth, one to two tablespoons of mineral or cooking oil.

HOW TO INDUCE VOMITING

In poisoning cases where induced vomiting is recommended, give the dog one tablespoon of 3 percent hydrogen peroxide for every ten pounds of body weight. Caution: Make sure it is 3 percent hydrogen peroxide. Fill a turkey baster or plastic syringe with the liquid (or a spoon if those aren't available) and squirt into the dog's mouth or cheek. Repeat up to three times, every fifteen minutes, until vomiting occurs. *After* vomiting has occurred, give the dog tablets of activated charcoal—one five-gram tablet for every ten pounds of weight.

NEVER INDUCE VOMITING IF . . .

the dog has already vomited, is unconscious, dazed, or disoriented; walking or moving in unusual ways; having convulsions, muscle contractions, twitching, or labored breathing; *or* if he has swallowed something sharp, something caustic like a cleaning solution, household chemical, petroleum product, acid, or alkali; *or* if he swallowed a product that says on the label not to induce vomiting.

IF YOU DON'T HAVE ACTIVATED CHARCOAL

A substitute for activated charcoal is a solution of one-fourth cup egg white and one-fourth cup milk for every ten pounds the dog weighs. Mix it up and squirt it into the dog's cheek using a plastic syringe or turkey baster. If those are not available, place by spoon into the dog's cheek.

For more information on dog poisoning:
Call your vet, your regional poison control center, or the ASPCA at 1-888-426-4435, or visit http://www.aspca.org/apcc. The ASPCA center is staffed with technicians and toxicologists

who can help pet owners deal with cases of poisoning. Be prepared to pay a fee for the consultation.

POISONOUS PLANTS

Many plants, including houseplants, can be deadly to dogs. Get rid of poisonous plants in your home and yard. English ivy, foxglove, and caladium appear on a long list of innocent-looking culprits. For a more complete list, see the Web site for The Humane Society of the United States at http://www.humanesociety.org.

If a dog should ingest parts of a poisonous plant, you might or might not see vomiting, diarrhea, or changes in behavior. But if you suspect that the dog might have eaten any part of a toxic plant, immediately call your vet or local poison control center. The staff might instruct you to induce vomiting. In cases where you can't identify the plant, you might need to take a sample of it to the vet.

Snake Bite

Of all domesticated animals, dogs receive the highest number of fatal snake bites. A bite from a venomous snake can cause paralysis, respiratory failure, and rapid death. Venomous snakes in the United States include rattlesnakes, coral snakes, cottonmouths, and copperheads. An old adage may help you remember the difference between venomous and nonvenomous snakes with their colorful bands: red on yellow, kill a fellow, red on black, venom lack. The point is that if the red band touches the yellow, that snake is poisonous.

You might witness your dog's encounter with a poisonous snake and can therefore help the vet treat the animal quickly by reporting what bit him. But you could just as easily *not* witness the bite, so it is important to know the symptoms.

Symptoms: Swelling around the bite, respiratory distress, disorientation, vomiting, drooling, muscle tremors, weakness or paralysis, shock, drop in blood pressure.

First-aid steps: *Do not* attempt to suck out venom. This introduces harmful bacteria into the wound. *Do not* apply a tourniquet, as it can cause major damage to surrounding tissue. *Do not* apply ice.

Keep the animal calm and quiet to reduce the circulation of the poison until you can get to the vet.

Please note: If your dog is at high risk for rattlesnake encounters, talk with your vet about a vaccine for rattlesnake bites.

Stings and Bites from Insects and Other Bugs

Dogs are often the victims of painful or life-threatening insect stings.

Symptoms: For yellow jackets, wasps, bees, and ants, there is painful redness and swelling, often on a bare-skin area such as the nose or paw pads. Face and neck swelling can also appear. A single sting can cause a deadly allergic reaction (anaphylactic shock) in some dogs. In nonallergic dogs, multiple stings can cause shock because of the heavy dose of toxins.

For scorpion bites, severe pain occurs in the area of the sting that lasts about one hour, then there can be numbness, redness, and swelling. The body can undergo seizures and exhibit tics, which are uncontrollable repetitive motions, and the dog can have problems moving the tongue and lips because of numbness.

For wood ticks the symptoms are local swelling, inflammation, and possible infection.

For black widow spiders there is tenderness in area around the bite; drooling; nervousness; pain in the muscles of the back, abdomen, and chest; abdominal rigidity (the classic sign of a black widow bite); chills, fever, labored breathing, shock. (Black widows are shiny black with a red hourglass-shaped mark on the belly. But there are other, harmless spiders that look very much like them.)

For brown recluse spider bites, pain occurs at the site of the bite, with localized swelling and redness of the tissue around the bite. However, the symptoms do not usually appear immediately. It could take up to six hours for them to develop. Within about twelve hours, a blister forms and evolves into a lesion resembling a bull's-eye. The skin dies and an ulcer develops at the site. In rare cases, the dog develops fever, seizures, vomiting, muscular-skeletal and joint pains, and kidney dysfunction. In the presence of those symptoms, the dog may die. (Brown recluses are dull brown with a violin-shaped mark on the lower part of body. The "neck" of the violin points backward or downward toward the abdomen. However, it is easy to confuse this spider with several similar-looking, harmless species.)

First-aid steps: Try to identify the insect and contact a veterinarian.

For bees, remove the stinger by scraping with a credit card or your fingernail. For all stings, spread a paste of baking soda and water on the sting site. Apply ice packs to the swollen area. Rub calamine lotion over the site to ease itching.

Seizure

Resulting from abnormal electrical activity in the brain, seizures can have many triggers, including a drop in blood sugar, infection, high temperature, poisoning, previous injury, distemper, or epilepsy. The condition can be congenital.

Symptoms: In a mild seizure, the dog's eyes might stare in a dazed manner or roll upward. In a moderate seizure, the dog collapses into a state of unconsciousness. Most likely, the legs will be rigidly outstretched. The dog might lose of control of his bowels and bladder and might salivate and move his limbs as if paddling in water. In the period following the seizure, the dog might seem confused and unable to hear or see even though he is once again conscious. The dog might engage in frantic pacing, eating, or drinking.

First-aid steps: Protect the dog from harming himself during and after the seizure. During the seizure, make sure the dog is in a safe location, moving him if necessary. Otherwise, *do not* disturb him in any way, as that may trigger more seizures. Ignore the popular misconception and *do not* pull out the tongue or place anything in his mouth. Make note of how long the seizure lasts and how many seizures there are so that you can report that information immediately to the vet.

Drowning

Most dogs are good swimmers, but some can run into trouble if they become fatigued in any number of situations, such as strong currents or floods, falling through ice, or not being able to get out of a swimming pool.

Symptoms: The dog will lose consciousness while in the water or shortly after. A dog might be drowning if he is in water holding its breath while frantically paddling. He might be coughing (from inhaling water) and struggling to keep from submerging. Although you may be able to rescue the dog from the water, he could vomit, lose consciousness, and die.

First-aid steps: Get water out of the lungs in the following way: Hold a small dog upside down by the rear legs. Hold a large dog upside down by the middle. Allow the water to run out of the nose and mouth. Then lay the dog down on his right side, with the head lower than the chest, and give him rescue breathing (see p. 81). If you don't get a pulse, start CPR (see pp. 81–82).

Burns

A tissue injury, a burn can be caused by heat, flame, electricity, or chemicals.

Caution: Always take immediate action to protect yourself and the dog if the cause of the burn is still present. Extinguish all flames and get yourself and the dog away from any further danger, such as sources of heat, electricity, or chemicals. For all types of burns, *do not* apply ointments, creams, butter, any other substance, bandages, or dressings to the injury site. *Do not* try to remove burned skin or hair. *Do not* deliberately puncture blisters. *Do not* place the dog in water that isn't flowing.

Thermal Burns

Because dogs fear flames, most of them won't get too close to a fire. But the source of thermal burn could be contact with a hot surface or something on fire.

Symptoms: In a first-degree thermal burn (least severe) there is typically red skin and pain. A second-degree burn (more severe) destroys the deep layer of skin and nerve endings; thus, the dog might not feel pain. There might be redness, peeling skin, blisters, or charring. In a third-degree burn (most severe), the thickness of the skin is destroyed and the tissue takes on a white or charred coloring. The hair might be burned off or still be present but falls off easily. If the burn is deep, the muscle and bone can be exposed. Second- and third-degree burns need immediate veterinary care.

First-aid steps: Wash your hands. Make a cold-water compress by drenching sterile gauze pads or the cleanest cloth you have available with normal saline or clean, cold water. Refresh the compress frequently, re-soaking it in cold water. The goal is to keep the injury site wet and cool and to not introduce germs onto the site. You can apply an ice or cold pack, but for no more than ten minutes at a time.

Give the dog lots of water (unless he's vomiting) to combat possible dehydration. Provide warmth with blankets. Watch for signs of shock and treat if necessary.

Chemical Burn on Tongue

Often the result of the animal licking some substance (like household cleaners or bleach).

Symptoms: The tongue might look red or white, swollen, or raw around the edges, and be painful. Other symptoms are drooling, excessive swallowing, and pawing at or around the mouth.

First-aid steps: Flush the dog's mouth with copious amounts of water. If the chemical was an acid, rinse with one quart of water mixed with one teaspoon of bicarbonate of soda.

Chemical Burn on Skin

Symptoms: These are the same as thermal burns above.

First-aid steps: Rinse the affected area with flowing water for at least fifteen minutes.

Caution: If possible, wear protective gloves. *Do not* get the substance on yourself or on other parts of the dog—especially not in your or the dog's eyes, nose, or mouth. *Do not* inhale a chemical powder or residue.

Chemicals in the Eye

Symptoms: Eye closed, squinting, pawing or rubbing at eye, redness, swelling, sensitivity to light, excess tear production.

First-aid steps: Flush the eye with a saline solution for fifteen minutes. Make the saline solution by dissolving two teaspoons of table salt in one quart of water. If you are not able to prepare this, use flowing water, although it might be irritating to the eye.

Electric Burn and Electric Shock

These kinds of burns most often occur when a dog chews on an electrical cord. The dog can receive a burn to the mouth, or worse, a shock to the heart from the electrical current running through the body. Such a shock can cause the heart rhythm to change, circulatory collapse, cardiac arrest, and death.

Symptoms: The dog is lying on the floor near an electric cord or outlet, perhaps unconscious. He can have involuntary muscle contractions that don't allow his mouth to release the electric cord. The dog might have coughing, drooling, labored breathing, and burns in his mouth.

First-aid steps: *Do not* touch the dog if he's still in contact with a cord or appliance of any kind. Turn off the main power to the building and then pull the plug out of the wall. Give the dog CPR. Mouth burns might be treated by flushing with copious amounts of flowing water, but first contact a vet for instructions.

EMBEDDED COLLARS

A dog suffering from an embedded collar is a gruesome and heartbreaking sight. This horror occurs when someone places a collar on a puppy, then, as the puppy grows, no one ever loosens or replaces the collar. The too-tight collar slowly strangles the growing dog. Also, the flesh expands, but the collar does not, so it cuts into the tissue, causing a deep and painful laceration that rings the throat.

Rescue workers cringe when they must deal with an embedded collar case, because they know that the treatment and recovery will be difficult and painful.

Do not attempt to remove an embedded collar yourself. Get the pooch to a veterinarian as quickly as possible. Sometimes surgical removal is necessary. Proper aftercare of the wound is critical and usually includes warm compresses, hydrogen peroxide washes, antibiotic ointment, and perhaps painkillers, as per your vet's instructions. Until healing is complete, you might need to use a harness instead of a collar on your dog.

As a general rule, make sure you can always slip just two fingers under your dog's collar, so that it is a snug but comfortable fit. For growing puppies check on the fit once a week.

Until we stop harming all other living beings, we are still savages.

—Thomas Edison

Excessive Heat Exposure

A homeless dog will roam the streets for hours on end looking for food, avoiding cars, and seeking shelter. Owned but neglected dogs are sometimes chained in a spot with no shade. On a dry, hot day, this poses the risk of sunstroke. Should the body temperature reach 105 to 106 degrees Fahrenheit, organ damage can occur. Should the body temperature exceed 106, there can be liver and kidney failure, brain damage, intestinal hemorrhaging, blood vessel damage, and blood clotting, leading to death.

A different condition, heat stroke, can afflict a dog that has been confined in a hot area, such as a car or a concrete or asphalt surface, or who has exercised too much in hot or humid weather. Groomers can cause heat stroke by muzzling a dog under a hair dryer.

Symptoms: Heavy panting, labored breathing, dilated pupils, bright red tongue and gums, drooling, vomiting, increased pulse rate, dizziness, weakness, collapse, convulsions.

First-aid steps: Move the dog to a cool area. In a bathtub or with a garden hose, wet the dog with cool (not cold) water for up to two minutes. If bath or hose water is not available, wet the dog as much as possible. If you can, turn an electric fan on the dog and apply ice packs or cloths soaked in alcohol to the paw pads and insides of the legs.

Caution: Keep in mind that if the dog is in some shock, the skin can feel cold and clammy, but the core temperature can still be high. Nevertheless, be very careful about continuing the cooling process for longer than two minutes, as you might lower the dog's temperature too much. Contact the vet as soon as possible for further instructions. Your vet might advise that you check the dog's temperature (see the sidebar below, "To Take a Dog's Temperature"), and continue the cooling process until the temperature drops to around 103.5 degrees. Stop the cooling procedures at that point.

TO TAKE A DOG'S TEMPERATURE

First, leash or otherwise restrain the dog so that it cannot run away. It's best to have a helper. *Do not* let the dog sit down throughout the procedure. Use a rectal thermometer, digital and unbreakable, if possible. Lubricate it with K-Y Jelly. Speak soothingly and keep the dog calm. Taking the temperature shouldn't be painful but might be uncomfortable. Raise the pooch's tail.

Again, *do not* let him sit down or get away from you throughout the procedure. Gently slip the thermometer into the anus. A slight twisting motion will help it go in. Hold it in place for about three minutes or the amount of time specified on the thermometer packaging. After that time, remove and wipe clean with a tissue. Read it according to package directions.

Caution: If you are using a glass thermometer, and the dog sits down or gets away from you, the thermometer could break and leave a piece inside the dog. If a thermometer of any kind is not whole when you take it out, get to a vet without delay.

SHORT SNOUTS SUFFER IN THE HEAT

Dogs cool themselves differently from humans. They only perspire through their paw pads. Panting helps them cool off by evaporating water from their mouths and noses. Breeds with shorter snouts can suffer from hot weather far worse than longer-nosed dogs, because the surface areas inside their noses and mouths are much smaller, allowing for less evaporation of water and thus, less cooling.

Excessive Cold Exposure

Dogs left in the cold are susceptible to many of the same problems a person would experience. Should his body temperature fall below the canine normal of 101 to 102.5 degrees Fahrenheit, the dog can quickly enter hypothermia. Short-coated breeds and older and younger animals are most likely to succumb to frigid weather. A homeless dog who has been roaming cold streets can have ice balls form around his feet and toes. Salted roads can also lead to cracked footpads, which are extremely painful.

Prevention: Never leave a dog outdoors in temperatures that would be uncomfortable for a human. Even a snug doghouse is not enough protection.

Symptoms: Shivering, difficulty breathing, lethargy, weakness, pale or bluish gums, paralysis leading to collapse. For ice balls on the paws and cracked paw pads, expect limping or bloody footprints, licking and biting at paw pads.

First-aid steps: Get the dog to a warm place. Wrap him in a blanket, coat, or whatever is available. Dry the dog if he is wet. Contact a vet for instructions. For ice balls, gently warm the feet with warm water. Soak in warm water if necessary. For cracked paw pads, get the dog to a vet, who might recommend application of a product such as New-Skin, Liquid Bandage, or Robby's Skin Protector, and wrapping for protection.

DIARRHEA

Diarrhea is one of the first health issues you're likely to face when you rescue or adopt a dog. Some of the more common causes are stress, a change in diet, eating something spoiled, or intestinal parasites. Many serious illnesses might also be the cause, as discussed throughout this chapter and in chapter 7.

The stool can range from soft to liquid, and might occur several times per day, even waking the dog (and you) during the night. Contact your vet if the diarrhea persists for more than twenty-four hours, if it looks black and tarry (indicating blood is present), or if the dog is vomiting, lethargic, or has a fever.

For that initial twenty-four hours, some vets recommend withholding food to give the digestive system a rest, while encouraging drinking water to avoid dehydration. Some vets recommend a bland diet of two parts plain, boiled white rice mixed with either one part cottage cheese or one part boiled chicken. There are also commercial bland diet foods available.

Viruses and Bacteria

A number of contagious canine viruses and bacteria can sicken, maim, or kill your dog. Regular vaccinations, a wholesome diet, and a healthy lifestyle can prevent most of the common illnesses. Because they often lack such preventive care, homeless dogs, as well as those that are owned but neglected, have lowered immunity and thus are at higher risk for catching infectious diseases.

As soon as possible, take your rescued or adopted pooch to a vet for a thorough exam. Unless you have documented proof that he already has received vaccinations, have your vet administer them. Sometimes people assume that if a homeless dog is a healthy-looking adult wearing a collar, he has already been vaccinated by a previous owner, but that is not always the case.

Below you'll find brief descriptions, symptoms, and possible treatment strategies vets recommend for the most common canine viruses and bacteria.

Please note: There is little, if any, effective first aid you can offer for the diseases described below. Most are life threatening and highly contagious to other dogs. If your pooch displays suspicious symptoms, get immediate veterinary attention.

CANINE VACCINATIONS MOST VETS RECOMMEND

Most veterinarians believe that a regular vaccination program plays a critical role in canine health. The rabies vaccine is required by law. However, other shots are up to the owner's discretion.

Vaccine recommendations are currently hotly debated. It is a subject you might want to research and discuss with your vet. In response to concerns about possible health risks, some vets are giving certain vaccinations less frequently than in the past.

DHPP is a standard vaccine against four viruses: canine distemper virus, canine adenovirus, parainfluenza, and canine parvovirus. Dogs that will be going to a boarding kennel or a groomer might need the vaccine against bordetella. In certain parts of the country, vaccines are recommended for leptospirosis and Lyme disease. Other possibilities are the vaccine for hepatitis and coronavirus.

HOW DO DOGS CATCH CONTAGIOUS DISEASES?

Dogs can catch contagious diseases if they come into contact with the urine, feces, blood, saliva, or nasal or eye secretions of an infected dog. But disease transmission does not require direct dog-to-dog contact. It might happen during a walk at the park if your dog sniffs at a bush that an infected dog has marked, or if he drinks water from a bowl used by a dog carrying one of the contagious illnesses. Some illnesses, such as leptospirosis and giardia, are not passed from dog to dog but are caused by microorganisms that might inhabit stagnant ponds, wetlands, or other slow-moving bodies of water. Other diseases are transmitted by bites from ticks, mosquitoes, certain types of flies, and other insects.

WARNING! PARVO IS HIGHLY CONTAGIOUS

Parvovirus, or parvo, one of the deadliest canine illnesses, is also one of the most contagious. Carried in infected dogs' droppings, it can survive in contaminated ground for nine months or more. It resists most disinfectants. Extremes of heat and cold do not kill it. Some dogs might be silent carriers of the virus, exhibiting no symptoms while they busily infect other dogs, unbeknownst to the owners. You can even take parvo home to your dog on your hands, shoes, or car tires!

HOW TO PROTECT YOUR DOG FROM CONTAGIOUS DISEASES

Make sure your dog is properly vaccinated. Most of the time, vaccinations work. They are highly effective prevention. However, just in case your dog is one of the few whose vaccination didn't "take," it doesn't hurt to make some common-sense efforts to give your dog extra protection, as follows:

Keep your dog's immune system perky with a healthy diet, clean drinking water, protection from extremes of weather, and minimal emotional stress. You can minimize stress with a reliable daily routine, plenty of exercise, playtime, chewing opportunities, and of course, generous helpings of TLC.

Never let your dog interact with a dog you suspect is ill.

If you yourself interact with a dog that seems ill, wash your hands and change your clothing and shoes before hanging out with your own dogs. (See the sidebar below, "Why, When, How to Quarantine.")

If you walk through an area where a sick dog has been, disinfect your shoes by wiping them with a solution of one part bleach to thirty parts water.

When out for walks it can be difficult to keep your dog from "reading messages" left by fellow canines. Your dog naturally wants to sniff their droppings and urine marks. But stay alert. Try not to let the dog lick, taste, or eat these temptations. (Some dogs of our acquaintance seem to believe that's the whole reason for taking a walk!)

WHY, WHEN, AND HOW TO QUARANTINE

If you suspect your dog might have a contagious illness, be a good citizen and don't take him out in public. The dog doesn't have to come into direct contact with other dogs to make them sick. Some diseases are easily transmitted through contact with the urine, feces, and other bodily products of an ill pooch.

In multiple-dog households where one or more is ill with a contagious disease, first make sure all your dogs have had their vaccinations. If any of them are younger than two years, ask your vet if you should bring them in for a booster shot. Even for mature, vaccinated dogs, ask your vet if your dog should have a titre blood test for parvovirus to make sure the vaccine is in effect.

Most vaccinations are tremendously effective, but just in case, protect your other dogs by isolating the contagious dog. Keep him in a separate room during his illness and then for at least a month after the dog recovers.

If possible, don't let the sick dog use the same part of the yard as the others for at least a month after recovery. Don't let him use the same food, water bowls, bedding, or toys. Immediately pick up the sick dog's droppings.

After interacting with the patient, wash your hands and change your clothing and shoes before interacting with the other dogs. Chlorine bleach is one of the few disinfectants that kill parvo. It could be harmful to your skin and health, but some veterinary experts suggest that after interacting with an infected dog, you should wash your hands with soap and water, then with a mild solution of one part bleach to thirty parts water (for example, four ounces of bleach in one gallon of water), then rinse off with plain water. A possibly healthier alternative is to wear protective gloves and wash or discard them after each use.

Disinfect your shoes by wiping them with the bleach solution.

After the dog has recovered, disinfect his quarters and the yard as much as possible. For example, you might mop the floor, walls, his crate, doghouse, and other hard surfaces with the bleach solution. Wash the dog's bedding in hot water and a little bleach.

If a pooch with parvo has been in your yard, you will need to disinfect your yard before allowing other dogs to enter. If you have other dogs, an extreme but effective step is to soak the whole yard with the bleach solution. This will kill all plants, grass, weeds, and other living things. Another possibility is to nuke only part of the yard in this way, and keep your dogs out of the rest of the yard for six months.

Obviously, these are drastic and bothersome solutions to the problem. The easiest and most effective method for prevention is vaccination.

Caution: Bleach bleaches! It can permanently damage wood, fabric, carpeting, and many other materials. It's best to first apply a bit of the solution to a small test spot and see how it goes. *Never* put bleach on your dog.

Distemper

In the past, this was feared as the most deadly canine virus. Although parvovirus might now occupy that notorious position, distemper still kills thousands of dogs every year (see the sidebar "Warning! Parvo Is Highly Contagious," p. 99).

Puppies are more likely than adults to get distemper. It can be a difficult illness to diagnose because its symptoms vary widely. There might be a temporary fever, lack of appetite, or mild lethargy. Or there might also be nose and eye discharges, coughing, vomiting, diarrhea, and persistent fever.

Even if a dog survives distemper's initial stage, he might go on to develop seizures, ambulatory problems like walking in circles, or tics. For example, involuntary muscle contractions cause some dogs that have had distemper to appear to be constantly chewing gum. Later the dog might sustain retinal damage, eye discoloration, or extreme toughening of the nose skin and paw pads.

There is no real cure for distemper. Your veterinarian can try to help your dog through the disease with supportive care that might include intravenous fluids to prevent dehydration and antibiotics to prevent secondary infections. Typically such treatment is expensive and difficult, but it can be successful. If the dog survives, the neurological problems might be permanent, but the other symptoms are usually cured.

Infectious Canine Hepatitis

While it is busily attacking the eyes, kidneys, liver, and blood vessels, the hepatitis virus might at first give no clues to its presence. For a few days there might be a cough, lack of appetite or energy, or a low fever. A couple of weeks later there might be a bluish discoloration of the eye known as "blue eye."

In mild cases, the dog recovers and is then immune to the virus for the rest of its life. In severe cases, hepatitis might cause liver, kidney, lung, brain, or spinal damage, internal bleeding or inflammation of the mouth, tonsils, or eyes, leading to shock and death.

There is no cure for hepatitis. It is commonly treated with intravenous fluids for rehydration and support, medications to lighten the liver's workload, and sometimes antibiotics to prevent secondary infections.

The vaccine for hepatitis is highly effective, and standard practice is for vets to give it along with other routine vaccinations. As a result, the disease is now rarely seen in the United States.

Leptospirosis

A variety of bacteria collectively known as leptospirosis can cause serious illness or death in dogs. The microorganisms can be encountered in the urine of infected animals and in stagnant water contaminated with urine. They can also be transmitted during mating, through bites, or by the dog eating an infected carcass. Cows, raccoons, rats, and mice are often sources of the illness.

The bacteria enter the body through mucous membranes, such as in the mouth, ears, and nose, or through cuts or abrasions on the dog's skin. After reaching the bloodstream, they multiply quickly to invade the spleen, liver, kidneys, eyes, and nervous and reproductive systems.

Depending on the severity of the infection, symptoms might include a fever, shivering, muscle tenderness, vomiting, heightened thirst, dehydration, hypothermia, lethargy, and kidney or liver failure. Although many dogs are able to recover, some die, and some develop such ailments as chronic kidney failure. Dogs that are not killed by the disease will continue to be contagious to other dogs for a period of months or even years.

Treatment usually centers on antibiotics, rehydration, medication to control vomiting, and intravenous fluids to help flush the kidneys.

Some newer vaccines might be effective for prevention. However, leptospirosis is no longer common to dogs in urban areas, so if you live in a city, your vet will probably not recommend the vaccine. If you live in an area where cattle, wildlife, and rodents are prevalent, ask your vet if your dog should be vaccinated.

Other precautions include eliminating rodents from your home and yard, keeping your dog out of stagnant water such as ponds and puddles, excluding him from closed-up and rodent-frequented areas like storage sheds and barns, and preventing the dog from ingesting animal carcasses.

Caution: Leptospirosis is one of the few diseases that is directly communicable from dogs to humans.

Parvovirus

One of dogkind's top killers, parvo usually attacks the digestive tract. Puppies are especially susceptible to the virus, which prefers to lodge in rapidly dividing cells. Destroying the cells, parvo makes the animal unable to absorb nutrients.

Symptoms include high fever, lack of energy and appetite, vomiting, and distinctively foul-smelling, bloody, liquid diarrhea. The results are often dehydration, shock, and death. And, unfortunately, a dog that has managed to survive a bout with parvo can contract it again.

Treatment must be immediate and aggressive, including hospitalization, intravenous fluids for massive rehydration, added electrolytes to maintain energy, antibiotics, and drugs to fight vomiting. In severe cases blood transfusions might be necessary to combat anemia.

Please note: Black-and-tan-colored breeds such as rottweilers and Doberman pinschers are more susceptible to parvo and have less chance of recovering from it than other breeds. However, the disease can strike any breed at any time.

Parainfluenza

A sort of doggie cold or flu, parainfluenza causes a mild infection of the respiratory tract. Contact with the nasal fluids of a dog carrying the virus can cause it. It can lower immunity and set the stage for secondary illnesses to take hold.

Symptoms include cough, nasal discharge, cough that can produce phlegm, and fever. It is highly contagious.

Fortunately, parainfluenza is easily managed with help from your veterinarian and is rarely fatal. However, in recent years a newer "dog flu" has appeared. It can be more serious, and there have been fatalities, but most dogs recover within a few weeks.

Bordetella

Tracheobronchitis, or kennel cough, is a catch-all term for infections of the upper respiratory system. Bordetella is a form of kennel cough but far from the only one. The vaccine required by boarding kennels and groomers is only for bordetella.

Dogs can most easily contract this disease when they lodge in close quarters with other dogs, such as in a kennel. It is caused by a bacterium that lodges in the respiratory tract. Dogs develop a severe cough, sometimes followed by gagging or retching. There might also be discharge from the nose or irritation of the eyes.

When caught in time, bordetella is easily treatable with antibiotics and cough suppressants and is usually not life threatening. Therefore, most vets do not administer the vaccine on a routine basis. Usually they rec-ommend it only if the dog is going to be boarded or kept in close confinement with large numbers of other dogs.

A nasal squirt rather than a hypodermic syringe is often used to administer the vaccine, which is only effective for about six months.

If your pooch gets kennel cough, remember to protect other dogs by keeping him away from them until the dog is well, to avoid spreading the illness. Try to protect the dog too from respiratory irritants like sprays, vapors, dust, chemical odors, and cigarette smoke. Make sure he drinks plenty of water, and be prepared to give him soft food if it seems that dry kibble makes the cough worse. Cut back on the dog's exercise—take him for leash walks instead of letting him run. Consider using a harness instead of a collar while walking to avoid irritating his throat. To help calm the cough, try steam; take the dog into the bathroom for a few minutes with the shower running hot water, or use a humidifier in the room where he sleeps.

West Nile Virus

Thank goodness here's one we don't have to worry about very much—yet. Although West Nile virus is slowly spreading across the United States, as of now it mainly affects horses and wild birds. There have been only rare cases of it in dogs.

Fortunately, it cannot be passed straight from animal to animal or from animals to people. Mosquitoes pick up the virus by feeding on animals carrying the disease and then transfer it while feeding on another animal.

West Nile brings on encephalitis, or brain swelling. Symptoms include lethargy, lack of appetite, tremors, convulsions, walking difficulty, walking in circles, and holding the head in odd ways. Young or elderly dogs are more susceptible to the virus, as are those with compromised immune systems.

HOW TO REMOVE A TICK (WARNING: THIS IS GROSS)

After trips to tick-inhabited places, perform tick checks. Or, if you live in a tick-prone area, make it a daily habit. Carefully examine every bit of your pooch's skin. One way to do this is to slowly run your fingers all over his body, as if you're performing a light massage, with enough pressure so that you can feel any small bump. Or you might push the fur against the grain to expose the skin and peruse it visually.

Ticks range from the size of a pinhead to about a quarter of an inch. The larger ones, of course, are easier to find. But some of the more dangerous ones are tiny. The black-legged tick, or deer tick, that transmits Lyme disease starts out life the size of a poppy seed, barely visible to the naked eye, and grows to the size of a sesame seed. Before a tick attaches itself to the skin, it is brown or black in color and relatively flat in shape. After attaching and drinking blood, it plumps up to look like a small pea or kernel of corn stuck on your dog's skin. Its color when filled with blood can be brown, purplish, pink, or yellow. When they attach, they bury their heads into the skin. Sometimes you can see their legs sticking out above the skin. (Sorry, but we did warn you this was gross.)

Your job is to get as much of the tick as possible out of your dog. Leaving the head behind can cause a skin infection, various diseases, or at least itch and irritation.

To remove the little pest, part the dog's fur so that you can get a clear shot. Use tweezers to grasp the tick as close to the skin as possible without pinching your dog. Make sure you have included the tick's head within the tweezer's grasp. Apply *gentle* pressure to the tweezers, without squeezing or crushing the tick. You don't want to squeeze the sucked-up blood back into your dog. *Slowly* pull the tick up and out in a smooth, continuous motion. If you live in an area prone to Lyme disease, place the tick in a tightly sealed container, such as a glass jar or plastic storage box, and take it to your vet for a lab test. If not, flush the parasite down the toilet.

Examine the bite spot to see if there's anything brown or black left in your dog's skin. If so, it might be the head, and you should call your vet to report it. The vet might want you to come in to get the head removed.

Don't forget to wash your hands thoroughly after removing a tick, and apply an antiseptic such as alcohol or Betadine to the bite spot on the dog's skin.

Caution: *Do not* attempt to burn off a tick. That is an old folk method that some people still use, but it can result in burns to yourself and to your dog.

Please note: One vet recommends pushing the tick inward very gently for about fifteen to twenty seconds before removing it, to make the tick's mouth parts relax so it comes out more easily.

HOW TO KEEP YOUR DOG (ALMOST) TICK-FREE

The easiest and surest method to keep your dog free of tick-borne disease is to use one of the liquid products such as Frontline, K9 Advantix, and others that are applied along the dog's neck and spine, one spot at a time, so that it spreads out all over the skin. These products also repel fleas. The product soaks into the skin and poisons the pest when it bites your dog. If all goes well, the insecticide kills the parasite before it has time to infect your dog with a nasty disease.

Most of these products' instructions call for application once per month. Many veterinarians recommend that if you want to apply one of these products after bathing your dog, you should wait twenty-four to forty-eight hours after the bath to give the natural skin oils a chance to return. Skin oils help the product spread more evenly and make it more effective.

Sprays and powders can also work, but must be applied frequently.

A number of pesticide products in spray, liquid, and powder form can kill fleas and ticks on indoor and outdoor surfaces. By law, certain chemicals may

only be applied by a licensed exterminator. Others are for consumer use. Follow all instructions carefully, and protect yourself with gloves, mask, and eye goggles during application.

Unless they contain the powerful insecticide amitraz, tick/flea collars are generally not considered to be as effective as other options.

Please note: No chemicals are 100 percent safe. For example, some vets warn that topical sprays and powders can be toxic to pets as well as humans. Research carefully and discuss options with your vet to find the right pest-control methods for you, your dog, and your household.

Natural Pest Control
Many pooch owners swear by natural pest-control alternatives and believe it's hazardous to both canine and human health to use chemical pesticides and insecticides. Some natural parasite control options include a mild solution of eucalyptus oil sprayed on the dog daily, and repellents for house and yard that are applied to baseboards or sprinkled on grass, such as boric acid (indoors), diatomaceous earth, orange oil, and eucalyptus oil.

PROTECTING YOURSELF AGAINST TICKS

One hazard of dog ownership is that if your dog gets ticks, so might you. To avoid the little critters when you're out in grassy, weedy, or overgrown areas, or in an area with wildlife, wear light clothing so that you can spot ticks more easily. Cover as much of yourself as possible. Tuck your pant legs into your socks. Do frequent, all-over tick checks on yourself and family members.

Lyme Disease

Ticks can kill. Certain illnesses, such as Lyme disease, are caused by ticks, which is the only way to become infected. Actually, Lyme disease is not exactly caused by ticks, but by bacteria that ticks sometimes carry. If a tick bites an animal that is carrying the illness, the tick picks up the bacteria and then takes them to the next animal it bites.

One of the most common symptoms of Lyme disease is limping, often on a front leg. There might be swelling of the lymph node in that leg and a fever of 103 degrees. The pain can become so severe that the dog no longer uses the leg. Joint and muscle pain throughout the body can even cause the dog to stop moving altogether. Over a period of just a few days, the dog can go from perfectly healthy to completely immobile. Sometimes the bacteria can attack the heart and nerves as well.

Unfortunately Lyme disease can mimic several other illnesses, and vice versa, so it is often misdiagnosed. Proper diagnosis is important because treatment is usually easy and successful if it is caught in time. Certain antibiotics are highly effective. Without prompt treatment, the heart, joint, and nerve tissues can suffer permanent damage.

The Lyme disease vaccination is neither foolproof nor mandatory. Veterinarians warn that it is not 100 percent effective, and most do not recommend this vaccination except in heavily Lyme-prone areas.

As with most illness, prevention is the best medicine. Try to keep your dog tick free. In some parts of the United States, Lyme disease is more common than in others. If you live in an area where it is more prevalent, be extra cautious.

Ehrlichiosis (Tick Fever)

Another tick-borne illness, ehrlichiosis is caused by a variety of organisms known collectively as *Ehrlichia*. The brown dog tick transmits *Ehrlichia*. It picks up the organism when it feeds on the blood of an infected animal, then moves on to feed on the next animal and passes along the disease in the process. Brown dog ticks are found throughout the United States, and almost every state has reported at least one case of it.

Often ehrlichiosis manifests in three phases. The first phase begins one to three weeks after the tick bite. It lasts two to four weeks, during which the disease attacks the liver, lymph nodes, spleen, blood, and bone marrow. Symptoms include fever, lethargy, lack of appetite, trouble breathing, bruising, joint pain, and stiffness.

In the second phase, sometimes the dog is able to fend off the disease and recover. If the animal does not recover, however, the disease may go on to the third phase. Unfortunately, recovery does not provide permanent immunity. A future tick bite could reinfect the dog.

In the third, or chronic, phase, one to four months after the tick bite, symptoms include fever, anemia, weight loss, bleeding, eye inflammation, swelling of the rear legs, and neurological problems. From this phase forward, symptoms might come and go, worsening during times of stress.

Ehrlichiosis can be accompanied by other diseases such as babesiosis or haemobartonellosis, which can all be transmitted during the same tick bite. Your veterinarian will order a blood test or perhaps two tests performed two weeks apart if any of these diseases is suspected.

Treatment during the first phase with antibiotics and sometimes additional medications is simple and generally successful. In severe cases, the dog might need intravenous fluids or blood transfusions. Unfortunately, during the chronic phase, treatment is more difficult and less successful.

No vaccine exists for ehrlichiosis. The best prevention is to protect your dog from ticks. (See the sidebar "How to Keep Your Dog (Almost) Tick-Free" on p. 104.) In heavily infested areas of the country, some vets prescribe a daily dose of antibiotics so that if your dog is bitten by a carrier tick, the disease-causing organism will be destroyed when it enters the bloodstream.

CAN MY DOG MAKE ME SICK?

Most canine illnesses are not directly communicable to humans. Some exceptions are rabies, leptospirosis, sarcoptic mange, and ringworm.

Rabies

For anyone who read or saw Steven King's *Cujo*, a novel and film about a rabid Saint Bernard, rabies is a terrifying word. In reality, very few dogs in the United States contract rabies. It is more likely to be found in wild animals, such as raccoons, skunks, bats, foxes, and coyotes. Raccoons account for about 40 percent of the cases, according to the U.S. Centers for Disease Control (CDC). Of domestic animals, cats are most often diagnosed with the disease, possibly because less than 10 percent of cats are vaccinated against rabies, and because more cats than dogs are allowed to roam freely and encounter wild creatures. The CDC cites widespread canine vaccination as one reason for the decline of the disease in dogs.

The best way to protect your dog from rabies is to vaccinate him, and to keep the dog from interacting with wild critters. That's a good idea anyway, given that your dog might not come out on the winning side of such encounters.

The rabies virus is contained in the saliva of infected animals and is usually transmitted by bites. Slowly, it attacks the nervous system. It might take weeks for symptoms to appear. In the initial stage there might be a fever and nervousness. Docile animals might become aggressive and, strangely, aggressive animals might become friendly. The disease progresses to cause such maladies as viciousness, disorientation, seizures, inability to swallow, choking, and paralysis.

If you suspect that your dog has been bitten by a wild animal, administer first aid and contact your vet immediately, even though it is unlikely that a vaccinated dog will contract the disease. If you see a bite wound on a dog you are rescuing, consult a veterinarian on how to proceed. Remember that calm behavior on the part of the dog is no guarantee that he doesn't have rabies.

Diagnosis is difficult because there is no blood test for the disease. Only an analysis of brain tissue can give a definitive answer, and extracting the tissue would be fatal to the dog. Sadly, in the rare cases where rabies is strongly suspected, euthanasia is the only choice. Although there is treatment available for humans who have the disease, the drug that is used in the injections has not been properly tested for animals.

Vaccinating your dog against rabies is legally required in almost every state and is the best, most responsible way to protect him from this frightening illness.

Dogs' lives are too short. Their only fault, really.
—novelist Agnes Sligh Turnbull

Jody Cramer

Katie Tina after.

Happily Ever After True Story Number Six:

Katie Tina

· ·

It was an ordinary looking stroller being pushed by a tall redhead named Jody Cramer. But instead of walking toward the playground, Jody and her stroller bumped along into the fenced dog park. There, she pulled back the stroller's pink hood to reveal a face—not the soft cheeks of a baby but the muzzle of a black-and-brown dog. Everyone in the dog park, both human and canine, watched as Jody gathered Katie Tina into her arms and gently placed her onto the ground.

As the dog stood beside her stroller, it became clear why she was a special-needs dog. She had only three legs, and the toes of her front paw had been amputated. Yet her tail wagged with an energetic force and her toothy smile radiated breathless joy. Katie Tina almost tipped over as she mingled with the party of dogs, but it was

Jody Cramer

Katie Tina before.

clear to see that even in her awkward, debilitated body, this was a dog that adored living.

Christi Payne, director of Compassion Without Borders, an animal rescue organization, assisted in Katie Tina's rescue. A woman had sent her photos of a dog hiding beneath a car. "The photos were so haunting I was unable to sleep that night," Christi remembered. "The bone on the dog's right foreleg was exposed, severed, and sticking out. The toes on the opposite foot were swollen, infected, and cut. I immediately asked the woman to go back to get the dog and take her to a veterinarian." Christi was later told how Katie Tina gladly hoisted herself into the woman's car, then greeted the staff at the veterinary hospital with her high-energy tail and smiling face.

Christi said, "Three days and two operations later, Katie Tina was a new dog. She had to have her front leg, which was horrifically infected, amputated—along with the toes on the other front foot. Amazingly, a few days later, she was running around and playing, showing no signs of distress whatsoever!"

Having two special-needs dogs already, Jody was not looking to adopt another one. But when she heard about Katie Tina, Jody said, "This dog needs me." Whether their wounds are emotional or physical, Jody's dogs are with her because few people have the financial means or the time commitment she is able to provide.

"My little dog, Miss Bean, was found in a dump missing an eye, then put into a cage for three years before her rescue," she explained. "My gentle dog, Woody, who at fourteen died this past spring, was so emotionally traumatized before I adopted him that he hid under my bed all the time."

Jody located a specialist who was able to design and create a special boot to fit Katie Tina's front paw. The boot helps her to better balance on her three legs so she can participate in her favorite activity—bowling. "Katie Tina isn't too interested in catching balls in her mouth," Jody reported, "but she loves it when I throw them across the lawn like a bowling ball."

Back at the dog park, Katie Tina is a magnet for questions and comments. What happened to her leg? Why is she wearing that thing on her foot? Where did you get that darling stroller? Patiently, Jody answers all their questions while skillfully advocating adopting rescued dogs. Jody said, "Katie Tina is such an ambassador for all homeless dogs. I can't tell you how many people, once they hear Katie's story, have decided to avoid breeders when adopting their next dog."

For Jody, providing a home for a rescued dog gives her infinite rewards. Something as simple as a warm blanket shows the substantial difference her home is making for Katie Tina. When Katie Tina first arrived at Jody's house, rather than sniffing other dog residents or searching for food bowls, this injured dog quickly identified the softest places to lie down—sofas, overstuffed chairs, pillows, even piles of laundry. Never again would Katie Tina rest her once-sore body on a hard surface. And each night, as she curls herself up on her Winnie-the-Pooh bed, Jody covers her with a pink blanket that somehow manages to stay tucked in around Katie's body until morning.

7.
Long-Term Health Needs of Rescued Dogs

Some Common, Long-Term Health Problems:
How to Prevent Them, Spot Them, and Deal with Them

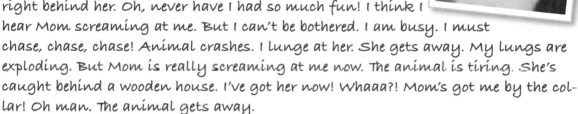

Kellie: Dog versus Deer

We have entered the grassland, and Mom unhooks my leash. I sense something wonderful! What do I see? Gotta get a closer look. My legs start flying over the grass. I'm chasing the largest, most scared animal I've ever seen! It is running like the wind! And I am right on its heels. She crashes into the fence. Then she runs in the other direction, and I am flying right behind her. Oh, never have I had so much fun! I think I hear Mom screaming at me. But I can't be bothered. I am busy. I must chase, chase, chase! Animal crashes. I lunge at her. She gets away. My lungs are exploding. But Mom is really screaming at me now. The animal is tiring. She's caught behind a wooden house. I've got her now! Whaaa?! Mom's got me by the collar! Oh man. The animal gets away.

The longer-term health needs of rescued dogs are not very different from those of purchased dogs. Sometimes a homeless dog's deprivations can create a chronic malady. For example, malnutrition can weaken the teeth. But given a loving home and proper care, most needy pooches bounce back from whatever horrors they have endured.

All dogs—pedigreed or mutt, abandoned or cherished—are subject to health problems. In this chapter we describe some of the more common ones you might face, and offer a health maintenance guide to help you prevent them.

Not to hurt our humble
brethren [the animals]
is our first duty to them,
but to stop there is not enough.
We have a higher mission:
to be of service to them
whenever they require it.
—St. Francis of Assisi

Routine Maintenance—A Guide for Lifetime Health

To keep your dog healthy, a schedule of routine maintenance goes a long way.

Vaccinations

Keep your pets up to date according to your vet's recommendations. (See chapter 6, pp. 98–102, for more information on vaccinations.)

Regular Vet Checkups

Your vet stays familiar with your dog (and vice versa), takes vitals, and gathers baseline information to be able to recognize abnormalities should they arise. Most vets recommend one or two visits per year.

Write It Down

When you go to the vet, take a notebook and pen to jot down questions you have for the vet, and the vet's opinions and advice. Use the notebook as a health journal to keep track of your dog's weight, other vital information, medical history, and treatment schedules. You can also make quick notes on changes in eating habits, stools, urination, vomiting, and other symptoms, so that you can notice trends and remember when they started.

Home Health Checks and Maintenance

Perform your own basic exams of your dog on a routine basis. During the veterinary exam, ask the vet to demonstrate how to monitor and maintain your pooch, following the guidelines below.

Ears

Be an ear sniffer. Smell your dog's ears when they're healthy so that you can recognize trouble when they're not. The odor should not be unpleasant or yeasty.

Clean weekly. Some dogs need it more often than others. Use a cleaning solution you can get from your vet. Squirt it into one ear and don't let the dog shake it out until you've massaged it in for a few seconds. Then let the dog shake. With a soft tissue or makeup pad, gently mop out any liquid or debris. Repeat the process on the other ear. Caution: *Never* probe deep into the ears with a swab or anything else.

Between cleanings, if you see wax building up in the ears, clean more often. Check regularly for foreign bodies such as foxtails (see the sidebar "Killer Seeds—The Dangers of Foxtails," p. 132). If your dog often shakes her head, leans it to one side, or paws at or rubs her ears, get her to the vet.

Eyes

They should look clear, free of redness, swelling, or excessive drainage or mucus. They should fit normally into the sockets with no bulging or shrunken appearance. Some dogs might have more eye drainage than others. Determine what's normal for your dog. A little mucus in the mornings or after eating is not unusual. Gently wipe away with a clean tissue or makeup pad, moistened with clean water if necessary. If your dog's eye is bloodshot, or she begins pawing at or rubbing an eye or seems overly sensitive to light, or she's bumping into things, see your vet. (See the description of glaucoma, which can quickly cause blindness, pp. 131–132.)

Teeth and Gums

Brush your dog's teeth and give her safe chewing opportunities every day or at least a few times a week. Get to know how your dog's mouth looks and smells normally. Check throughout the mouth and gums for lesions, ulcers, or changes in color. Check the teeth for cracks, breaks, or other abnormalities. Unusually bad breath or a drastic change in odor is a good reason to see the vet.

To brush, use a washcloth or gauze pad wrapped around your finger, or a special doggie toothbrush, rubbery fingertip brush, or dental sponge—all of which you can purchase from your pet store or vet. Use only special doggie toothpaste, because the human kind can be harmful. Brush in circular, massaging motions, but don't brush upward, because that can drive debris under the gums. Make sure to get every tooth, from the little front ones all the way to the big back molars. (See the sidebar "Health Maintenance for the Skittish Dog," p. 114, on how to accustom your dog to tooth brushing and other routine maintenance tasks.)

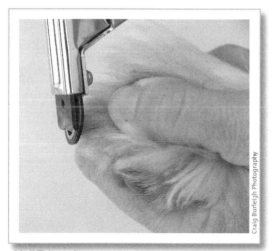

Nail Trimming.

Nails

Check frequently for splits and tears. Check nail beds for inflammation or bleeding. Keep nails trimmed to near the quick line. Different dogs' nails grow at different rates. Some pooches might need pedicures once a week, others once a month.

To trim, gently hold your dog's paw in one hand and the doggie nail clippers in the other. *Do not* use any instrument other than doggie nail clippers. Look at the underside of the nail to find the quick, the blood vessel running lengthwise through the middle of the nail. If you can't see it clearly, use a magnifying glass and get better lighting—even a flashlight. The nail should be trimmed to just beyond the end of the quick. Position the clippers at a forty-five-degree angle to the nail, slanted upward. Snip off a little at a time—slivers instead of chunks—to make sure you don't hit the quick. Not clipping enough is better than clipping too much.

If you do clip too much, it will bleed—a lot. Your dog might freak out, cry, and frantically lick at the blood, but it's not serious. Stay calm, apply a disinfectant like Betadine, and press gently with sterile gauze pads to stop the bleeding. Or use a styptic product like Kwik Stop Styptic Powder or CutStop Styptic Pads.

Paws and Paw Pads

Check frequently for wounds, foxtails, and thorns. Don't forget the webbing between the toes. Gently squeeze and manipulate all parts of the paw to check for soreness or injury.

Limbs and Tail

Keep an eye out for limping or for biting or licking at the limbs or tail. During your routine home checks, *gently and lightly* manipulate the joints to test their range of movement and to see if there's any soreness or sensitivity.

Whole Body

Once a week or so, perform an all-over check. Lightly massage your pooch from nose to tail, feeling for lumps, swelling, soreness, or sensitivity.

Skin and Coat

Know your dog's odor. If it changes or becomes unpleasant, bathe her more often. A persistent bad odor could indicate a health problem.

While you're doing the whole-body check, examine the skin for parasites (primarily fleas and ticks), lesions, redness, inflammation, oozing, matted fur, and foreign bodies like foxtails and thorns. The coat should look and feel lustrous and full. Although coat texture varies from dog to dog, it should never be dry, dull, or contain dandruff.

Bathing

Most dogs need a bath once or twice a month. Some have oilier or allergy-prone skin that needs bathing more often. If your dog's skin and coat are normal, use a good-quality, canine-formulated shampoo. Otherwise, your vet might recommend a medicated shampoo. When bathing, use warm or lukewarm water, especially in cold weather. Take care not to get shampoo in the dog's eyes. Massage the shampoo all over the dog's body, including her belly, paws, and tail. Rinse off completely. Leftover shampoo can dry out your dog's skin and coat. Dry your dog thoroughly with clean towels. After every bath, clean ears (as described above) to remove any water.

Parasite Control

Whatever methods you use for flea and tick abatement (see chapter 6, p. 104, for possibilities), regular and thorough dosage and application are key. On your calendar or in your doggie health journal, keep track of doses and applications to know when the next ones are due.

Brushing and Clipping

Most dogs love to be brushed. That's reason enough to do it. Another good reason is that it cuts down on shedding, which means less vacuuming. But most important, it's great for your dog's health. Brushing prevents matted fur, helps air out the skin and coat, spreads beneficial natural oils, and stimulates the dog's blood circulation, almost like a massage. Try to brush daily or at least a couple times a week. Wash the brush at least once a week.

If your dog has long hair that needs to be clipped, get it done regularly to prevent matting, skin and eye inflammations, and other problems.

Anal Sacs

Dogs have a pair of tiny glands in "anal sacs" on the exterior of the anus that make smelly secretions. Usually this happens quietly when the dog defecates, and you, thankfully, are none the wiser. However, some dogs' anal glands do not evacuate enough on their own, and need to be expressed manually. If your pooch often "scoots," dragging her bottom along the floor, frequently licks her anus, or emits a pungently foul odor from that vicinity, the dog probably needs her anal glands expressed. Otherwise, they could become impacted and infected. This happens to be the authors' least favorite pooch maintenance item, which is why we have our vets or groomers do it. If you take it on yourself, ask your vet to show you the correct method. Generally, you will put your fingers on each side of the anus, pressing upward and inward. (See why we're willing to pay to get out of this?)

Nutrition

With your vet, determine an ideal weight for your dog and keep her there. Feed your dog a high-quality pet food or home-cooked dog meals (with your vet's OK). Many health problems can be corrected or at least improved by proper nutrition, including the right food and, sometimes, supplements. Don't make sudden diet changes. If you change foods or add supplements, introduce them over a period of days or weeks, with gradually increasing amounts. For most dogs, especially larger ones, feeding twice a day is best. *Always* keep plenty of fresh, clean water available.

Exercise

Exercise your dog daily, as it is one of the single most important ingredients for canine health. It offers the same whole body benefits that it does to humans, including weight control, strength building, immunity boosting, and stress reduction. Your pooch will tell you how much is too little or too much. If she's still play-bowing and barking excitedly after twenty minutes of fetching the ball, keep going. If the dog is panting hard and lagging behind at the end of a two-mile walk, try a shorter walk the next day.

Stress Reduction

Stress can damage doggie health as much as it does our own. To manage it (for both you and your dog), try to keep a regular daily routine. Your pooch feels more secure if she knows more or less when she'll get to eat, exercise, play, and hang out with you. Your dog also needs to know that there's an established, reliable pack order, in which every family member enjoys a safe, respected position. Never allow bullying or aggression between canines or humans in your household. Dysfunctional families can be as hard on our dogs as on us! Daily exercise, safe chewing opportunities, and lots of time with you are other essentials for lowering stress.

Time with You

Spending time with your dog might be the most valuable contribution you can make to her lifelong health. Dogs are supremely social animals. Their drive to bond is so strong that they almost can't thrive without it. And over the millennia they've been bred to crave bonds with humans. You don't need to clear your schedule to make time for your pooch. She's delighted to keep you and your family company while you wash the dishes, do homework, garden, or even nap. The more time she gets with her beloved pack, the stronger she'll grow in body, mind, and spirit.

OLDER, WISER, AND A LITTLE NEEDIER

As your dog grows older, routine health maintenance tasks become more important and must be done more frequently. For example, senior pooches tend to need more baths than younger ones, because their skin's natural oils and resistance to bacteria aren't as efficient. Nails need trimming more often because the dogs are less active and thus don't file them down as they walk or run. A lifetime of wear and tear leaves teeth and gums more vulnerable. The incidence of many ailments ranging from tumors to diabetes increases with age.

There are also emotional changes. Some pooches might become quiet and withdrawn; others might grow more dependent and clingy.

Allot more time to a senior pooch. Extra TLC boosts morale and helps ease aches and pains. Also, your diligent care and watchfulness can mean early detection of many maladies, thus bringing more successful treatment and better health for your best friend.

HEALTH MAINTENANCE FOR THE SKITTISH DOG

Why should a worried dog want you to pry open her mouth and stick a toothbrush in it? Or whack at her nails with scary clippers? Simple—because she'll get lots of petting, praise, and yummy things to eat. Bribery works wonders to get your pooch to agree to almost any procedure.

First, set the mood. Choose a calm time of day when family activity is at a minimum, and maybe after the dog has exercised or eaten. Sit in a comfortable, well-lit spot, perhaps where you normally snuggle with her, whether it's the sofa, the dog's bed, or the rug. While you cuddle, have beside you the equipment for the task—for example, toothbrush, toothpaste, nail clippers, ear cleaning solution—where the dog can see and sniff them. Pick up the tools, but don't attempt to use them yet. Give

the dog praise, petting, and treats. Gently handle her paws and claws one by one. Continue with the praise and treats.

Some pooches might dash away and hide at the mere sight of grooming tools. Don't force the issue. Just act casual and perform this exercise for several days, moving the tools gradually closer to the dog until she barely notices them anymore.

For nail clipping, sit in your snuggle spot as usual with the clippers beside you. Give the dog a treat and, while she's chewing, pick up the clippers and touch them gently to a paw. The dog might yank her paw away. Keep trying for as many days as it takes. When the dog becomes comfortable with the clippers on her paw, hold a claw and touch the clippers to it but don't clip. Using this gradual approach, take baby steps toward your goal. Keep trying until you can make the clip. Remember to dispense lots of praise and treats.

The same strategy can work for other tasks, like tooth brushing. Sitting in your snuggle spot, dip your finger in something yummy like chicken broth, and touch it to your dog's teeth. Next, using a flavored doggie toothpaste, touch the toothbrush to her teeth but don't brush. Eventually the dog will become more focused on the intriguing flavors, treats, and praise than on her fear, and she might even enjoy this one-on-one time with you.

DEMONSTRATION ON THE MEDICATION

Whenever your vet prescribes a medication—whether it's a pill, liquid, ointment, or eye drops—while you're still in the exam room, ask the vet to show you how to administer it to your dog. The same goes for any procedures, such as cleaning or bandaging a wound, that you're asked to perform at home.

GOT SKUNKED?

Dogs are fascinated by wild animals—sometimes a little too much so—and often get skunked. The age-old remedy of applying tomato juice to a dog sprayed by a skunk most often just leaves your dog smelling like skunked tomatoes! Aside from over-the-counter skunk stink remedies, which can be purchased online and at most pet supply stores, you probably already have the items you need right in your kitchen and medicine cabinet.

Mix together one quart of hydrogen peroxide, one-fourth cup of baking soda, and one teaspoon of antigrease dish soap. Use immediately. Do not store any leftovers. With a washcloth, work the solution into your dog's coat, carefully avoiding the eyes. Rinse the solution thoroughly and repeat.

Descriptions of Common Longer-Term Ailments

Whether you've adopted a dog for keeps, or you're caring for a rescue until you can find a forever home for her, you're likely to encounter pooch health issues. In this section you'll find thumbnail sketches of some of the more common illnesses to give you a quick look at symptoms and treatment options.

Please note: The symptoms listed are just possibilities. Your dog might exhibit none of the symptoms discussed or might have different ones. The treatments listed are also only some of the possibilities a vet might recommend, depending on your dog's particular case. Use this chapter as a preliminary guide, not as a diagnostic reference or as a treatment plan. Always consult a veterinarian.

Malnutrition

Most homeless dogs are hungry. Even owned dogs can suffer from dietary deficiencies or starvation because of neglectful owners. Some might stay alive by scavenging and begging. Depending on how long the dog was homeless or neglected, her degree of malnutrition might be light or severe.

The dog's appearance can clue you in. A thin and bony dog needs more and better food. When ribs and bones show prominently through the coat, malnutrition is serious. A severely starved dog is emaciated. She'll look like a walking bag of bones, with a grotesque, skeletal appearance. Few sights are more heartrending.

Symptoms: Ribs and bones are showing, along with skin inflammation, oozing, inflamed eyes, pale gums, dull coat, hair loss, vomiting, unusually foul-smelling droppings, and lethargy.

Please note: Not all malnourished dogs will exhibit all these symptoms. We have met severely starved dogs who were not lethargic but affectionate and playful. The natural and almost irrepressible canine zest for life can sometimes be deceptive.

Ironically, an overweight dog is also considered malnourished. Some dogs in need appear as if they've been getting too much food. Perhaps the food they are scavenging or receiving from Good Samaritans is high in fat and unhealthy. Even a dog who is (or was) owned might be too heavy because of improper feeding.

Most dogs can recover easily from a poor or scanty diet, but it is very important to follow your veterinarian's instructions. Many vets will recommend a canine-formulated multivitamin, along with the following:

For light malnutrition, offer normal-portion meals twice a day. For more severe cases, offer several *small* meals per day of easily digestible puppy or growth-formulated food. After a couple of weeks, as the dog begins to put on weight, taper off to two normal-portion meals per day.

Caution: Feeding a malnourished dog too much, too fast can cause heart and liver damage. Again, make sure to follow your vet's advice.

For overweight dogs, see the following sidebar, "Fido or Lardo? Is Your Pooch Too Fat?"

Other Reasons a Dog Might Be Skinny

Many medical conditions can cause a dog to lose weight, including cancer, kidney disease, bowel obstruction, dental problems, anemia, and pancreatitis, to name a few. Extreme weight loss, whatever the cause, can be life threatening. Your vet can help you determine why your rescue is underweight and how to treat the condition.

FIDO OR LARDO? IS YOUR POOCH TOO FAT?

Obesity isn't just a human problem. Some vets consider it to be the top medical issue for American dogs, affecting everything from hormonal to orthopedic health.

It works the same as in humans. Obesity results when the intake of calories exceeds the calories burned—eating too much, exercising too little. The body stores the excess calories as fat. Even a tiny bit each day adds up to weight gain over time.

Most owners will not notice how chunky their pooches are getting until they take them into the vet for some other issue, or they realize that their dogs are huffing and puffing during a walk, or they notice they seem to suffer in warmer temperatures. If you have trouble feeling your pooch's ribs through her skin, she needs to lose weight.

After an exam that includes blood and urine tests to rule out any underlying disease, the vet might determine your pet's ideal weight and recommend putting Rover on a diet. A doggie slimming plan might include the following: calculating current caloric intake and planning a lower one; increasing exercise as tolerated; changing the type of dog food and snacks; providing lots of clean water, more fiber, and veggie snacks to diminish appetite; and regular weigh-ins.

Achieving a target weight can take anywhere from eight to twelve months.

And it will require cooperation from the entire family. No sneaking goodies on the sly. Everyone needs to understand the serious health consequences of canine obesity.

A DOG'S FAVORITE SUBJECT—FOOD!

A broad selection of packaged dog foods awaits you on pet store shelves. How do you decide which one is best for your dog?

First, read labels. Ask your vet what percentages of carbohydrate, fiber, and fat are right for your particular pooch, and look for those percentages on the labels. Avoid foods whose primary ingredient is "animal by-products." (We'd rather not think about what that might be!) "Meal" is another word that can be translated as unappetizing body parts.

It is generally acknowledged that foods without artificial flavorings, colorings, or synthetic preservatives are a better choice. Keep in mind, though, that foods using natural preservatives such as vitamins E and C might have a shorter shelf life.

Look for the manufacturer's phone number on the package. It indicates that they are open to consumer questions and feedback.

Unfortunately, it can be a process of trial and error. Over time, a food that isn't right for your pooch can bring on a variety of problems including dull coat, dry skin, and gas. You might try switching foods (gradually) to see it if helps.

THE BENEFITS OF HOME COOKING

Many of us are too busy to even *think* about cooking for our dogs. But there can be enormous benefits. For one thing, you know exactly what's in it and how it was prepared. And your dog gets fresh, wholesome fare, instead of something that comes out of a bag or can.

Should you just slide food off your plate into your dog's bowl? Unfortunately, no. What you eat could be harmful to your dog. Instead, invest in a book on home cooking for your canine best friend. And don't forget to talk with your vet about it.

BARBARA'S BASIC BLEND

This is a basic home-cooking recipe and feeding guide contributed by our book's behavior and training consultant, Barbara O'Connor, whose large, rescued canine family (eight at current count) is the lucky, lifelong, thriving recipient of her gourmet pooch cuisine.

4 cups short-grain rice
1 cup pearl barley
1 cup millet
3 pounds ground turkey or chicken
1 cup each chopped parsley, carrots, spinach, and Swiss chard
4 cloves garlic, ground or finely chopped

Combine rice, barley, and millet in large soup pot and cover with water. Bring to a boil, then cover with a lid and simmer for 1 hour. Add more water if needed. Stir frequently.

Add ground turkey or chicken and stir to mix well. Cook 10 more minutes.

Add the chopped vegetables and stir to mix well. Cook 15 more minutes.

After cooling, use immediately, or pour into standard-size ice cube trays, and place in freezer. Once frozen, release from tray into freezer bags. Store in freezer and thaw out as needed. (Warning: Homemade dog meals do not last nearly as long as packaged chow, even in the freezer. Observe the same food safety precautions you would for human consumption.)

Feeding Guide

	1 to 25 lbs	26 to 51 lbs	51 to 70 lbs	71 to 100 lbs	100+ lbs
Puppy	2–12 cubes	10–18 cubes	14–24 cubes	14–30 cubes	24–36 cubes
Adult	2–8 cubes	6–12 cubes	8–18 cubes	14–24 cubes	28–34 cubes
Senior	2–6 cubes	4–8 cubes	6–14 cubes	12–20 cubes	18–30 cubes

Musculoskeletal

Osteoarthritis

The inflammation of a joint, this is also known as *degenerative joint disease*. Through normal wear and tear on the joint, the cartilage deteriorates, causing painful changes in the bone. This can also be instigated or made worse by an injury.

Symptoms: Limping; difficulty climbing stairs, rising after lying down, or getting in and out of cars; a change in gait; shrinkage of the muscles of the affected limbs; enlargement of the muscles that bear more weight; biting at painful joints.

Prevention: Exercise, good nutrition, and weight control help to prevent and treat.

Treatment: Anti-inflammatory drugs, pain relievers.

Hip Dysplasia

This involves abnormal changes and gradual degeneration of the hip joint.

Symptoms: Limited movement, a swaying motion in the gait, difficulty climbing stairs or rising after lying down, yelping with pain during exertion involving the hips.

Prevention: Genetic condition that is difficult to prevent. Exacerbated by careless inbreeding of purebreds. Ask your vet if your dog's breed or breed mix might predispose it to dysplasia, and watch for the signs.

Treatment: Weight reduction, surgery, anti-inflammatory drugs, pain relievers, reasonable and consistent exercise.

Elbow Dysplasia

This term is used for a group of disorders that affect the elbow joint. It can cause stiffness, pain, and lameness, worsening over a dog's lifetime.

Symptoms: A stiff gait, lameness, pain, swelling in elbow, less willingness to walk or run. Usually afflicts males and larger breeds.

Prevention: Strong genetic component. Can be triggered or exacerbated by repeated movements, such as jumping off a truck or a deck.

Treatment: Anti-inflammatory drugs, pain relievers, rest, restricted activity, surgery in younger dogs, reasonable and consistent exercise.

Ruptured Cruciate Ligament

Rupture of one of the two (front or back, but usually the front) cruciate ligaments that cross inside the knee. Caused by a sudden injury or blow to the knee.

Symptoms: Acute pain and lameness. Or in older, overweight dogs, slowly evolving lameness because of progressive stretching or tearing of the ligament.

Prevention: Avoid exertion a dog is unaccustomed to and sudden, extreme limb extensions or movement. Avoid letting the dog run on uneven terrain; for example, in yards with gopher holes.

Treatment: Rest, anti-inflammatory drugs, pain relievers, surgery.

Collapsed Disc, Disc Extrusion, and Disc Rupture

A collapsed (or herniated) disc occurs in the spine between a pair of vertebrae. In some cases the "jelly" (shock-absorbing material) becomes calcified and hard. Trauma causes the hardened jelly to bulge or explode into the spinal canal, creating pressure and pain. In disc extrusion, discs calcify and deteriorate, even rupture, in the first year of the dog's life.

Symptoms: Weakness of limbs; intense pain; arching of back in pain; unwillingness to turn the head; ataxia, or "drunk walk," progressing to paralysis; neurological dysfunction.

Prevention: Weight control, moderate daily exercise, training dog not to pull or jerk on leash. Harsh discipline with choke collar can exacerbate this condition.

Treatment: Rest and restricted activity, anti-inflammatory drugs, surgery. Use a chest harness instead of a neck collar.

NUTRITIONAL SUPPLEMENTS FOR ORTHOPEDIC PROBLEMS

Vets often recommend the nutritional supplement glucosamine and sometimes chondroitin for orthopedic prob-lems, along with other therapies. Recent studies suggest they can be helpful, especially in the early stages.

WHY DOES MY PUPPY LIMP?

It's not just older dogs who limp and hobble. Either through genes or injury, puppies and young dogs also might suffer from muscular/skeletal disorders. Hip dysplasia, elbow dysplasia, injury, or paw pad wounds might be causing the problem. Among other possibilities are epiphyseal fractures and panosteitis, described below. At the first sign of trouble, get your puppy to a vet.

Epiphyseal Fractures: Commonly observed in growing dogs less than one year old. At the end of each long bone, such as the femur (thigh bone) or humerus (upper front leg), there are soft areas where growth takes place. These epiphyseal growth plates contain immature, noncalcified cells that make them soft and spongy. As the weakest part of the bone, growth plates are more easily fractured than other bone.

Panosteitis: Painful bone disease common in young, large-breed dogs. Causes intermittent lameness that can switch from one leg to another. Possibly genetic. Males get it more often than females. Lasts from two to eighteen months—sometimes longer—but usually goes away on its own, leaving no permanent damage. Sometimes mistaken for elbow or hip dysplasia, or vice versa.

JUMP IN, THE WATER'S THERAPEUTIC!

Swimming is terrific exercise for both humans and dogs. For pooches suffering from limited movement or certain kinds of pain, it can be especially beneficial. Many doggie swim centers around the country are offering the services of canine physical therapists who guide patients through special aqua exercises to address ailments. In warm water, muscles relax. The weightlessness helps restore range of motion. The activity stimulates the flow of blood and oxygen, which promotes healing. Plus, once they get past any initial doubts, most dogs have fun—and that's healing too.

If you think your dog might benefit, talk about it with your vet and ask for the name of a recommended swim center.

Caution: Doggie swim therapy can do a cannonball in your pocketbook. It's not always cheap. But it can greatly improve the quality and even length of your dog's life.

HANDICAPPED DOGS

Many dogs with disabilities such as partial paralysis or a missing limb lead full, busy lives. Take a look at Web sites like http://www.handicappedpets.com to find all sorts of equipment for the care of handicapped pets.

Brain

Epilepsy

With this condition, uncoordinated nerve and muscle responses culminate in seizure. (But not all seizures are caused by epilepsy.) Seizures are recurring and the disorder is chronic.

Symptoms: Staring into space or upward eye gaze, involuntary contracting of the muscles and/or shaking and jerking of the body and limbs (because of haphazard electrical activity in the brain), loss of consciousness, involuntary vocalization (not pain), facial twitching, drooling, involuntary urination and defecation, jaw clamping.

Caution: The following can be especially life threatening: multiple seizures within twenty-four hours, or a cluster of seizures with little or no recovery time.

Prevention: Be aware of triggers that may interrupt normal brain activity, such as low blood sugar, ingestion of insecticides and other toxins, diminished thyroid output, and viral or bacterial infections (like distemper). Possible genetic component.

Treatment: Antiseizure medications.

(For more information on how to deal with seizures, see chapter 6, p. 93.)

Cognitive Dysfunction Syndrome

This progressive aging of the dog's brain—chemical and physiological changes—cause mental deterioration. It is sometimes likened to human dementia.

Symptoms: Behavioral changes, decrease in responsiveness, increased sleep time, confusion, lack of recognition of familiar people, reduced interest in surroundings and food, loss of control of bladder and bowel, increase in panting, increased difficulty navigating familiar routes in the environment.

Prevention: No known prevention. Some dog owners believe in providing mental stimulation, lots of positive interaction, good nutrition, and lowering stress.

Treatment: Medication, adherence to a regular routine and surroundings. Also follow the preventive measures above.

Heart

Mitral Insufficiency

This thickening and deformity of the mitral valve leads to the valve leaking. It can develop over many years.

Symptoms: Increased respiratory rate, panting, tiring easily, coughing, loss of appetite. A murmur may be heard. If heart failure occurs, signs include abdomen swelling, fainting, and abnormal heart rate and rhythms.

Prevention: None known. Sometimes genetic.

Treatment: No treatment unless the dog develops heart failure. Salt restriction, treatment with drugs when/if heart failure develops.

Dilated Cardiomyopathy

This condition causes the heart chambers to become thin, weak, overstressed, and enlarged. Blood can back up into the lungs, causing pulmonary edema/congestive heart failure. It most often affects large and giant breeds such as Doberman pinschers, Great Danes, and boxers. It frequently causes arrhythmias and sudden death.

Symptoms: Pale gums, increased heart rate and respirations with labored breathing, episodic periods of weakness, coughing, fainting, ascites (fluid in the abdomen), loss of appetite, lethargy, pain and paralysis in the rear legs.

Prevention: Genetics are likely a factor.

Treatment: Antiarrhythmia drugs, drugs to strengthen the contractility of the heart muscle and improve heart function. Almost always fatal, but with proper treatment might be controlled for some period of time.

Congestive Heart Failure

With this condition, the heart grows weak and ineffective in pumping of oxygenated blood throughout the body. It causes fatigue and, in most cases, accumulation of fluid in the tissues of the lungs, chest cavity, and abdominal cavity. It can affect any breed, but in giant breeds it can be triggered by dilated cardiomyopathy or valvular disease.

Symptoms: Labored breathing, exercise intolerance, weight loss, coughing.

Prevention: Not preventable; however, early diagnosis can help. Avoid high-salt foods and snacks, excessive heat and humidity, and extreme physical exercise.

Treatment: Low-sodium diets, diuretics (to decrease fluid retention), bronchial dilators and nitroglycerine paste (to decrease the work of the heart).

Heartworm

This parasite lives in the right ventricle and adjacent blood vessels of the heart and is transmitted by mosquitoes. It can cause congestive heart failure and lung, liver, kidney, and circulatory disease. Without treatment, almost always cripples or kills.

Symptoms: Tiring easily, exercise intolerance, coughing, labored breathing, vomiting, weight loss, bulging chest, fainting.

Prevention: If you live in an area with a lot of mosquitoes, talk with your vet about heartworm preventive medication. Although heartworm is most common in certain regions, cases have been reported in all fifty states.

Treatment: Expensive and risky but often effective. Daily injections of an arsenic compound. Severely restricted physical activity for one to two months (to prevent dead heartworms in the bloodstream from damaging organs).

Caution: *Do not* give your dog heartworm preventive medication until your vet performs a blood test to see if the parasite is present. If it is, the preventive medication can be dangerous to the dog.

Lungs

Respiratory Infections

Infections in the respiratory system are caused by any of a variety of fungal, bacterial, or viral factors, or through exposure and inhalation of a foreign agent such as smoke, dust, or allergens.

Symptoms: Dry cough, fever, loss of appetite, lethargy, nasal secretions.

Prevention: Strong immune system, avoidance of triggers described above, good nutrition, low-stress environment, intranasal vaccines for certain types.

Treatment: Adequate hydration, rest, antibiotics.

Pneumonia

Infection—caused by bacteria, virus, fungus, or parasites—can lead to a condition of the lungs involving fluid buildup.

Symptoms: Rapid, labored breathing, cough, elevated temperature (often over 104 degrees Fahrenheit), bluish-gray tongue, gums, and lips.

Prevention: Good nutrition, strong immune system, clean environment. Don't ignore upper respiratory infections, as they can progress to pneumonia. Keep your dog away from sick dogs.

Treatment: Elimination or control of factors that precipitated the pneumonia, antibiotics, diuretics, rehydration, oxygenation, control of fever.

Kidneys

Chronic and Acute Renal (Kidney) Failure

With the shutdown of kidney function, the kidneys lose their ability to filter toxins from the blood or to retain valuable electrolytes and minerals. Chronic failure can be brought on by congenital abnormalities, cancer, blockages, autoimmune disorders, medications, trauma, or infection, both bacterial and fungal. Acute failure can be caused by high blood pressure, poisoning (by antifreeze or rat poison), trauma, or by a virus or bacterial infection such as leptospirosis. Early detection and treatment of acute renal failure can sometimes restore full function.

Symptoms: For chronic failure, symptoms include increased thirst, increased urine output, squatting but not urinating, vomiting, lethargy, weight loss, lack of interest in food, pain (often upon physical examination of the kidney area), possibly elevated blood pressure, blood in the urine. For acute failure, symptoms include dehydration, arching of the back along with a stiff-legged gait, and a decrease or an absence of urine output.

Prevention: Early detection of any urinary problems, good diet, exercise, plenty of clean water. However, for some causes of kidney failure there is no prevention.

Treatment: Low-protein and low-sodium diet, adequate hydration, B-complex and C vitamins, antiulcer medication, antibiotics. Dialysis and transplants are not often great options because they are time consuming, difficult for the dog, and expensive.

Kidney Infection

This often occurs when bacteria from a lower urinary tract infection (UTI) moves upward along the urethra to the kidney. It can also be a result of bacteria in the blood from dental disease.

Symptoms: Loss of appetite, weight loss, thirst, increased water intake.

Prevention: Excellent nutrition, exercise, plenty of clean water, avoidance of injury to kidneys (trauma or ingesting of toxins), strong immune system.

Treatment: Antibiotics, adequate hydration, dietary management to ensure adequate caloric intake, some protein restriction.

Please note: Hepatitis, a disease of the liver, is covered in chapter six. For certain liver maladies, some vets recommend supplementation with vitamin E for its antioxidant properties.

Gastrointestinal (Digestive)

Gastritis (Acute or Chronic)
This inflammation of the stomach lining can be caused by spoiled food, a foreign body, shock, food allergy, ingestion of a toxin or certain steroids, antibiotics or aspirin, or infection caused by a parasite, bacterium, or virus.

Symptoms: Vomiting, weakness, loss of appetite, weight loss, diarrhea. In acute gastritis, the duration of vomiting seldom lasts more than seven days. In chronic gastritis, intermittent vomiting may last up to two weeks. Chronic gastritis is often seen in cases of cancer or inflammatory bowel disease.

Prevention: Elimination of foods and drugs that trigger episodes.

Treatment: Rest, nothing by mouth for hours, then the introduction of bland diet and water, anti-emetics to reduce vomiting, medication to protectively coat the gastrointestinal tract, antacids.

Outside of a dog, a book is probably man's best friend, and inside of a dog, it's too dark to read.

—Groucho Marx

Enteritis
This inflammation of the intestines most often occurs in puppies. It can damage bone marrow and heart tissues. The causes are bacteria, viruses such as parvo, protozoa, intestinal parasites, or ingestion of a foreign substance.

Caution: Dogs can die within twenty-four hours if not treated.

Symptoms: Depression, vomiting, foul-smelling feces, puppies stop suckling, diarrhea, fever, weight loss, feces streaked with blood and/or mucus, back arched and abdomen pulled in because of pain. Dobermans and rottweilers might be more susceptible.

Prevention: Strong immune system. Control parasites, vaccinate for diseases like parvo, and control the environment so that you can watch what the dog ingests.

Treatment: Rehydration, medications to control vomiting and diarrhea.

Inflammatory Bowel Disease
This involves chronic irritation of the stomach or intestines.

Symptoms: Persistent vomiting, chronic diarrhea, poor appetite, weight loss.

Prevention: None known.

Treatment: Diet changes (high protein or a different protein from what the dog is accustomed to eating), medications to reduce inflammation.

Please note: Other common gastrointestinal problems include parasites, discussed below; ingestion of foreign objects, covered in chapter 6, pp. 82–83; and bloat, or gastric dilatation-volvulus (the second most fatal dog ailment), also covered in chapter 6, pp. 89–90.

INCONTINENCE
If your dog has the opportunity for frequent potty breaks but is still making

urinary or bowel "mistakes" indoors, visit the vet. The problem might be medical rather than behavioral, and could be easily solved. For example, some spayed females can have urinary leakage, which often can be cured successfully with medication.

In dogs with myelopathy (degeneration of the nerve tissue in the spine), steroids often help to some degree with bowel control. Some owners also consult holistic veterinarians for treatment options ranging from acupuncture to herbs.

However, chronic medical conditions—including simple old age—can create incurable incontinence. Here are a few tips on how to cope:

Routine is more important now than ever. Feeding and exercising your dog at the same times every day can help regulate her elimination functions. According to the dog's abilities and stamina, make sure she gets adequate exercise. This helps tone sphincters and other muscles involved in urine and bowel control.

Restrict your dog to an area of the house with flooring that is easily cleaned. If you have small children, make sure they cannot enter that area, which might be unsanitary. Cover your dog's bedding with incontinence pads, available at pet stores and some drugstores. Diapers are another option, but they can cause chafing. You might look into special beds for incontinent dogs, such as the SleePee Time bed, available at http://www.sleepeetime.com.

Never let your dog lie in urine or feces. Aside from the unpleasantness for both you and your dog, it is unhygienic and can cause a number of health problems. Keep your dog clean—don't let waste products remain on the fur or skin. If your schedule does not allow for prompt cleaning of your incontinent dog and its environment, and there are no other options, at some point you might have to consider euthanasia. This is a last resort, and should only be employed when your dog's quality of life is greatly diminished.

Urinary

Urinary Tract Infection (UTI)
As its name implies, this is an infection of the urinary tract.

Symptoms: Fever, frequent urination attempts producing scant urine, straining to urinate, pain upon urination, perpetual licking in the genital area, bloody or cloudy urine.

Prevention: Adequate intake of clean water, proper nutrition and diet.

Treatment: Antibiotics, pain relievers, anti-inflammatories.

Reproductive Organs

Pyometra
This potentially fatal condition is an abscessed (pus-filled) uterus. Bacteria and toxins leak through the uterine walls into the bloodstream.

Symptoms: Typically found in older female dogs just finishing a heat cycle. Loss of appetite, increased thirst and drinking of water, vaginal discharge of foul-smelling pus.

Prevention: Spaying (removal of uterus and ovaries—ovariohysterectomy).

Treatment: Surgery to remove the uterus and ovaries, antibiotics, pain relievers.

Prostatitis

This inflammation of the prostate gland, which may be acute or chronic, is most often caused by a bacterial urinary tract infection that leads to an abscess in the prostate.

Symptoms: In acute prostatitis, symptoms include depression, lethargy, fever, straining to defecate, or tenderness or pain in the abdomen. In chronic prostatitis, symptoms might be blood or pus leaking from the penis or found in the urine. Either high or low blood sugar is a possibility. In chronic prostatitis, the animal might show no symptoms.

Prevention: Neutering (removal of testicles—castration). If your dog develops a UTI, see the vet to prevent the bacteria from moving up into the prostate tissue.

Treatment: Antibiotics, intravenous fluids, surgery.

Endocrine System

Hypothyroidism

This condition diminished function of the thyroid gland—causes decreased production of the thyroid hormone and a lowered metabolism rate. Some sources assert that 90 percent of new cases occur because of a weakened immune system. Pollutants and allergens may be triggers. A higher incidence of hypothyroidism occurs in certain breeds, including Labradors, cocker spaniels, golden retrievers, Doberman pinschers, and Airedales. It is sometimes caused by the dog's immune system attacking the thyroid tissues (autoimmune thyroiditis).

Symptoms: Lethargy, dry skin, hair loss, intolerance to cold, depression, extreme behavior changes (including aggressiveness), seizures, decreased heart rate, weight gain, bacterial infections of the skin, ear infections.

Prevention: None known. Genetic component.

Treatment: Drug therapy involving a daily dose of a synthetic thyroid hormone.

Diabetes

The most common is Type 1 diabetes mellitus, which occurs when the pancreas does not produce enough insulin. Type 2 diabetes mellitus occurs when the insulin produced is sufficient, but there is a problem with the body's ability to use it. Type 1 diabetes mellitus usually affects middle-aged dogs.

Symptoms: Increased thirst, weight loss in the presence of a good appetite, increased frequency of urination, sudden onset of blindness.

Prevention: Type 1 is not preventable; however, the risk for Type 2 may be reduced with weight management and proper diet.

Treatment: Daily injections of insulin, high-fiber diet, exercise, weight management.

Immune System

Atopy

An allergy that shows up on the skin, this is also known as *allergic inhalant dermatitis*. Dog allergies often manifest as skin conditions. Atopy is the most common. Triggers include ragweed, feathers, trees, shrubs, grasses, mold, dust mites, pollen, and even animal dander. Atopy worsens in allergic dogs with each successive allergy season.

Symptoms: Extreme itching with excessive chewing, biting, licking, rubbing the skin (so much so that in some cases, incisor teeth are worn to the gum line).

Prevention: Minimize exposure to the allergens. For example, dust and clean your home more often to reduce mold allergens, dust, and dust mites. Keep dogs indoors during the allergy season's heavy pollen periods. Possible genetic component.

Treatment: Antihistamines, corticosteriods, fatty acid supplements, hyposensitization (allergy testing and allergen injections).

Cancer

Cancer can occur in almost any part of the body, but we discuss a few of the most common ones here.

Lymphoma or Canine Lymphosarcoma (LSA)

A malignancy that rapidly grows in lymph tissue, LSA can occur in any area of the dog's body where there is lymph tissue, including almost every organ, as well as skin, bone marrow, and the gastrointestinal tract. It typically affects middle-aged dogs. Untreated, life expectancy after diagnosis is about two months.

Symptoms: Loss of appetite, vomiting, diarrhea, presence of one or more palpable lymph nodes, weight loss, depression, increased thirst and drinking, increased urination.

Prevention: Avoid exposure to known carcinogens. There is a possible genetic component.

Treatment: Chemotherapy and radiation therapies.

Mammary Cancer

This involves malignant nodules or aggressive tumors in breasts and occurs most frequently in nonspayed middle-aged females.

Symptoms: One or more hard, pea-sized tumors (often around the fourth or fifth nipple from the dog's front legs toward the back). Tumors often grow rapidly, are irregularly shaped, firm, and not easily moved from their attachment to the underlying tissue. Sometimes there is bleeding or ulceration of the affected nipple or tissue.

Prevention: Spaying drastically reduces risk.

Treatment: Surgical removal of the tumor to test for malignancy. Antihormonal drug regimens, radical mastectomy of all nipples and breast tissue.

Lipomas

A lipoma is a nonmalignant fatty tumor. (We've included it here because many people suspect cancer when they find a lipoma on their dog.) It commonly grows under the skin and attaches itself to muscle or connective tissue. It can appear virtually anywhere, but most often on the trunk. Depending on its location, the lipoma might restrict range of movement. Although it can grow enormous, it rarely becomes malignant, but if it does it is called an *infiltrative lipoma* and can spread throughout the body.

Symptoms: Appear as spherical or oval lumps, bumps, and swelled areas. Very soft and moveable under the skin. Infiltrative lipomas are irregularly shaped, and sometimes painful.

Prevention: No known prevention. Should be closely monitored, and not allowed to become so large that they interfere with movement.

Treatment: Surgery (if necessary).

HOW TO KNOW IF YOUR DOG IS IN PAIN

Not showing pain is hardwired into dogs' brains. Why? Because a show of pain in the wild signals weakness and can make an injured animal a target for predators. Hiding pain is a survival strategy. You can tell if your dog is suffering by the following:

- Favoring and protecting a limb or body area
- Yelping, crying out, or whimpering
- Biting, nipping, chewing, or licking at a limb or body area
- Limping—when a limb is injured, often the dog will not bear weight on it
- Pawing at an eye or ear
- Hunching over, spine arched, belly tight or drawn inward (abdominal pain)
- Trembling, anxiety, depression, aggression—any behavioral changes
- Stumbling and collapsing—indicates serious crisis. See vet immediately.

Know what is normal for your dog, so that you can recognize the abnormal. When your dog shows you she is in discomfort or pain, take action, so that she learns that communicating with you brings about a quick response and relief.

External Parasites and Other Skin Problems

Flea Allergy Dermatitis

Inflammation of the skin (dermatitis) is an allergic response to the saliva of fleas. A secondary skin infection can result in severe cases.

Symptoms: Excessive itching, incessant biting of the hind parts, lesions as a result of gnawing or chewing at a flea bite site.

Prevention: Flea eradication.

Treatment: Antibiotic and antifungal medications, steroids, flea control.

Hot Spots, Moist Eczema, or Pyotraumatic Dermatitis

These conditions are localized bacterial infections on the skin and are often seen in dogs with heavy, thick coats such as German shepherds or golden retrievers. Moisture under the dog's coat gets trapped, establishing an environment ripe for bacterial infection. Spots can develop pus, emit a foul smell, rapidly spread over the skin, and become painful.

Symptoms: Redness, pain, oozing, itchiness. Skin at the infected site may feel warm to the touch. Dog licks and bites at skin.

Prevention: Regular grooming (brushing/trimming) and regular baths (perhaps with medicated shampoo). Try to keep the dog from biting or licking. Check frequently for matted hair and skin lesions.

Treatment: Shave hair from site, clean with gentle skin cleanser and water, apply cool compresses several times daily; frequent bathing with medicated shampoo until condition subsides, antibiotics, Elizabethan collar (if licking or biting at skin), steroids.

Lick Granulomas or Acral Lick Dermatitis

Constant licking causes a lesion that can't heal. The lesion thickens, deepens, and widens. Possible reasons for licking include boredom, allergies that cause the initial itching, insect stings or bites, joint pain, hypothyroidism, psychological stress (such as a new baby, new housemates, or new dog). Some suggest lick granulomas are the result of a type of canine obsessive-compulsive behavior, not easily corrected. If you block access to the granuloma, the dog might start a new site.

Symptoms: Constant licking, ulcerated lesion that may ooze fluid or blood and doesn't readily heal.

Prevention: Low stress, plenty of exercise, mental stimulation, early intervention.

Treatment: Laser surgery of the lesion, antibiotics, topical medications, behavioral therapy to deal with psychological issues, antianxiety medications.

Demodectic Mange

A condition of the skin infested with the *Demodex* mite. Causes loss of hair. *Demodex* mites are always present to some degree on all dogs and are usually harmless, but stress and other factors can lower immunity, causing the mites' effects to proliferate. This typically affects puppies between the ages of three to twelve months. It's also known as red mange, puppy mange, and follicular mange.

Symptoms: Hair loss around eyes, mouth, and on legs. A secondary infection will have itchy, crusty, reddish skin, sometimes greasy and oozing.

Prevention: Low stress, regular good grooming, good nutrition, adequate exercise.

Treatment: Baths with medicated shampoo, medicated ointment for hair loss areas. Mild cases sometimes resolve themselves if stress is reduced. Advanced cases may require antibiotics and insecticidal dips.

Please note: *Demodex* is not communicable to humans or to other dogs.

Sarcoptic Mange

This skin condition is caused by the *Sarcoptes scabei* mite that burrows into the skin, lays eggs, then in a few days the cycle repeats itself, spreading the disease over the body. The oozing sores may harbor bacteria that cause a secondary infection.

Symptoms: Hair loss on ears, face, legs, and elbows. Crusty ear tips. Red pustules, yellow crusts, swollen lymph nodes, excessive itching that causes the dog to aggressively bite and lick the itchy sites.

Prevention: Regular good grooming, nutrition, and exercise; avoidance of contact with sites where other dogs (potentially infected with mange) congregate; and avoidance of areas where foxes may be present (foxes can harbor the mites).

Treatment: Oral and/or topical medications.

Please note: Sarcoptic mites cannot live for very long on humans, but they can cause us temporary itching. Dogs can easily infect each other with the condition. If one dog has it, make sure to treat all dogs in the household.

Ringworm

This highly contagious fungus infects the scalp, nails, and body. Ringworm can be spread from animals to people, from people to animals, and from people to people. Pets and people can also acquire it from contaminated objects, especially soil.

Symptoms: Circular patches of hair loss, minor lesions, round, scaly, inflamed patches on the skin.

Prevention: Early detection, vigorous and frequent hand washing.

Treatment: Oral medication, topical antifungal creams, medicated shampoos, keeping dog's hair clipped, antiseptic dipping.

Pyoderma

This bacterial infection causes lesions on the surface of the skin, just beneath it, or much deeper.

Symptoms: Intense itching. Painful red and draining pustule-type lesions.

Prevention: Regular grooming to guard against the formation of matted fur, frequent checking of the dog's skin for signs of infection or inflammation.

Treatment: Antibiotics, antibacterial shampoos, medications to deal with immune system suppression or underlying skin disease.

NUTRITIONAL SUPPLEMENTS FOR THE SKIN

Some skin problems can improve dramatically with the addition of fatty acids to the diet. Many veterinarians recommend Omega-3 and Omega-6 supplements for good results. Talk with your vet about what supplements might be helpful to your dog.

WARNING! DON'T DOUBLE UP ON DEWORMERS

Check with your vet before administering a deworming medication if your dog is also receiving a heartworm preventative.

Intestinal Parasites

It's not unusual for dogs to harbor intestinal parasites. Homeless dogs can be even more vulnerable because of their exposure to contaminated areas or other infected animals. And the stress of homelessness or even new surroundings after rescue can cause otherwise dormant parasites to flourish. We discuss some of the most common ones below. Because the symptoms, prevention, and treatment are so similar for them all, we present that information first. Then you'll find descrip-

tions of each parasite along with any unique or specific details.

Symptoms: Diarrhea (perhaps bloody), weight loss, dry coat, lackluster appearance, vomiting, mucus on feces, weakness, poor stamina, anemia, presence of worms in feces or around anus.

Prevention: Keep the yard and house free of fleas, especially dog bedding and carpeting. Avoid areas where the soil might be contaminated by feces of infected dogs. Regular pickup of feces at home.

Treatment: Prompt and periodic deworming with medication, aggressive cleanup of dog environment, especially where there are feces, and frequent hand washing.

Tapeworm

A dog gets infected with the common type of tapeworm *Dipylidium caninum* when it swallows a flea that has tapeworm larvae inside it. The tapeworm hooks itself onto the small intestine and remains there while growing to roughly eight inches.

Symptoms: As the tapeworm reproduces, segments might exit the body and move around the anus, in feces, or stick to the anal hair and dry up. They look like flat, half-inch-long white noodles, or when dry, like grains of rice.

Prevention: Avoid a different type of tapeworm—*Echinococcus*—by not allowing the dog to eat small rodents that might be hosting the parasite.

Hookworm

These bloodsuckers attach themselves to the lining of the small intestine. They are acquired by ingesting hookworm eggs from infested soil. Eggs can also be transmitted from mother to puppy through the mother's milk.

Roundworm

This parasite infests the intestines of puppies; generally it does not affect adults. Roundworms reproduce in great numbers reaching a length of seven inches. Pups can die from a severe infestation. Transmission is fecal–oral and is often passed from mother to pup.

Symptoms: Potbellied look, poor growth, presence of worms in stool or vomit.

Whipworm

Infestation occurs when a dog ingests the parasite and it attaches itself to the dog's large intestine and then reproduces.

Symptoms: Whipworms look like pieces of thread with one enlarged end.

Treatment: Feces examination may not readily reveal whipworm, so several samples must be tested.

Giardia

A protozoan parasite, giardia infests the small intestine, interferes with food absorption, and weakens the immune system. It is passed by infected animals through their feces onto the ground or into bodies of water where others can contract it.

Symptoms: Smelly, greasy, light-colored diarrhea and weight loss despite a normal appetite.

Prevention: Regular pickup of feces in the dog's environment. Avoid areas where many feces of other animals are present. Avoid animals infected with giardia. Do not let your dog enter or drink from freshwater bodies such as ponds, lakes, rivers, creeks, and so on.

Treatment: Antiprotozoan medication, aggressive disinfection of the dog's environment using cleaning solutions (for example, ammonia) that are specific for giardia, bathing with medicinal shampoo (because parasites can stick to the fur).

Please note: Giardia is easily transmitted to humans and other animals. If your dog gets it, please see quarantine and disinfection procedures in chapter 6, pp. 98–100.

Coccidia

Protozoan parasites, coccidia attach themselves to the intestinal tract. They are most commonly seen in puppies under six months or in adults who have compromised immune systems or are under stress (for example, if they are homeless or in a new home).

Symptoms: Diarrhea (maybe bloody), vomiting, loss of appetite, dehydration.

Prevention: Insect and small rodent control. Protect food and water from contamination by such carriers as cockroaches, flies, and mice. Resistant to many disinfectants. Sterilize other contaminated objects with steam cleaning, boiling water, or a solution of 10 percent ammonia.

Treatment: Medication does not kill the coccidia but inhibits their ability to reproduce until the animal's immune system can strengthen enough to combat them.

DO I HAVE TO DO EVERYTHING MY VET SAYS?

Your relationship with your vet should be a partnership working for the health of your dog. No one knows your dog and its needs as well as you do. On the other paw, most of us haven't completed veterinary school, earned a veterinary license, or treated hundreds of dogs, as our vets have. Working together as a team is the best approach.

There will be times when you feel your vet is wrong. If so, talk about options. For example, maybe your vet is recommending surgery for your older pet, but you don't feel the dog is up to it. This might be a time when your own daily observations and familiarity with your pet give you better insight than the clinical data your vet must rely on.

With the right kind of vet-client relationship, you and your vet will both consider each other's opinions and cooperate to decide what is best for your pooch. If you feel unsure, don't hesitate to visit other vets or veterinary specialists for additional opinions.

Eyes

Injuries

An injury is any trauma to the eye, such as scratches, scrapes, cuts, bruises, and contact with chemicals or other irritants. This can proceed to become a corneal ulcer—a lesion with infection and pus—and some injuries can result in blindness.

Symptoms: Squinting, oozing, a bloodshot sclera (white part), rubbing or pawing at the eye, increased blinking, watery eyes, pain. Breeds such as bloodhounds, with their drooping eyelids' large pockets, and Pekingese, whose eyes slightly jut forward, suffer a higher risk for eye injury.

Prevention: Don't let a dog hang her head out of the car window, since irritants and foreign objects may hit her eyes. Make sure your dog avoids cat chasing (they aim for the eyes), encounters with wildlife, and contact with aggressive dogs. Groom so that there is no hair hanging into the eyes. Keep caustic or abrasive liquids and substances out of the dog's reach.

Treatment: Eye washes, anti-inflammatory and pain medications, antibiotic ointments or drops. Sometimes surgery is necessary to repair or remove a damaged eye.

Cataracts

This disruption of the normal arrangement of fibers in the lens can impair vision to the point of blindness. Cataracts can develop after an infection (especially with certain viruses such as parvo) and often affect older dogs, but they can develop at any age.

Symptoms: Cloudy appearance of the lenses, signs of impaired vision, such as bumping into furniture or walls. Inherited in some breeds, such as the Old English sheepdog, golden retriever, Boston terrier, Siberian husky, standard poodle.

Prevention: Can be caused by poor nutrition. Strong genetic component. Sometimes brought on by untreated diabetes.

Treatment: Surgical removal of cataracts.

Please note: Not all dogs with cloudy-looking eyes have cataracts. Nuclear sclerosis is a normal, age-related, harmless change in the eye that appears very similar to cataracts but causes no appreciable loss of vision.

Glaucoma

A condition involving increased fluid pressure in the eye. It can cause blindness, in some cases within hours.

Symptoms: Squinting. Redness around the rim of eye. Cloudy, large pupils. Eye might seem to bulge or protrude. Can be very painful. Dog might paw at it, rub it on the floor, furniture, or you. Higher incidence in certain breeds such as the chow chow, miniature poodle, basset hound, wirehaired fox terrier, and Boston terrier, to name a few.

Prevention: No known prevention. Eye exams, good eye hygiene, avoid eye inflammations and infections.

Treatment: Reduce eye pressure with medication and sometimes surgery.

Caution: Glaucoma is considered to be an emergency. Blindness can occur within hours. Any of the symptoms above warrant an immediate trip to the vet.

Foxtails.

KILLER SEEDS—THE DANGERS OF FOXTAILS

Foxtails are the plant world's curse on canines. Little barbs, they bear the seeds of certain grasses commonly thought of as weeds and known collectively as foxtails. The barbs can get into eyes, ears, nose, throat, paws, urethra, anus—virtually anywhere on the dog's body. They not only cause pain and inflammation but can also trigger infection, require surgical removal, or even become life threatening.

If a dog is squinting or pawing at a watery eye, constantly licking at a particular spot, sneezing, coughing, or gagging, suspect a foxtail. Once a foxtail is lodged on the dog, it can enter the bloodstream and migrate, posing tremendous health hazards.

Eradicate these grasses from your yard. Annual plants, they sprout in the spring, so if you remove them before they dry and drop their seeds, they cannot spread. After a couple of seasons, with a little work, your yard can be foxtail-free. Also avoid walking or exercising your pooch in foxtail-invaded areas. Frequently check for the barbs on your dog. Remove them by pulling straight out. Don't break off any pieces that might remain lodged in the skin. Take those innocent-looking seeds seriously; they can be dangerous.

Ears

Infections

Inflammation of the external ear canal, caused by bacteria, fungus, or allergy, can be painful. It's the most common ear problem in dogs.

Symptoms: Redness, pawing or biting at the ear, shaking of the head, sometimes a foul-smelling yellow or black discharge.

Prevention: Keep ears clean.

Treatment: Antibiotics, antifungal medication, anti-inflammatory drugs. Can sometimes be resistant to antibiotics.

Mites

Tiny parasites resembling crabs. Can cause painful secondary bacterial or yeast infections in the ear canal, most often in puppies. Quite contagious between pets.

Symptoms: Head shaking, scratching, excessive wax, a thick, blackish or reddish discharge.

Prevention: Avoid exposure to infested animals. Maintain strict sanitation to eliminate mites from pet environment. Keep ears clean. Check frequently for strong, rancid smell and discharge in ear canal.

Treatment: Cleaning of the ears, anti-mite medication.

The Teeth and Mouth

Calculus and Gingivitis

Bacteria thrive on remnants of food in the mouth and harden into plaque deposits or calculus. It builds up along the gum, forming pockets, which create a favorable environment for the growth of bacteria. It can lead to gingivitis, an inflammation of the gums. It can also destroy the roots of the teeth, attack bone, and enter the circulatory system, damaging heart valves, the liver, and kidneys.

Symptoms: Yellow or brown buildup around teeth at the gum line; painful red, swollen, receding, or bleeding gums; bad breath; mouth sensitivity and difficulty chewing; pus at the gum line; pawing at the mouth; drooling; teeth that are loose or missing; nausea; lack of appetite; lethargy; coughing; breathing problems.

Prevention: Daily tooth brushing, specially formulated pet food that reduces plaque buildup, regular vet exams. If you're feeding your dog packaged dog foods, make it dry kibble and hard biscuits; keep soft canned foods to a minimum.

Treatment: Antibiotics, vet cleaning of teeth and gums, removal of calculus and dead tissue, possible tooth extraction. Feed the dog dry kibble rather than soft canned foods.

Caution: Some nondental diseases can mimic gingivitis. Consult your vet.

Breaks and Cracks

Broken and cracked canine teeth are often the result of either direct trauma, such as being hit by a rock or car, or chewing hard objects. The most common tooth breakage occurs in the upper fang tooth and the upper fourth premolar. At the site of the fractured tooth, bacteria form and move along the root canal to infect the bloodstream, tooth, and bone (possibly causing an abscess).

Symptoms: Pain, bad breath, pus, bleeding gums, lethargy, nausea, pawing at mouth.

Prevention: Only give toys that soften as they are chewed (rawhide bones, for example). Keep up daily tooth brushing and vet exams.

Treatment: Root canal therapy (pulp of tooth is removed), repair of fractures, tooth extraction; antibiotics, pain medication.

IF IT FEELS GOOD, CHEW IT!

Dogs need to chew. This is not only an irresistible behavioral urge, but it is also essential to overall health. It massages and strengthens gums and teeth, as well as the mouth and jaw muscles, stimulating blood circulation. It helps to loosen and remove plaque. Think of it as doggie dental flossing. And for puppies, it helps to relieve the discomfort of teething.

It's also a great stress and boredom reliever. When dogs chew, the movement of the jaw triggers the release of endorphin, or "happiness," hormones, creating a sense of relaxation and well-being. It's kind of like a pooch mini vacation or spa session.

Give your best friend safe chewing opportunities every day, or at least several times per week. This not only improves health, but will also distract your dog from your shoes!

WARNING: CHEW TOY HAZARDS

Finding a safe doggie chew product can be frustrating. For one thing, pooches can be picky. Yours might be interested only if it squeaks, rolls, or smells edible.

Then you enter the maze of hazards. Some chew products are too hard and can break or crack teeth. Rule of thumb: If it hurts when you tap it on your knee, it's too hard—for example, the hard Nylabones and similar products (although dogs love them!). The softer Gumabones are safer, but strong chewers can pulverize them in minutes.

A more dog-safe chew will have some "give" to it, like rawhides. However, they can cause trouble too. The dog can rip off and swallow a large piece (especially the knot on the ends of some rawhides) that then gets stuck in the digestive tract. Ask your vet to recommend the right size rawhide for your dog. Some recommend giving rawhides for just fifteen or twenty minutes at a time, under supervision. Also, make sure to use only rawhides made in the United States. Those made elsewhere are sometimes treated with chemicals that can be toxic.

Greenies have been in the news, too. Reportedly, some dogs swallowed pieces of them that lodged in the digestive tract and didn't break down,

causing death. The manufacturer began making Greenies softer to be more digestible.

Many dogs love plastic or soft cloth squeaky toys. These can provide hours of entertainment, but again, are not without their hazards. The squeakers inside can be swallowed and obstruct the digestive tract.

Even the classic tennis ball is suspect. The coatings can be toxic, abrasive to tooth enamel, and they have been known to get stuck whole in the throats of larger dogs.

Real animal bones can splinter and pierce tissue. Some vets recommend large, boiled beef bones. You can buy them prepared or boil them yourself, but first check with your vet about how to go about it, and whether or not it's right for your dog.

Possibly safer chew options include hard rubbery products, such as Kongs (you can stuff them with peanut butter, treats, or a special Kong spray-in filling to make them more appealing); twisted, knotted rope toys; and real meat tendon chews. But dogs, being what they are, might find a way to hurt themselves with these or anything else.

The bottom line is to talk with your vet about what chews are best for your pooch, and keep a close eye on your dog while she's enjoying them. Make sure that no splinters are breaking off, and that the dog doesn't attempt to swallow any large pieces or hazardous items like squeakers.

Paws

Paw Pads

Injuries can range from moderate to severe blisters, calluses, ulcers, chemical or thermal burns, abrasions and lacerations.

Symptoms: Limping, pain, bleeding, pus.

Prevention: Paw pads are covered by a special, thicker type of skin designed for heavy wear, tear, and shock absorption. But they are not indestructible, and once an injury occurs on the pad, it can be slow to heal. Avoid rocky, sharp, hot, or icy surfaces, and trash-strewn areas. If such places are unavoidable, use dog booties, found at most pet stores. Examine dog's paws frequently, including the nail beds and between the toes.

Treatment: Wound care, antibiotics, medicated dressings, ointments, splints and pads to relieve pressure, confinement.

Claws and Dew Claws

The most common problem with doggie toenails is that they can break, split, or be clipped or torn to the quick. They can snag on something and be ripped off completely. If allowed to grow too long, they can cause the dog to limp or stagger, or even cause harmful changes in the bone structure. Dew claws are the nails that are located on the inside of the paw, connected to the limb by loose skin. Allowed to grow too long, dew claws can curl in a circle, tear and bleed profusely, and even penetrate into the toe pad. All such events cause severe pain, bleeding, and infection.

Symptoms: Licking of a toe, a bleeding toenail, a missing toenail, a cracked or broken toenail. Can be very painful.

Prevention: Regular clipping. Regular examination of nails and nail beds.

Treatment: Removal of torn portions or removal of entire nail, antibiotics.

THE HOLISTIC DOG—ALTERNATIVE MEDICINE

From flower essences and herbs to massage and acupuncture, holistic medicine offers new approaches to pooch health care. Some licensed vets refer to themselves as *holistic* veterinarians, specializing in alternative modes of care. Others are beginning to incorporate a few nontraditional methods into their practices. For example, vets today often use nutrition and certain supplements—such as glucosamine for orthopedic ailments—as preventive measures or even cures.

Some of the other types of holistic therapies, such as acupuncture, are less widely accepted, yet might be of interest to you in caring for your pet. As is the case with all treatment options, do your homework, learn all you can, and consult a qualified professional for guidance. (See the Recommended Books List on p. 225 for titles on the subject.)

Death

On average, humans live several decades and dogs make it to only one or two. Chances are that at some point we'll have to deal with the departures of our four-footed best friends. Here's a guide that might help.

Saying Good-bye—How to Make the Right Decision

As if dealing with a dog's death weren't difficult enough, often we have to make the decision ourselves as to *when* it's going to happen. A pooch's severe illness or injury might force us to consider ending her life in a humane, painless way, rather than allowing the dog to linger and suffer—especially if there is little hope she'll get better. Weigh the following questions:

What are the dog's life expectancy and chances for recovery?

Is the dog in pain? Can the pain be controlled?

Do the dog's medications allow her to be alert and aware of her surroundings?

Is the dog still able to interact with you, your family, and other pets? Does she seem interested in doing so?

What is the dog's life like now compared to her life before the illness or injury?

Is the dog able to participate in any activities that give her pleasure?

How many good days are there compared to bad ones?

If you do decide to euthanize your dog, give some thought to preparation. Is your dog comfortable enough that you could set aside a period of time to say good-bye—perhaps a last day together with the family? Or would it be best for your dog and you to proceed as quickly as possible?

An "Easy Death"—How Humane Euthanasia Is Performed

Euthanasia means "good death" or "easy death." It lives up to its name. The procedure is quick and painless, allowing your dog's life to end in a peaceful way.

You might make an appointment to take your dog to the vet's office, or arrange for a vet to come to your home. Some, but not all, will perform house calls for this need, perhaps charging an extra fee.

Beforehand, the vet will ask you to sign authorization documents. You will also be asked whether you wish to be present. This is a personal choice. Your presence can be helpful to your dog in almost all circumstances, including this final one, but witnessing your dog's death can be overwhelming. Finally, you will be asked how you would like for the vet to deal with the remains. (See below for more information.)

Before the procedure begins, make sure that your vet plans to give your dog an intravenous injection of a sedative *prior to* the injection of the euthanasia drug. Not all vets include this in their process, but most recommend it to ensure a stress-free send-off for your pet.

When you are ready, the vet should administer the sedative and wait a few moments for it to take effect. The dog will relax and fall asleep or into a semiconscious state. The vet will then inject a high concentration of a barbiturate anesthetic. Within seconds, this drug will reach the heart and cause it to slow and then stop. Your vet will perform a few simple tests to make certain the procedure is complete.

Sometimes vets will cover the body. If you do not want your pet covered, you might see involuntary movements of the muscles or hear gasps as the lungs contract, for as long as a couple of minutes. This does not indicate consciousness or pain—it's a sign that the brain has shut off and is no longer controlling the body. There might also be emissions from the bladder or bowel.

Some people wish to stay with their dog's body for a few moments after death, and others don't. At this point, you've done your best for your dear friend, and that choice is up to you.

Necessary Arrangements—Burial and Cremation

In years gone by, pets were often laid to rest in graves dug by their owners in the backyard. Today, personal preferences, urban life, or sometimes even city ordinances might prohibit home burials. If so, your vet can refer you to companies that offer pet burial or cremation services. Costs vary widely depending on options you choose—from tens of dollars into the hundreds.

Your vet can also dispose of your dog's remains, but keep in mind that sometimes this is by means of companies that render (boil down) animal carcasses into fat for use in commercial products. Discuss your choices with your vet.

Friends Forever—Dealing with Loss

Here are some ideas for dealing with the death of a dog:

Allow yourself to grieve. It's a gradual healing process. Give it time. Absorbing loss goes at its own pace—for some of us more slowly than for others.

The death of a dog can feel similar to the death of a child. As your dog's guardian, you functioned much like a parent, with the associated sense of responsibility. You might blame yourself for your dog's demise. "If only I had done this, or if only I hadn't done that." These feelings are common and normal, but not always accurate. Be realistic about how much you could have affected the outcome.

Keep in mind that no one makes perfect decisions or gives perfect care—especially under stressful or emotional circumstances. If you truly made a mistake, consider it a valuable lesson learned. Remember that your dog would not blame you and would not want you to be hard on yourself.

Don't let anyone rush you into adopting another dog. Sometimes it's best to wait awhile to simply "be" with the memories of your departed friend. On the other paw, if you feel ready to plunge in right away, go for it. Is it disloyal? No way. A new friend might be just what you need, and your previous pooch would only want you to be happy!

Tune out those who speak to you in ignorance, saying things like, "It's just a dog" or, "You can get another one." Seek out those who understand that pets are family.

Some sort of memorial ceremony might help—as elaborate as a formal funeral or as simple as a stroll through a park that your pooch enjoyed.

Other rituals can also be healing. As often as you need, you might light a candle in your friend's memory and meditate on the flame as a symbol of your dog's inextinguishable warmth and brightness. Every day, think of one funny thing that your pooch did. This helps you refocus on the happy parts of her life instead of the difficult times at the end.

Consider making a donation to an animal welfare organization, perhaps one that posts the names of departed pets, as a memorial to yours.

Don't overlook the grieving of other family members, including pets. They'll feel it too. Sometimes the best way to help yourself is to help others. Give lots of extra hugs, take longer walks and playtimes, make special meals, or just hang out.

If your feelings become overwhelming, consider visiting a grief counselor, preferably one knowledgeable about pet loss, or joining a pet loss support group.

Grief can cause not only emotional changes but also physical ones—tummy trouble, insomnia, high blood pressure, or anything in between. Preoccupation with loss can also lead to accidents ranging from stubbed toes to car wrecks. When you're grieving, be extra good to yourself to stay safe and healthy. Your beloved best friend would want it that way.

> If there are no dogs in Heaven, then when I die I want to go where they went.
>
> —Author Unknown

Abigail Plumley

Bubbles, Abigail, and Pretty.

Happily Ever After True Story Number Seven:

Bubbles

• •

With the Golden Gate Bridge in the distance and acres of green grass beneath her paws, Bubbles tears through the wind, racing like a champion, her sleek tan-and-white body a blur to the cameraman who was trying in vain to film her. Another dog, not quite as fast as Bubbles, tried his best to play her game. But Bubbles is too caught up in the moment and the wonderful sensations that course through her young body. Running, breathing, barking. All of it is like a gift for this dog because, not too long ago, she was a victim of one of the worst storms ever to hit the United States—Hurricane Katrina.

After the storm, volunteers from all over the country traveled to the Gulf Coast to help rescue animals left behind. For weeks, they pulled dogs, cats, reptiles, and birds from flooded homes. As time passed, animals still caught in the devastation were rarely found alive.

On October 20, 2005, fifty-two days after the storm subsided, a woman heard the low growl of a dog. It was coming from inside a house that had not yet been checked. She dared not go in alone, so she called the Southern

Courtesy of Southern Animal Foundation.

Moments after Bubbles is discovered, an SAF volunteer uses a "come-along" to gently coax the emaciated dog from the bathtub she had been living in since the hurricane hit.

Animal Foundation (SAF) for help. At 10:30 p.m. the rescuers arrived. Dr. Missy Jackson and four others waded through contaminated floodwaters carrying their equipment: food, water, and a catch pole. This group had experienced many heartbreaking rescues, but what they found inside this house was quite simply a miracle.

"She was lying inside an old rusted bathtub," said Dr. Jackson. Flashlights revealed what almost looked like a skeleton. It seemed only the dog's brown eyes were left alive. "We brought her out of the tub and it was so sad. Poor little thing. She was very frightened, but very sweet and trusting." Dr. Jackson observed terrible sores on the dog's pressure points. "They were like bedsores. I suspect she had been in that tub for over a month, waiting for her family to come home."

Later that night, back in the SAF office, the dog was placed on a thick, warm blanket. But as Dr. Jackson sat at the computer to type up the evening's events, the dog painfully stood up and wobbled over to the desk. "Very gently, she moved herself between my knees and rested her head on my lap," the vet said. "I think she finally felt safe."

During the next four months, the staff and volunteers at SAF nursed the dog back to health. As she grew stronger, her energetic, happy personality bubbled to the surface. She needed a name. Someone suggested "Bubbles."

Looking back on the catastrophe of Katrina and the suffering the storm caused for thousands of animals, Bubbles was truly a miracle survivor. The story of her rescue spread. Soon she was flown to Los Angeles and San Francisco where she was featured in press events. She filmed public service announcements with actor Kevin Nealon to help spread the word that many of the saved animals from the Gulf Coast now needed homes. And Bubbles was one of them.

Colleen Kessler and Gary Schick fostered Bubbles. A husband-and-wife team, they founded the organization Peace, Love & Pets to help animal victims of Katrina.

"We fell madly in love with her," said Colleen. "She was perfectly trained—sit, down, come, off, no. She was great in the car, could play a neat game of tag, and loved to cuddle, especially in the early morning." Then why couldn't Colleen and Gary adopt Bubbles? "We were fancying keeping her, until we let the cats out." Maybe it was just "cat curiosity," but Bubbles's antics upon spying the two senior citizen felines made it clear that she needed a catless home.

In Phoenix, Arizona, Abigail Plumley and her family were looking for a dog to adopt. Their rescued dalmatian, Pretty, seemed ready for a sister. After meeting the Plumleys and Pretty, Colleen knew she had found Bubbles her forever home.

Abigail said, "We are the winners, having Bubbles in our family. Knowing what she went through, giving her this loving home has been so rewarding."

And for Bubbles, the love was not one-sided. Maybe it was because of the TLC Bubbles received at the clinic in New Orleans. Or perhaps it was Colleen and Gary and the affection they showered upon her. But somewhere along the way, Bubbles blossomed into a nurturer.

Abigail describes Bubbles's generous spirit with this story: "Pretty had a bad ear infection, so as I was cleaning her ears, she started to cry. When I finished, Bubbles started to lick Pretty's ears as if consoling her and petting her, as if to reassure her that everything was all right."

Nowadays, when Bubbles needs reassurance, she snuggles between Abigail's knees, where she rests her head on Abigail's lap, quietly at peace in a place she feels safe.

8.
Understanding Your Rescued Dog: Building Up to Great Behavior
Developing Communication and Laying the Groundwork for Effective Training

Kellie: I Shall Become Zephyr
I am back in the car, and my stomach is creeping closer to my mouth. And then, the door opens and out I go. There are people holding dogs on leashes. Mom is talking to me, so I better try to listen. She wants me to walk next to her. Okay, I get the picture. Walk close to Mom. Stop. She said another word. Oh! I know that word! Sit! I'm sitting! In a circle we walk, sit, walk, sit. Sometimes Mom gives my leash a yank. Sorry, Mom. I'll try to do better. The lady in charge has a stunning dog named Zephyr. He is so smart! He understands the sounds that people make. I wish I could do that. Next thing I know, all the dogs are playing and sniffing. Class is dismissed.

We asked Barbara O'Connor to write chapters 8 and 9 with us. She contributed behavior, health, and safety information to other parts of the book as well. For three decades Barbara taught classes at the San Bruno Dog Obedience School in San Bruno, California, and trained thousands of private clients and their dogs. Her specialty is dogs that others deem nontrainable. She has personally rescued, retrained, and rehomed hundreds of them.

What can you expect from your rescued dog? The unexpected!

The terms *homeless*, *stray*, or *rescued* dogs call up contradictory images in our heads: gregarious and grateful . . . clever and conniving . . . feral and ferocious. All pooch personalities are shaped by their individual life experiences and genetic makeup. Dogs in need—whether they're found on the street, in a neglectful owner's backyard, or at a shelter—can be as different as night and day.

Like humans, canines react to adversity and change in a variety of ways. Arriving in your home, some dogs might become fearful, suspicious, withdrawn, or aloof. Others might be ultraneedy and clingy, unable to be apart from you for even a few minutes. In contrast, dogs who have had to fend for themselves for a long time might be cheerily independent, seeming to care not one bit about your opinion of their behavior. Undernourished dogs might be obsessive about food, resorting to theft off countertops, or even aggression. Then there are those lucky ones who are able to bounce right back, quickly fitting in, forgiving and forgetting all that went before.

Whether you are adopting a pooch yourself or rehoming a rescue, part of your job is to help the dog become a good canine citizen. This is for his own sake as well as that of the humans and other pets in his life. Poorly behaved dogs usually are not happy ones. Oftentimes, their indiscretions are a way of acting out emotions ranging from insecurity to fear to anger. And a decently behaved dog has the best chance of being accepted into a home and enjoying a happy, healthy, long life.

Half the battle in training your dog is to understand him, to lay the groundwork for strong relationships between the dog, yourself, and other family members, and to keep him safe and cherished in the process. This chapter is devoted to those endeavors. In the next chapter, we offer specific training strategies.

Please note: One style does not fit all. In this chapter and in chapter 9, you'll find some training options. Not all dog owners or professional trainers use or recommend these methods. In fact, some might disagree strongly with ideas we present. Your key to success will be to learn as much as possible about dogs and training from numerous sources, and most important, to study and understand your dog, yourself, and your household. The best solutions will be custom fit to the needs of your own "pack."

The average dog is a nicer person than the average person.
—Andy Rooney

IS IT ALWAYS YOUR FAULT?

A popular way to explain bad dog behavior is to blame the owner. The assumption is that given proper training and care, the dog would be fine. We agree that it is usually the owner's fault—or the fault of a previous owner—but not always. Other factors can affect canine behavior. Basic temperament is partly predetermined by genes. A puppy's treatment by his mother and his rank in the litter can also play important roles. Just like humans, some pooch moms and siblings are nicer than others. And sometimes, undiscovered health problems can cause unwanted behaviors.

I try to remember that dogs do not wake up in the morning with the sole purpose of seeing how much they can mess up my day! They are simply dogs, and do what is natural to them until they understand what is appropriate to their new family unit."
—Rita Martinez, CPDT, Rescues Are Special

Getting to Know You

The first step on the road to good behavior is to understand your dog. His breed or mix of breeds, past experiences, age, and health all play a role in his temperament. With many rescues, very little is known of their past. As for breed, sometimes it can be anyone's guess. Understanding dogs in general, and your rescue in particular, will require your patient observational skills.

How to "Read" a Dog

Don't speak "Dog"? Here's a translation guide:

Friendly: Ears perked up, eyes wide open, alert, soft look. Mouth relaxed, possibly slightly open, "smiling." Relaxed body posture, or possible wiggling of whole rear end. Tail is up or out straight from body wagging. Maybe some vocal whimpering, yapping, short high barks, or happy howling.

Happy and Playful: Ears perked up and forward or relaxed. Eyes wide open with a sparkle. Mouth relaxed and slightly open, teeth covered unless "smiling" wide. Tail wagging, vocalizing with excited barking, soft play-growling or yodeling. Excited, jumping up and down, bouncing. Running in circles, or forward and back, as an invitation to play. Hackles may be up in excitement.

Play Bow: Might bark or other vocalization, run in circles, stop, then lower front end, while rear end goes up in the air, wiggling. Tail up and wagging, ears up.

Alert: Prelude to another behavior. Tail out, ears forward, mouth closed, stands tall and forward. Hackles may be up in anticipation.

Neutral or Relaxed: Ears up, mouth may be open. Closed is more common. Corners of mouth relaxed. Tail down.

Submissive: Ears down, flattened against head. Eyes are narrowed to slits or wide open with the whites showing. Lips pulled back from teeth in a "grin." Nuzzling, licking, or both, the face of another dog or human. Body is lowered to the ground; front paw may be raised to show further submission. May roll on back, exposing belly. May leak or dribble urine. Possible emptying of anal glands. Tail down between legs or flattened onto belly. A short tail is plastered against butt. Possible low, worried whining, yelping, whimpering in fear.

Defensive: For example, a cornered dog. Will attack as a last resort. May be growling or whining. Ears back, wrinkled nose, corner of mouth back, may expose teeth in a snarl. Body lowered, with tail tucked.

Guarding: Ears perked up forward, eyes wide open, alert. Mouth is slightly open, teeth bared. May be snapping or gnashing. Body is tense, rigid, standing very tall in an aggressive or dominant stance. Hackles up. Tail is rigid, held straight out from body, may be fluffed. Loud, alert bark, growl snarl.

Offensive: Dangerous, aggressive. May be growling. Ready to attack if ears forward or back, eyes narrow or staring in a challenge, nose wrinkled, lips open, drawn back to expose teeth bared in a snarl, corners of mouth forward. Stands tall and forward with hackles up over neck and hindquarters, sometimes up and down back. Tail straight out from body, and fluffed up.

Feelings

Throughout the ages, great thinkers from Pythagoras to Leonardo da Vinci to Albert Einstein have observed that many animals have responses akin to those of humans. Recently, researchers have found that the brain structure of our fellow mammals is quite similar to our own. As Dr. Allen Schoen, DVM, stated on www.catsplay.com, "Our dogs and cats have the same neurotransmitters we do, and the same neuro-hormones—and at the same parts of the brain. Why shouldn't they feel emotions?"

According to researchers Paul Morris and Christine Doe of the University of Portsmouth in the United Kingdom, "The data clearly suggest that complex emotions are present in a wider range of species than once thought and that animals do indeed have rich emotional lives."

Never underestimate a dog's capacity for emotion, and its effect on his life and on yours. Most people find that their canine companions can experience joy, sadness, love, anger, forgiveness, resentment, selflessness, selfishness, charity, and greed. That hero's welcome you get from your pooch when you come home is sheer love. The dog that refuses to eat for days after the death of an owner or a fellow pet might be grieving.

The complexity of canine emotion is nothing short of a gift to humanity. The flip side of that gift, however, is our burden of responsibility. Knowing that our dogs can experience loneliness, we can't dump them in the backyard for long days. Knowing they're fearful, we can't let the dog-park bully rough them up. Knowing they love us, we can't abandon them when they're sick or old.

As with any gift, we must honor, develop, and enjoy the great font of feeling within our best friends.

TAKING CARE OF EACH OTHER

(a true story from trainer Barbara O'Connor)

Every morning the little fox terrier brought Mark's slippers to his side of the bed. She knew just how to set them so all he had to do was get his feet into them. Most days it was a difficult task, for he was ninety-four years old. As he walked slowly to the front door, Foxy eagerly awaited him there. He opened the door, and in one leap she was out and down the two steps. She slowed to grab the newspaper, then turned and leaped back into the house. She pushed the door shut behind her and ran to Mark, sitting at the table. Standing on

her hind legs, Foxy presented the paper directly into Mark's trembling hand.

Whatever he dropped, she would fetch up and present. When the phone rang, she'd bring Mark the receiver. Hearing the mail truck, she'd run to the side door, where a rope on the latch enabled her to open it and take the mail from Dick the letter carrier. Then she'd dash back and present it to Mark.

He loved her so much! Before Foxy, he dreaded waking up. Now he laughed again. Three years earlier on his daily walk, he had found the dog in the gutter, almost dead from the cold and wet. He nursed her back to health and she thrived. Now she took care of him. You'd never convince Mark that dogs don't have emotions.

Trust

One of the most important building blocks for great pooch behavior is its trust in you. Some people believe that a rescued pooch, especially, will be devoted just because you provide chow and shelter. Certainly it doesn't hurt for a pooch to see you as a source of food and creature comforts. But there's more to it than that.

For an adopted dog that had a rough go of it pre-rescue, you might have to overcome fears instilled by neglect or abuse. It might take the dog awhile to accept that you're a different kind of human who will never hurt him.

Another step toward trust comes when your rescue sees you as a powerful protector and ally. When there's a threat he shouldn't have to handle, like a neighbor's kids lobbing rocks at him over the fence, you take swift action to stop it.

Even beyond those basics, there's another whole dimension. You earn your dog's deepest trust when he observes you being reliable, fair, and consistent on an hourly, daily basis. Your attitude is critical. Calm, cheerful, and sure of yourself, you're a good leader. You set reasonable rules for both yourself and your pooch. You live up to your end of the bargain, and help your dog live up to his end. Only then will he look to you for guidance.

Finally, when the dog senses that you not only love him, but also respect him as a valued family/pack member, you bind the dog to you forever, heart and soul.

I hope to be the kind of person my dog thinks I am.
—Unknown Author

Quality Time

The top thing you can do to improve your dog's behavior—and his life—is to spend time with him. That's the fastest path to mutual understanding and trust.

An amazing thing happens when you're together: Your dog trains himself. Although Rowdy's rambunctious behavior might indicate otherwise, the truth is that he watches your every move. You are your dog's universe, and his job is to navigate that realm. Your canine friend is on constant alert to your body language, moods, likes, and dislikes. In the course of a normal day spent with him, even if you don't take the time for a formal training session, you'll be teaching Rowdy during every minute. Your dog watches for subtle cues that you might not even know you're giving: You tense when Rowdy looms over your kitten; you smile when he nuzzles your daughter's hand.

Being together, you can take advantage of dozens of casual training opportunities. For instance, have Rowdy sit and stay before you give him his food bowl, or as you put on his leash for a walk. This develops his patience and self-control. When you open a door, have your dog wait till you give him permission to proceed. This discourages dashing outside, in case the dog finds the front door left open someday. Socialize your dog by exposing him to all sorts of people of every size, shape, and race, wearing every type of dress and accessories. Walk him by noisy construction sites, playgrounds with shrieking kids, and get him used to all different kinds of environments.

Don't forget to play with your dog every chance you get. Canine packs bond by clowning around. They also enjoy lots of friendly physical contact, so don't skimp on snuggles. Last but not least, canine packs just hang out, passing the time together. Whatever you're doing, having your best friend nearby can strengthen your ties and brighten the day for you both.

A Dog Is a Dog

One of the kindest things you can do for your dog is to remember that she is, after all, a dog. Some of a dog's behavior will seem very human, but she has important needs and motivations that are uniquely canine. Respect and fulfill those and you'll have a happier, healthier dog.

Doggie needs include chewing (discussed in chapter 7, pp. 133–134) and digging, discussed in chapter 9, pp. 168–169. Here are a couple more:

Sniffing

A dog's nose cells contain about twenty-five times more smell receptors than ours do. It's estimated that a canine sense of smell is fifty to one hundred times better than ours. On a park picnic bench a dog can tell who sat there and what they ate—yesterday. It's a pity to let such a phenomenal skill go to waste.

Right in your neighborhood, dogs love to "read the newspaper." From the urine marks left by other dogs, your pooch can tell if they are male or female, spayed or neutered, purebred or mixed, young or old, tall or short, and friend or foe. When you take your dog for walks, make sure to allow leisure time for this hobby. For part of the outing, let your dog lead you while he follows his nose. Don't allow the dog to drag you (see the section on leash pulling in chapter 9, pp. 163–164). Just stay attuned to his movements and relax.

Another way to celebrate your dog's sniffing skill is to get involved in organized tracking and scent work, or play sniffing games at home. (See chapter 11, pp. 216–217.)

Barking

Some dogs really enjoy barking. Unfortunately most neighbors do not. You can channel this noisy urge by teaching your pooch to bark on command, then getting him to do so at appropriate times and places (see the sidebar below "Speak! Barking on Command").

WHY DO DOGS DESTROY THINGS?

On TV nature shows, you can see how wolves and other wild canines dine. With no knives or forks, the carcasses of prey aren't always easy to eat. Sinews, muscle tendons, and bones can be hard and tough. Dogs must rip off pieces they can chew and swallow to stay alive. It takes a lot of fang action and jaw power to do that. By instinct, your dog practices this skill on his toys, his chews, the sticks he finds in the yard,

or sometimes, if unsupervised, your belongings.

SPEAK! BARKING ON COMMAND

Imagine being forced into silence for the rest of your life. We all like expressing ourselves. But there's always a right time and place. To channel your dog's urge to bark, teach him to "speak" when you ask, then give the command for fun now and then.

Tie your pooch's leash to something stationary, and hold his favorite treat just out of his reach. Chatter excitedly. Out of frustration, he barks. Quickly, say, "Luke, speak. Good speak," and give him the treat. Repeat several times. Eventually the dog will make the connection that he doesn't get the treat till he speaks, and will do so on command.

Please note: Obviously, it's best to practice and use this trick where you're well out of earshot of anyone it might disturb.

Basic Training Guidelines

Here are some steps to take toward a great relationship with your pooch:

Ask a Pro

Try to sign up for obedience classes as soon as possible after you rescue/adopt your dog. Even if you already know how to train, a class is a great way to socialize your dog with other dogs and people, and you just might learn something new.

Try to get a reputable, professional trainer/behaviorist's advice early on. A pro with years of paws-on experience has probably encountered your rescue's exact behaviors before, and knows tried-and-true ways to improve them.

The trainer can take an honest look at your pooch because he or she is not as emotionally involved as you are. Before rescue/adoption, the trainer can perform temperament testing on that adorable fluffball whom you think is positively perfect. A trainer can make objective evaluations of how you and your family members interact with the pooch, and how your lifestyle or your home's setup might need to change.

By noticing subtle clues your dog gives, a trainer can often predict problems that haven't materialized yet and suggest preventive strategies.

How to Find Good Trainers and Obedience Classes

For recommendations, ask people you see walking well-behaved dogs. Also ask friends, family, your vet, local shelters, and rescue organizations.

After you've made a list of trainers, interview each on the phone. Stick to the ones with excellent reputations and broad experience. Arrange a meeting and look for humane and fair methods that you feel you will be able to use yourself with your pooch. Ask to meet the trainers' dogs. Are they well trained but also well loved? Do they seem to be having fun, responding enthusiastically to commands? Or are they fearfully submissive? Good trainers should have a genuine love of dogs, a sense of humor, a wide range of training options to fit different situations, and good communication skills. They should be observant, patient, and flexible, recognizing that each dog needs a tailor-made approach, and thus be willing to try several methods until they find the right one.

Ask trainers if they have a group class at your level. Before signing up, leave your pooch at home and attend one of the classes just to watch. Does the instructor have control and the students' attention? Are the students, both human and canine, enjoying themselves? How are the dogs behaving? Are a variety of methods used to meet each dog's individual needs? Are lesson handouts available?

Tuition for group classes runs from about $50 to $125 for eight weeks. Drop-in advanced classes cost about $7 to $10. Fees for private lessons can range from about $75 to $150, depending on the distance the trainer must travel.

What's Reasonable to Expect from Your Dog?

At first, not much. Your pooch might arrive with few if any social skills. But with patient guidance from their humans, most dogs can learn some basic manners. These manners don't just make your life easier; they also help keep your dog safe. It won't happen overnight—and it will never be perfect. But given time, you and your best friend should be able to live together with some modicum of ease. Here are some goals:

Well socialized—gets along peaceably with household members, other pets, visitors, people in public, pets in public, the vet, the groomer

Comes when called

Walks smoothly on leash

Does not jump on people

Does not bark excessively

While you sleep, stays quiet or at least out of trouble. (Might require crating, but should be quiet in crate.)

Does not chew inappropriately

Does not dig inappropriately

What Can Your Pooch Expect from You?

Your dog is your best bud. He is also your pupil and follower. You're not just his best pal; you're his teacher and leader. Your dog's life is in your hands. Will you live up to that sacred trust? Think about qualities that make the best teachers and leaders. Most people with happy, thriving dogs can be described in the following ways: fair, firm, reliable, consistent, nurturing, forgiving, fun-loving, safeguard the interests of others as much as their own, consider the big picture, move past failures and build on small successes.

DOING NOTHING IS GOOD— POSITIVE REINFORCEMENT

Your dog is lying there drowsily, watching you fold laundry. In a soft voice, without looking up, you say, "Good boy, Rowdy. Good quiet. Good dog." Why praise Rowdy when he's doing nothing? *Because* he's doing nothing! Doing nothing, calmly and quietly, is a skill you want to encourage. It doesn't come easily to all dogs. A bit of praise now and then, just to let the dog know he's doing something right, for a change, can keep his paws on the right path and boost his confidence besides.

You can use the same strategy for other subtle displays of good behavior.

Let's say Rowdy's nemesis the squirrel darts past the window, but Rowdy is too absorbed in the rawhide he's chewing on to bark. Tell him, "Rowdy, good quiet. Good chew."

Positive reinforcement—acknowledging that your dog is being good—is just as important, if not more so, than correcting him when he's not so good.

Socialization

Many behavior problems stem from a dog's lack of exposure to unfamiliar people, places, and other animals. A common cure for these problems is socialization. It means becoming accustomed to a wide variety of experiences. Your dog not only gets used to the particular new situations you put him in, he also learns how to cope with newness itself—overcoming mistrust of the unusual—thus lowering his anxiety when the next unfamiliar experience comes along.

Socialization is one of the biggest favors you can do for your dog and for yourself. You'll build your dog's confidence and social skills, which deter dozens of unwanted behaviors. Plus the two of you will get to know each other better and just plain have fun.

Take your dog anywhere he's allowed, starting out with quiet, easily controlled environments such as a shopping mall parking lot. Walk your dog near shoppers, at a bit of a distance, to see how he reacts. If the dog is quiet and comfortable, go closer. If all goes well, and you're sure the dog's not fearful or aggressive, let people pet him—one person at a time, never in a group, which could be intimidating. Visit a pet store to see how the dog does around the clerks, shoppers, and other dogs on leash. Once he's comfortable, check out more challenging settings. Hang out across the street from a busy construction site with heavy equipment in operation. Join a crowd at a street fair. Attend pet-friendly fund-raisers hosted by rescue organizations or pet stores, where Rowdy can meet other four-footers. Eventually you can try a dog park, dog beach, or other off-leash dog areas.

At home, have guests over. Dogs who are perfectly friendly in public might behave very differently on their own turf. Territorial drives might make Rowdy suspicious or even aggressive toward visitors. By introducing your dog to strangers at home, you're getting him used to the idea that if you say so, it's OK for your friends, family, and repair workers to enter your pack's den.

Gradual socialization in as many situations as possible—in your home and in public—can work like a magic wand to prevent or wave away many pooch problems.

CRUISIN' TOGETHER

One of the best ways to begin socializing an inexperienced, shy, or fearful dog is to take him for car rides. He's exposed to the big, wide world from a safe distance in your comfy vehicle. For a dog it can seem like a magic carpet ride—cruising through all manner of interesting smells, sights, and sounds without having to deal with them.

> *Well-mannered dogs enjoy a much richer life—they go more places and have more company than the untrained dog.*
> —*Rita Martinez, CPDT, Rescues Are Special*

Basic Commands

In obedience school, with a private trainer, and/or on your own, here are some basic commands you and your dog should learn. Please note: Words for commands vary from trainer to trainer; it doesn't matter as long as you're consistent with the words you use for your dog.

No—the dog stops doing whatever he is doing

Watch—looks at your face

Sit—sits straight with front paws and bottom on the floor

Down—lies down

Stand—stands with all four paws on the ground

Stay—maintains a "sit," "down," or "stand" position until released

Wait—a looser version of stay; free to move about but not past a certain point (for example, doesn't go through a doorway, doesn't jump out the open hatch of a car)

OK—A release word (similar to "at ease" in the military); dog is released from a "stay" or "wait"—lets dog go from the previous command

Come here—comes to you

Come—comes to you, sits directly in front of and facing you, and stays until you release him

Heel—walks close to your side, never surging ahead or lagging behind

Leave it—does not sniff or touch a particular object, animal, or person

Drop it—drops whatever is in his mouth

Off—stops jumping on you or others, or gets off furniture or other defined item

Out—leaves a room, part of the yard, or other defined area

Hand Signals

Many dog trainers accompany vocal commands with hand signals, so that the dog learns both and learns to respond to either. You can choose any signals you want, or follow the ones used by your dog trainer or obedience instructor. For example, say, "Rowdy, down," and hold out your hand, palm facing down. Or say, "Rowdy, stay," and hold up your hand, palm toward him in a "stop" motion. It's quite impressive to watch a well-trained pooch and his silent human work entirely off hand signals.

JUST SAY THE WORD

Here's one low-hassle way to teach your dog simple commands and tricks: Wait till she's just about to perform the desired movement on her own, choose a word to represent it, then say the dog's name and say the word.

For example, Rowdy is drawing in his hindquarters, getting ready to sit. Say, "Rowdy, sit." He's trotting up to you. Say, "Rowdy, come here." He's stretching out his front legs, with his back end up in the air. Say, "Rowdy, bow." As he completes each action—which he was going to do anyway—don't forget to praise: "Rowdy, good sit (or come or bow)!" Perhaps give him a treat.

Top Training Tips

The first few months with a new dog aren't always easy. The settling-in period requires saintly patience and eagle-eye supervision to keep the pooch safe and to stop naughty habits from taking hold. Perseverance and a sense of humor can see you through.

- Always praise when Rowdy seeks you out, especially if he is looking at you.
- Say your dog's name before every command so he'll know you're talking to him. It's especially important in multi-dog households. But try to avoid using the dog's name when you're reprimanding him so he won't associate his name with unpleasantness.
- Try to be specific in your commands and praise. This will help your dog identify exactly which behaviors you do or don't want. Instead of just saying, "No," when the dog runs to the window and barks excessively, say, "Quiet." As soon as he complies, instead of just saying, "Rowdy, good boy," say, "Rowdy, good quiet." The dog will begin to realize that the problem wasn't being near the window—it was the barking.
- Avoid giving a command more than once at a time. If you say, "Rowdy, sit," and he doesn't do so, do not keep saying it until he does. That teaches a dog that he doesn't have to do it until you've said it nine times. Instead, silently show Rowdy what to do, repeating whatever procedure you've used to teach him the command. (For example, luring the dog into a sitting position with a treat, or gently pulling up on the leash and lightly pressing your palm down on his rump.) If the dog is not on leash, put the leash on and follow the same procedure. The second Rowdy sits, even if you had to guide him into it, praise him using the name of the command: "Rowdy, good sit!" Maybe give your dog a treat.

Now his attention is on you—a perfect moment to repeat and positively reinforce the training exercise until he gets it right.

- Use any words you like for commands. Just make them short, easy words the dog can understand, and words that don't sound too much like other commands.

- Any negative reaction or correction from you should end the instant Rowdy stops an unwanted behavior. And immediately after it ends, praise the dog. Such precision defines exactly what the dog was doing wrong, and when he started doing right.

- Never carry grudges. Once an incident of unwanted behavior ends, it's over. Even if your dog altered your best suit or remodeled your kitchen cabinets, don't let your pooch know you're still fuming. Five minutes after a dog's naughty deed, he has forgotten about it. Continuing to pout or punish the dog is pointless and counterproductive.

- Never issue a command you can't enforce. For example, you spot Rowdy disconnecting your garden hose. Just then your boss from work calls with important questions. You ask your boss to hold and yell out the window, "Rowdy, leave it!" but Rowdy keeps chewing. You have to get back to your boss and answer questions while Rowdy decimates the hose. You've just taught Rowdy that it's OK to ignore you.

- If you don't have the time or the energy to deal with a misbehavior right then, pretend you didn't see it. Do not let your dog see that you've seen it. In his mind that signals inconsistency—sometimes what he's doing is wrong, and some-

times it's OK, depending on how busy or tired you are. Dogs learn to exploit that fact in no time.

- Never start a battle you can't win. For example, if your one-hundred-twenty-pound pooch refuses to enter the tub for his bath, don't try to outmuscle the dog. Once he digs in its paws, you'll just tire yourself and teach the dog that your puny frame is no match for his brawn. Or let's say your sneaky one has filched a steak from the table and growls when you try to get it back. Don't force it. Your dog has bigger teeth. But you have a bigger brain. Chapter 9 offers guidance on how to use smart thinking to deal with these situations.

- You can never be too patient. Aside from a caring heart, patience is probably the one quality you need most in dealing with any dog. Sometimes it's a matter of baby steps—with two forward and one back—but eventually, perseverance pays. You might have to correct Rowdy ninety-nine times about jumping on people, then the hundredth time, he gets it.

- Lengthen your fuse. Rowdy is likely to commit all manner of crimes. You get your dog a pricey orthopedic bed to help with his arthritis, and he shreds it. Why? You've knocked yourself out to rescue and care for the dog, and this is the thanks you get? Exasperation, frustration, and anger are perfectly normal reactions. But losing your temper shows the dog that you are easily flustered, not in control, and that maybe the dog had better take charge. The more you can apply your brain to solving problems instead of your emotions, the better the outcome. Don't yell and scream; plot and scheme.

- Always use the mildest possible correction when your dog misbehaves. If you respond harshly every time, you will harden your dog so that all he understands are harsh corrections.
- Understand your dog's needs, and fulfill them. Literally at your mercy, a dog has little ability to do for himself. If you cannot or will not meet your dog's needs, he will try to find a way. This is a major cause of unwanted and even dangerous behavior. But when your dog sees that you are a caring, capable manager, he will be able to relax, turn his focus on you, and repay you a thousand times over.

NO DUMB DOGS

Although we've often heard people say things like, "My dog is a knucklehead; he can't learn anything," we've found that pooches have drastically different personalities that make them appear smarter or dumber than others.

For example, some are more tuned in to you or more eager to please you. They're more responsive and interactive, which makes them seem smarter. The past experiences and emotional state of a dog also can affect his ability to concentrate on what he's being asked to do. An abused or neglected dog might be suspicious of an unfamiliar situation—something as innocuous as you throwing a ball for him to fetch. We've even known many dogs who were downright terrified of toys!

Time and time again we've seen lackluster pooches suddenly break out and shine when the moment was right—that is, when they felt safe, comfortable, and motivated.

In our opinion, there are no dumb dogs.

YOU *CAN* TEACH AN OLD DOG NEW TRICKS

For dogs, age is no barrier to learning. As long as the pooch is generally healthy, he can be taught, or retaught, as the case may be. It's true that older dogs might have developed more entrenched behaviors than younger ones, but on the plus side, they're usually more mellow and calm, making it easier for them to focus and cooperate.

ANGER MANAGEMENT

If you ever feel like punishing your dog with pain, don't. Kicking, hitting, slapping, swatting, spanking, poking, pinching, and other such acts not only are inhumane, they don't work. Violence destroys your relationship. Instead of seeking your approval, your best friend will simply fear your reprisal.

To your dog, your hands and body should be the source of all good things. He will crave—even worship—your physical presence. Once you use those tools to hurt the dog, you've lost an irreplaceable asset in your training strategy, not to mention your bond. You're no longer the wise, powerful alpha leader; you become nothing but a brute who has to resort to inflicting pain.

If you're losing your temper, please get immediate help. Most communities offer anger management resources ranging from telephone hotlines to low-cost therapy. While you examine your situation, seriously consider boarding your dog at a kennel, with a responsible friend or relative, or even rehoming him. Many pet rescue organizations are willing and able to help. Remember that violence toward animals often leads to violence toward humans. Don't delay in addressing this dangerous problem.

> If you are patient in one moment of anger, you will escape a hundred days of sorrow.
>
> —Chinese proverb

BELIEVE IN MAGIC

Did you know that to your dog, you are a wizard? How else could you produce things like steak, comfy sofas, and transportation to the beach, seemingly out of thin air? In your dog's eyes, you control the galaxy and can make anything happen. Take advantage of this fortunate misconception. Maintain the illusion that you are all powerful. Fulfill his doggie needs, never lose your cool, conjure up a little fun for the two of you every day—and you'll make life magical for you both.

TRAINING EQUIPMENT

Gradually, you are developing an understanding of your dog. You've signed up for obedience classes and/or hired a private trainer. At some point, you'll need to invest in training equipment. Your obedience class teacher or trainer can offer guidance. Here are some ideas to get you started.

ONE TOOL DOES NOT FIT ALL

There are many types of training equipment. Trainers and dog owners have a wide range of preferences. Always use what is best for a particular dog in a particular situation.

Also consider quality. Most training equipment is no longer made in the United States. Some of it can be of poor workmanship. For example, chain collars and leash clips can have faulty welding that fails and breaks when your dog yanks on it suddenly, leaving you with no control. As a general rule, seek American- or German-made products.

Your Voice

Your voice is the most powerful piece of equipment you'll ever have for training your dog, and it's portable! When the two of you develop a close relationship, your dog hangs on your every breath. He interprets every nuance. Think of yourself as a singer and learn to use your voice, packing it with information for your dog.

Develop four voices:

Casual: Your normal tone, used for the idle chitchat you do with your dog now and then whenever you're together. To your dog, that sound means that everything is all right and ordinary. Then, when something unusual or distressing happens, you can chitchat in the same relaxed tone to reassure the dog. For example, you can use it when you're trimming his nails, or the vet is examining his sore paw, or during a thunderstorm.

Command: Not much different from your casual voice. Calm, low key. The softer, the better. *Do not* get in the habit of yelling loud and sharp orders at your dog. Great professional trainers are remarkably quiet with their own well-taught dogs. Just make sure to enunciate commands clearly, and separate them with brief pauses from anything else you are saying. If you chatter along in your reassuring casual voice then slip a command in the middle of it, it's not fair to expect Rowdy to pick up on it.

Praise: Sweet-talking, happy, fun, proud. Perhaps a little higher-pitched than the other voices, to mimic the cooing of a mother dog.

Correction: Sharp, distinct, but not angry. Deeper, and just a little louder than your command voice. The goal is to make it different enough that it grabs the dog's attention right away, but not so different that he senses you have lost control. A capable, confident leader doesn't have to roar.

The Crate

A crate is a plastic or wire box with ventilation holes or "windows" and a securely fastening door, designed to confine a dog safely. Other names include *kennel* and *transport kennel*. You might take one look at this tool and say, "That's a cage, a jail, a claustrophobia chamber! I would never do that to my dog!" Many of us who now frequently use crates had the same initial reaction, but we're glad we reconsidered.

Parents confine young children in cribs and playpens to keep them out of danger. Used correctly, a crate can serve the same purpose for your dog.

All domestic dog breeds are descended from the wolf. For shelter, wolves and other wild canines often dig small spaces into the dirt or snow. Inside, they curl up and relax. These dens are not large. They are barely bigger than the animal himself. Your dog retains the same instincts. Introduce her correctly to her crate, and she'll see it as comfort and refuge—her own private retreat or "room."

Why Use a Crate?

A crate gives you and Rowdy peace of mind.

It eliminates the chance that while you're busy, the dog will chew electrical cords, eat detergent, pull the aquarium down on himself, or sneak out the front door that someone left open during your dinner party.

It saves your shoes, clothing, furniture, rugs, and a houseful of items you'd never imagine a dog would want to shred.

It gives you freedom to leave the house without worrying about Rowdy's safety, or that his barking in the yard will disturb neighbors while you're away.

It's a secure place to put Rowdy when the dog-fearing carpenter is fixing the window frame that Rowdy chewed last week (when you dashed to the corner store for a few minutes and *didn't* put him in the crate).

It's a portable, comfortable place to keep Rowdy near you while you're getting him accustomed to visitors.

It's a safer way to travel in the car, protecting the dog from the impact of an accident or sudden braking.

It's one of the most useful tools for house-training pooches (see the sidebar, "House-training and Potty Breaks," chapter 5, p. 53).

It helps prepare Rowdy for the confinement he'll have to undergo at the groomer's, vet's office, boarding kennel, or visiting a friend's home.

It's a quiet, stress-free retreat for Rowdy, where he can take a snooze or enjoy his favorite toys or chews undisturbed.

It especially helps Rowdy when he's new to a household. He know he can go into his crate for some downtime, where he doesn't have to worry about all the new rules, or getting in trouble, or pleasing anybody. He can escape rambunctious other pets or children. He can de-stress and regroup.

How to Select a Crate

A crate should be big enough for your dog to stand up without his head or ears touching the ceiling, and long enough so he can easily turn around, lie down, or sit.

Look for well-known, American- or German-made brands.

You can choose between plastic or metal wire grid. The plastic ones are made of a smooth, molded material. The doors and the windows are enclosed with hard-wire grid panels that allow for ventilation and visibility. The metal kind are made entirely of the see-through, hard-wire grid material. Both types have swinging doors that fasten shut.

The plastic crates can provide more of a sheltered feeling and protection from drafts and chill. The metal wire crates give Rowdy a better view of what's happening around him, and more air flow. If you select the plastic crate, you can position it with the door side facing the room's activity, so that Rowdy can still see what's going on, and turn an electric fan on it if he's too warm. If you choose the metal wire crate, you can cover it with a blanket if you want Rowdy to feel more protected and cozy.

To use a crate for airplane travel, make sure that the labeling certifies that use.

Before you buy, familiarize yourself with how the crate assembles and operates. The plastic kind usually comes in two parts—a top shell and a bottom one—that fasten together with nuts and bolts or devices like snap tabs. For the fasteners, the more metal you see, the better. Plastic fasteners break more easily. Learn how to open and lock the door properly.

How to Introduce the Crate

The crate can be a lonely place, but the following steps make it a comfy, welcoming den for your dog.

Play the Great Crate Adventure Game: Arm yourself with your pooch's favorite treats. A popular item at trainer Barbara's house is homemade jerky (see the sidebar on p. 156 for the recipe). Make sure it's a treat Rowdy values highly and cannot resist. You will be using it sparingly—pieces about the size of a pea— just enough to keep your dog interested but not overfed.

Make a trail of treats around the entire exterior of the crate. While Rowdy snacks happily around the treat trail, and checks out the crate as he goes, your job is to have fun. Chatter excitedly about the great crate adventure. "Wow, look at that. It's your crate, Rowdy. With treats, too! Oh, boy! Good dog, Rowdy." The happier you sound, the happier the dog will be. Replenish the treat trail and repeat several times.

Make a trail of treats leading up to the crate entrance, following the same "fun" procedure. Repeat several times.

Make a treat trail that goes into the crate, all the way to the back. The *second* Rowdy enters, praise lavishly. "Good crate, Rowdy, good boy!" *Do not* shut the door. Let Rowdy decide when he wants to come out. Repeat several times. *Never* shut the door. Whenever the dog is inside the crate, keep up the happy talk. The second he leaves the crate, stop talking. This shows the dog that good things happen *inside* the crate.

Throw a treat in front of the crate and say, "Rowdy, get the treat," and praise him when he does so. Repeat, next tossing the treat to the middle of the crate, and then to the very back.

Remember to praise profusely whenever the dog is inside the crate, and stop when he comes out.

After about fifteen minutes of the game, stop and shut the crate door so that Rowdy can no longer enter. This is a bit of reverse psychology. Rowdy has now seen how great the crate can be. During this familiarization period, shutting the door makes the crate seem extra special, like forbidden fruit, something to look forward to.

Play the game several times a day.

Meanwhile, feed Rowdy all his meals inside the crate. Put his bowl at the very back of the crate. Leave the door open so that he can enter and exit at will. But remember to shut it again as soon as Rowdy comes out.

How to Get Your Dog to Hang Out Happily in the Crate

Once your dog seems completely comfortable entering and exiting his crate as described above, you can start getting him used to the idea of staying inside the crate.

Throw a large treat to the very back of the crate. Say, "Rowdy, get the treat." When he goes in, say, "Rowdy, good crate." Now shut the door briefly. The second Rowdy starts to turn around (after eating the treat), open the door and say, "Rowdy, come here!" He'll come out. Repeat several times.

For several days you've fed Rowdy his meals in the crate, and you've always made sure to place his bowl all the way in the back of the crate and you've left the door open while he was inside. Now, while Rowdy is busy eating, shut the door. When he has just finished eating, open it and let him come out when he pleases. Repeat with every meal for a few days.

Follow the procedure above, but this time, leave the door shut until Rowdy finishes eating. As the dog turns around to exit, say, "Wow, Rowdy, look, a treat!" Give Rowdy his favorite treat through the door of the crate. Say, "Rowdy, good boy, good crate!" Then, opening the door, say, "Rowdy, OK." The dog will exit the crate.

Using the same procedure, keep the door shut for a few seconds longer each time, until you've worked up to a minute, then a few minutes, then ten minutes. Never leave the room. Read a book, watch TV, eat, or do something else. Give Rowdy a treat at least every thirty seconds. Give the dog lots of praise: "Rowdy, good crate. Good boy." Gradually work up to an hour with Rowdy in the crate and you nearby. Repeat for several days.

At some point during the hour, leave the room for five seconds. Keep up constant happy talk so Rowdy will know you're still there. On the next occasion, make it fifteen seconds. Slowly work up to half an hour, then an hour.

Using this approach, eventually you should be able to leave Rowdy in the crate alone, and in the room alone, for a few hours at a time. (See the sidebar on p. 156, "Crate Safety—Don't Overuse the Crate.")

Please note: If Rowdy complains about being in the crate by barking, howling, or pawing at the door, ignore him. The second he stops complaining, reward him. *Never* open the crate door while the dog is complaining.

If you don't have several days to get Rowdy accustomed to his crate, and you have to be able to use it sooner, go through as much of the procedure above as you can in the time available. The main goal is to introduce the dog to his crate gradually and pleasantly. Don't just stuff the dog into it, shut the door, and leave.

CRATE SAFETY—DON'T OVERUSE THE CRATE

Crates are not meant for round-the-clock confinement. They are properly used as temporary containment to protect your dog and your belongings for brief periods while you cannot supervise him.

It's okay to crate your dog while you are sleeping, for up to ten hours.

For the waking hours, the limit is four hours at a time. If possible, give the dog potty breaks and exercise. If breaks aren't possible during the four hours, make sure to give the dog a potty break and exercise just before and just after crating.

CRATE SAFETY—SOME ASSEMBLY REQUIRED

Learn how to assemble the crate properly, and how to shut the door securely. On some crates it's all too easy to make a mistake in either process. An incorrectly assembled crate can allow your dog to squeeze through an opening or chew on a protruding part and get hurt in the process. A wrongly shut door can allow escape.

CRATE SAFETY—A DOG'S CRATE IS HIS CASTLE

All visitors, especially children, should *never* enter the crate, even when unoccupied by the dog, and *never* touch or bother the dog in any way while he is inside.

THE CRATE—CRUEL OR RESPONSIBLE?

You can almost count on criticism from family, friends, the plumber, the cable guy, and a host of others for your "cruelty" in putting your dog in "prison," aka, the crate. An interesting exercise is to think about how many dogs your crateless critics no longer have because they met untimely ends—perhaps shooting out the front door to get hit by a car in the street, or escaping lonely backyards, never to be seen again.

Brace yourself for criticism about other training tools and methods too. Everyone has an opinion. Often those opinions are based on notions about dogs craving free, unfettered lives. When you're hearing those critiques, keep in mind the millions of dogs who are relinquished, abandoned, neglected, abused, or killed every year because their "unfettered" behavior makes living with them difficult. Most important, remember how your pooch looked when he was "free" and starving in the park where you found him, or when he was at the shelter waiting for love that might never come. Then think about how your dog looks now. The proof, as they say, is in the pudding.

BARBARA'S HOMEMADE JERKY RECIPE

Trainer Barbara has found that homemade jerky can win over almost any dog to a new or intimidating experience. She takes thin slices of any meat or poultry and places them on a cookie sheet in the oven. She bakes them at 250 degrees for eight to ten minutes or until they're dried out. All unused portions are refrigerated to avoid spoiling.

TOYS VERSUS TREATS

If Rowdy is more motivated by toys and fun than by treats, when you're training, reward him with a special toy or chew that he receives only for that occasion, or play chase or fetch with him.

The Shake Can

A shake can, as described in this chapter and in chapter 9, p. 177, is a useful tool for interrupting and discouraging your dog's unwanted behavior. To make one, rinse out an empty soda can, remove the tab, and drop the tab plus ten pennies through the hole. Tape the hole shut with duct tape or heavy masking tape.

When you rattle the shake can, the noise startles your dog. To use a movie term, it does a "freeze frame" on the action, stopping your dog's behavior if even for a few seconds, thus giving you a chance to redirect him.

For example, if your dog starts barking inappropriately, say, "Rowdy, quiet." If the barking continues, rattle the can as you repeat, "Quiet." The instant he stops, even if it's just for a few seconds, praise him lavishly and say, "Rowdy, good quiet."

What if the shake can doesn't work on Rowdy because of his insensitivity to sound? Make a "shake bag" by preparing ten cans like the one described above. Drop all ten soda cans into one thirteen-gallon, tall kitchen garbage bag, making sure the cans are at the bottom of the bag. Get the air out of the bag and tie a knot at the top of the bag. You want the cans to be able to move up and down freely when you shake the shake bag.

The Spray Bottle

Another deterrent method is the spray bottle. Fill a *clean* household spray bottle with water. Consider adding twenty drops of Rescue Remedy to the water (see the sidebar below, "Flower Power"). It might have a calming effect. Caution: *Do not* use a bottle that has *ever* contained chemicals or cleaning solutions. *Do not* spray directly into the dog's eyes or ears. Aim for the neck or open mouth.

You might use this in place of the shake can, especially if the noise of the cans disturbs other family members or neighbors.

FLOWER POWER

In the 1930s British physician Edward Bach prepared thirty-eight flower-based liquid remedies, each for a specific emotional state. The most well-known is Rescue Remedy, which is for use in stressful or emergency situations. Many dog trainers and owners employ these products to help diminish the negative feelings that can cause unwanted behaviors in their pooches.

How to mix: To a one-ounce eyedropper bottle add ten drops of Rescue Remedy. Fill bottle with filtered or bottled water.

How to administer: Do not shake. Gently turn bottle upside down, then right side up. Give Rowdy one-half dropper four times a day or more. Put in food, on treats, and even directly on gums. Put twenty drops in a twelve-ounce spray bottle and mist over the top of the dog's body.

Training Collars

Martingale
Adjustable leather or nylon martingale-type collars with a buckle for easy on and off are excellent for walking and training. They are designed to slip and tighten if the dog is pulling, but not tight enough to choke.

Choke (Chain)
As the name implies, a choke collar tightens around your dog's neck if he pulls on the leash. Some people see this as cruel or inhumane. Used improperly, it certainly can be. It can also be physically harmful or even fatal (see the sidebar below, "Choke Collars Can Injure and Kill"). That being said, many responsible pet owners use the choke collar correctly as a humane and effective training aid. Before using this type of collar, ask a qualified trainer to show you how.

Prong (Pinch)
Although a prong collar looks like a medieval torture device, with metal sticks that appear to poke into the dog's neck, it is a humane training option. The prongs cannot wound or injure the dog. When your dog pulls on the leash, the collar will tighten to cause your dog discomfort but not pain. No matter how hard a dog pulls, the collar cannot tighten past a certain point. It cannot stop your dog's blood circulation or airflow. Although this type of collar looks scary, in some ways it is safer than a choke collar. For powerful pullers, a prong collar can work like magic as a training tool, paving the way for future use of a regular buckle collar.

Prong collars are a bit complicated, and at first they can be difficult to get on and off your dog. If you wish to use one, ask your trainer to show you how.

Caution: Because of the way they're designed, prong collars can and do come apart with no warning. This can be bad if you're standing on a busy street corner waiting to cross, and Rowdy spots a goose on the other side of the road. (Yes, this actually happened to us.) As a safeguard, you might place a traditional leather no-slip collar (looks like a leather chain choke) on Rowdy in addition to the prong collar. Clip the leash to both collars, so that you'll still be connected if the prong comes apart.

CHOKE COLLARS CAN INJURE AND KILL
Never ever, no matter what, leave a choke collar on an unsupervised dog. This collar lives up to its name when improperly used. Every year it strangles and kills untold numbers of pooches. A dog tied out with a choke collar can circle around a post or tree, making the leash, rope, or cable wrap too tight. That pulls on the choke collar, which squeezes around the dog's neck and cuts off his air. Even if the dog is not tied up, the rings or links on the collar can catch on something and have the same strangling effect. Use this collar *only* in your watchful presence, then remove it *immediately*.

Before walking Rowdy on a choke collar, get a trainer to show you how. Incorrect use can do serious damage both physically and psychologically.

Leashes

It seems counterintuitive, but a leash means freedom. Notice how excited your dog gets when you bring out his leash? Your dog knows the two of you are going *out*. He's thinking adventure, new smells, and fun with you. A leash also means you won't get a ticket for violating the leash law, and that your dog won't, in a moment of passion, chase a rabbit into a ravine and disappear for hours—or worse.

Moreover, the leash is like a communication line between you and your best friend, enabling the two of you to walk together as a smooth unit, almost as if you're holding hands—or paws, as the case may be.

Walking Leashes

Many different materials are available, but most people find that leather is easiest on the hands, preventing the blisters and burn that nylon or rope can cause. A length of about six feet keeps your dog close enough for easy control but allows him to range a bit. The width makes a difference in the weight of the leash and thus in its feel. In general you'll want a one-half- to one-inch width for dogs over forty pounds, and one-fourth- to one-half-inch for those under forty pounds. Make sure there is a loop at the end where you will hold the leash. Avoid loops with plastic or metal pieces, or rigid pieces of nylon or rough stitching that can chafe, scrape, or cut your hand.

Tab Leash

A piece of leash (eight to twelve inches) is attached to a clip for off-leash training in your house or yard. You can also use a piece of old leash with the clip intact.

Lunge Line

With this thirty-foot-long leash, you can teach off-leash exercises such as coming when called. Cotton web is best because nylon can burn your hands. Lunge lines made for horses are great for dogs over forty pounds, but smaller dogs need lighter lines. Your trainer can show you how the lunge line is used.

Chewproof Leash

Sometimes, you might want to tie your dog to a stationary object in the house to keep him near you and safe while you cook, pay bills, or help the kids with homework. Many dogs will chew through leather or nylon in about twenty-seven seconds flat on a slow day. Look for lines made of chain or cable. Make sure they're not so heavy that they cause your dog discomfort while he's sitting or standing.

Caution: Not recommended for walking your dog. *Never* leave a tied-up dog unattended. Clip leashes to your dog's collar. *Do not* wind them around the dog's neck to use as collars. However, if your dog's collar breaks or comes off while you're out walking, you can feed the leash's clip end through the handle end to form a loop that you can slip over the dog's neck, and use only as an *emergency* collar/leash combo.

SELF-RETRACTING LEASHES

A self-retracting leash is a cord or tape encased in a plastic holder. It extends to the length you want, to a maximum of about twenty-six feet. When you press the brake button it locks the desired length of cord or tape. There are pros and cons to this leash.

On the positive side, you can decide what length of leash you want and change it at will. It's a great tool with a well-mannered dog. And it's useful in obedience class for structured exercises such as "come."

On the negative side, you lose a great deal of control over your dog with these leashes, and the cords have been known to cut, strangle, and even cause amputations to humans and dogs. Research this type of leash thoroughly and discuss them with your trainer before using.

Muzzle

It's a good idea to keep a basket muzzle on hand, and to get your dog accustomed to it before it's needed. Unfortunately, there might come a moment when Rowdy is ill, injured, or in pain, and you must protect yourself and others from biting while he receives first-aid and medical care. The more familiar the dog is with the muzzle, the less traumatic it will be in an already-traumatic crisis.

Basket muzzles are preferable because Rowdy can breathe easily and even drink water through it. You can use a plastic basket muzzle for dogs thirty pounds and under. For larger dogs, you'll need the metal wire basket type.

To familiarize Rowdy with the muzzle, place it on the floor. Put his favorite treats all around and even inside it. Let him explore while you do happy talk.

Next, hold the muzzle in your hand at Rowdy's level. Place a treat in the very front of the muzzle. Encourage Rowdy with praise as he pokes his nose into it to get the treat. Say, "Rowdy, muzzle. Good boy!" Repeat every day for a period of weeks, during which you *never* strap the muzzle on.

Then begin fiddling with the straps while Rowdy eats the treat. If he remains relaxed, buckle the strap and give him treats through the muzzle, praise him, then unbuckle after just a few seconds. Repeat this step for another period of weeks, gradually increasing the amount of time the muzzle is on, until your dog is comfortable wearing it for ten minutes. Caution: *Never* leave a muzzle on for more than ten minutes (see chapter 6, pp. 79–80, for more on when and how to muzzle safely).

Electric Barking Collar and Electric Remote Collar

Electric Barking Collar

This device has helped many owners keep dogs who were mindless barkers. It automatically delivers a tingle, or "zing," when the dog barks for longer than a few seconds.

Electric Remote Collar

This collar delivers a tingle or zing when you push a button on a remote control. It can be used to reduce dangerous behaviors such as extreme chewing or escaping from the yard. Though it sounds cruel, it can save dogs' lives when no other method works.

Caution: Consult a qualified trainer to learn if, when, and how to use an electric collar, and use one *only* after you have tried every other training option.

DON'T COP OUT WITH ELECTRIC COLLARS

Never use barking collars or remote collars out of laziness. First, consult one or more qualified trainers about your pooch's problem behavior and try every other training option. Avoid using remote collars for minor problems—such as jumping on the sofa or begging for table food—that can be addressed in other ways. Hire an experienced trainer to show you if, when, and how to use it.

Controlling or Communicating?

Some people believe that dog training is for control freaks. Usually those are people who have never had a dog, or who only have dogs who were born easygoing, or whose dogs were trained by a previous owner, or whose dogs spend their whole lives outside with little human companionship, or whose dogs "run away" and end up on the street, in shelters, euthanized—or worse. Without some degree of training, it is almost impossible for most dogs to live companionably in a human household.

Never let anyone make you feel self-conscious or guilty about teaching your dog in a fair, kind way. By showing a dog what you expect and how to achieve it, you are eliminating a lot of the stress in his life. The dog doesn't have to walk on eggshells trying to figure out what you do or don't want. Also, it blazes trails for two-way communication, so that the dog can "talk" to you, as well.

Contrary to what some folks say, 99.9 percent of dogs *love* training when it's done in an upbeat, positive way. It stimulates and broadens their minds. It brings praise, treats, and time with their best friends. Life doesn't get much better than that.

Hilary.

Happily Ever After True Story Number Eight:
Hamster, Hilary, and Liesel

"Fighting for the underdog," is Shannon McKenzie's motto. When she founded her own non-profit organization in Minneapolis, Minnesota, to help overlooked animals, she named it Underdog Rescue and Placement. Beginning with two black kittens and a pit bull puppy named Lucy, Shannon has since placed fifteen hundred dogs and cats in new homes.

The work is exhausting and never-ending. And a recent week was no exception. She was alerted that a puppy mill was ready to dump a few breeders—female dogs that are impregnated over and over again, usually until their bodies give out. "It was an Amish puppy mill," said Shannon, "so, having no electricity, these dogs spent their entire lives in the dark—freezing in the winter and burning hot in the summer."

As soon as she got the call to come pick them up, Shannon didn't hesitate to make the five-hour drive.

Talking about the three dogs she had rescued that night, Shannon's voice cracked from lack of sleep. "Hamster, a tricolor cocker spaniel, is the most social and loving. Hilary is also a cocker spaniel, very sweet, but likes to steal things such as my cell phone. And Liesel is a poodle, who is so shy, but you can tell she wants to be my friend."

Even though each dog had borne multiple litters of puppies, their health was fairly good. Shannon immediately had them examined by a vet, heartworm tested, vaccinated, spayed, and groomed.

After having lived their entire lives in small cages, never enjoying the comfort of a human's touch, the three girls showed a surprising readiness to understand what living in a house with a real caregiver was all about. "Puppy mill dogs are never housebroken, but these girls figured it out within a week."

When asked what keeps her motivated to keep saving dogs when so many continue to suffer, Shannon simply said, "It's my passion. Most people can't stomach what I witness. And the trade-offs are tough. I have no social life. I'm always feeling some sort of heartache." But if she were to quit, Shannon added, the animals would not just go away.

How does she avoid burnout? "Here in Minneapolis, it's the network of wonderful women in the pet industry. Every weekend we get together and talk with each other about what we're doing. This is a good city for people who care about dogs, because we have a small-town feel, with a big heart for animals."

9.
Behavior Problems and Solutions
How to Prevent and Change Some of the More Common and Difficult Unwanted Behaviors
Written with trainer Barbara O'Connor

Kellie: All in the Family

I have him cornered. We are batting each other. He pats my nose. I pat his head. Then he does a surprise move, ducks under the table, and leaps over a chair. I must chase him! Got him! He is so warm. I especially like to sniff his furry tummy. I always forget that he's a cat and that he has claws. Oops! Just got reminded. Abby ignores us, chewing a toy. I bet she'd like to share it!

The behaviors considered in this chapter could belong to any dog. There are some that rescued pooches might be more likely to display, such as separation anxiety or food theft. But each dog is so unique, and the range of canine temperament is so broad, that it's impossible to predict a dog's behavior based on her origin or experiences. Thus, in this chapter we discuss the most common troubles we've encountered over the years among all the pesky pooches we've known and loved.

We've chosen not to detail the basics that you can learn while attending obedience classes, such as teaching your pooch to sit or heel on command. Instead we focus on a few of the stickier wickets.

In order to really enjoy a dog, one doesn't merely try to train him to be semihuman. The point of it is to open oneself to the possibility of becoming partly a dog.

—Edward Hoagland

Pulling on the Leash

It's unrealistic to expect an untrained dog to walk on leash without pulling. For most dogs, dragging a human is effortless. But it's not very comfortable for the human, and it can cause orthopedic problems for the dog. Every pooch deserves to be taught.

Before you go for a walk, absorb excess energy. Play an active game for ten to fifteen minutes. If you have a yard, encourage your dog to go potty there.

On the walk, think of the leash as a communication line. Use it to tell the dog that she has the most freedom and comfort when she's not pulling. Maintain a constant, normal walking gait. When Daisy pulls, tug back, just slightly overmatching her strength with a long, steady pressure. When you feel her slow or see her lean or step back, instantly release your pressure, and praise the dog. Repeat whenever Daisy pulls. *Always* release at her slightest give, and praise her.

At home, play "pressure games." Sit in a chair, with Daisy on leash. She pulls to leave. Tighten the leash just enough to stop her forward motion. As she stops, instantly release the tension. The leash goes slack. Praise profusely! Repeat several times.

This is a gradual training method that can take weeks or longer as you get the feel of it, and it is dependent on the dog's breed, temperament, prey drive, and history.

Here's another method: Find an open area like a grassy field in a park or an uncrowded parking lot. Start walking with Daisy at a normal pace. Relax and keep the leash slack. When she starts to pull, suddenly and smoothly turn and change direction. Daisy will hit the end of the leash, going the wrong way. Don't look at her or say anything. Just keep walking. As soon as Daisy follows you, praise her. Keep walking normally. But every single time she pulls, repeat the procedure. You might have to change direction twenty-five times while walking one hundred paces. To any observer you will look like a nut. Your dog, too, might think you've lost your marbles. It doesn't matter. What you're doing is getting Daisy to focus her attention on you and on which way you're going. When she doesn't, she gets the frustration of hitting a dead end.

After practicing this method in an open area, you can apply it on your routine walks as well. Again, don't expect overnight results. Leash pulling tends to be a stubborn problem that can take a while to improve.

Jumping On People

Obnoxious though it is, jumping on people is normal dog behavior. Puppies jump up on their moms to get attention. As they grow older and bigger, jumping becomes part of play. Most people do not mind puppies' paws on them till they start getting bigger. Meanwhile, they allow the habit to become engrained.

When a little puppy first arrives, he can be taught not to jump. When the puppy does jump on people to greet them, gently and consistently push him off and say, "Off." Once his paws are on the floor, pet and praise the puppy saying, "Dusty, good off!" Then redirect Dusty to play with a toy, and get him to think about something else. With consistent responses, Dusty will learn that he only gets attention when he greets without jumping.

Another way to teach any dog not to jump is to teach an alternate behavior. Dogs can't do two things at once, so teach Dusty to sit when people come to your house. He can't jump and sit at the same time. Give Dusty lavish praise when he sits. Soon he will learn how great it is when he sits to greet.

A third way to discourage jumping is to simply turn your back to Dusty when he jumps on you, or step to the side, or take a step backward. He learns that jumping on people deprives him of interaction with them

If the jumping behavior is more entrenched, you might also need to keep shake cans handy throughout the house. Whenever Shelby jumps on a human, she hears the unsettling rattle of a can, accompanied by the sharp word "off." The second her paws are on the floor, she'll hear the happy words, "Shelby, good off. Good dog. What a great girl!" with lots of petting and perhaps a toy.

On occasions when Shelby controls herself and manages for a few seconds *not* to jump on the person she's approaching, immediately pet and praise her. After weeks of consistent responses, Shelby discovers that she doesn't have to jump on anyone to get attention, and that things go a lot better when she doesn't.

Mouthing

Many dogs, usually young ones, are "mouthy." They put their jaws lightly or roughly around whatever is handy—your arm, fingers, ankle, toes, nose, ponytail, or jacket sleeve. It can be annoying, or even painful, and it's a potentially dangerous habit, indicating that the dog has not yet developed a bite inhibition around humans.

First, understand where the habit originates. When puppies play, they explore and familiarize themselves with each other using their mouths like we use our hands. Growing into adults, they continue developing these lifelong skills. Watch two dogs having fun and observe how mouthiness is a mainstay of play. Sometimes if a younger dog bites an older dog too hard, the older one responds by stopping the play, and pinning the young one down using her mouth, causing the youngster to submit. The submitting dog must go still, avoid eye contact, and tuck under her tail, or cautiously move just the tip of her tail. As they resume play, the younger dog has learned to be more respectful.

Though it's a normal part of puppy behavior, mouthing needs to be redirected to appropriate items—safe toys or chews.

For dogs six months and older, here's one technique for curbing the habit: First, get prepared. Stand somewhere with toys hidden nearby. Attach your dog's leash to her collar. When the dog mouths you, avoid screaming, thrashing, waving arms, or kicking. This just excites the dog more, and can further suppress her bite inhibition. Remain calm and motionless as you immediately say, sternly, "No!" and sharply pull up and away from your body with the leash. The dog should stop mouthing and look at you. Instantly produce a toy or chew and wave it at the dog's level, chatting happily, using her name, and toss it to the dog. With enough repetitions, your dog will learn to mouth the toys or chews instead of you.

With some dogs you can try exclaiming loudly by saying something like "Ow!" when she mouths you, then immediately give her a toy. Typically, this works only with mild-mannered, gentle-natured pooches, not the more active and assertive ones, who might only grow more stimulated by the sound of distress.

Please note: Mouthy dogs can make great retrievers when the drive is properly channeled. See chapter 11, p. 214, on how to encourage retrieving.

Nuisance Vocalizing

Excessive vocalization—barking, whining, and howling—can be a dog's worst enemy. It causes owners of rental housing to prohibit pooches. It causes neighbors to file police nuisance reports against dog owners. It causes many canines to be abandoned, relinquished to shelters, euthanized, and even beaten.

There can be many reasons why your dog is expressing herself. She might be excited about a smell in the air. She might be afraid of new surroundings, or of people, storms, or earthquakes. The dog might be guarding your property. She might be ill or in pain. When they have nothing better to do, dogs might enjoy recreational or boredom barking. Try to observe and understand why they're vocalizing, then consider the ideas below.

Fear Response

If you think your dog is noisy because she's afraid of something, try to figure out what that is. Look for sounds, sights, or smells that might seem threatening, or that she might associate with a previous unpleasant experience. If you can't eliminate the source of your dog's fear, try to desensitize the dog to it. Whenever the fear source is present, engage your dog in an activity she likes. She can be eating treats, playing with you, practicing obedience training with lots of rewards, or enjoying a favorite toy or chew that she only receives during that time. Slowly, the dog might begin to associate the dreaded sound, sight, or smell with that positive experience instead of fear.

If your dog barks, howls, or whines in fear at night when you're trying to sleep, put the dog where she'll feel safe, such as a crate covered with a light sheet in a quiet room. To mimic a heartbeat, cover a windup clock with a towel and place it just outside the crate (so that the dog can't chew it). Turn a radio on to some soft music. See the sidebar, "Flower Power," in chapter 8, p. 157, for information on a calming herbal mixture you might try.

Boredom Response

A dog left alone for long periods, indoors or out, might resort to barking to pass the time. It's a way of releasing tension and expressing frustration. And the sound of her own voice beats the sound of silence.

Your first goal is to reduce as much as possible the amount of time that your best friend is alone. When your dog has to be on her own, make the environment interesting (see chapter 11, p. 216). Remember that sleeping dogs don't bark, so try to give your pooch enough exercise before she's left alone so that she'll be too tuckered out to complain.

If your budget allows, consider doggie day care. It can be pricey, but it's a great alternative to the home-alone blues.

Overreaction Response

Some dogs are on a hair trigger. They overreact, making a lot of noise in the process.

Every day Mandy sees your mild-mannered, elderly neighbor take his morning constitutional. Mandy acts like he's a serial killer.

To ease her concerns, teach her that you are in control and that you will take care of everything. Before your neighbor goes by, put on Mandy's leash. When he appears, be calm and in control. Say, "Mandy, it's all right. Quiet." If she stops barking even for a few seconds, praise her and give her a treat. Entice her with another treat by holding it in front of your face, so that she is looking into your eyes. Say "Mandy, watch." Even if she only glances at you, say "Mandy, good watch," and give her the treat. Now say "Mandy, sit." Keep her attention on *you* instead of on your neighbor, by giving her a variety of commands and the rewards of petting, praise, and treats.

Repeat this exercise as many times as necessary over days or weeks until Mandy begins to associate that "dangerous" neighbor with something she really likes, instead of the threat she imagines he poses. The goal is to redirect Mandy's attention onto you.

Another option for overreactive barking is to use shake cans. Every morning a school bus drives by. The high-pitched shrieks and laughter of the kids on board send Mandy into a tizzy. Say, "Mandy, it's just the bus. Quiet." If she continues, rattle a shake can. The *instant* Mandy stops barking, praise her, and perhaps give her a treat. Repeat the exercise until she learns that the presence of the school bus means either the unpleasant rattle of the can, or the happy talk and treats—her choice—depending on whether she barks.

Warning Response

The doorbell rings and Pepito is in full flight, yapping like mad. The leash should already be on, as you knew that the pizza guy, Ralph, was on his way. Pick up the end of the flying leash and say, "Pepito, wait!" He keeps going and runs himself to the end of the leash, coming to an abrupt stop. He is momentarily silent as he looks sheepishly back at you. You exclaim, "Pepito, good wait!" Even though he didn't stop voluntarily, praise anyway so he'll begin to associate the action with the praise.

Attach his leash to something solid (stair railing, ring in wall, heavy furniture). Walk past him to the door. He tries to follows you. Say, "Pepito, wait." The leash stops him. Say; "Pepito, good boy!" Then do some happy talk. "Hey, Pepito, it's Ralph the pizza man! Good wait, Pepito. Good quiet."

As you open the door, ask Ralph to remain there for a moment. Pepito barks again. Turn and walk toward Pepito as if you are going to walk directly into him. Say, "Pepito, it's all right. Quiet!" He stops, because you have redirected his thinking again. As you turn toward Ralph, you repeat, "Pepito wait. Good wait, Pepito, good quiet."

Ralph hands you the pizza. Ask him to toss Pepito a treat. Show Pepito the treat while moving it to Ralph's hand. Ask Ralph to say, "Hey, Pepito, catch a treat?" Ralph cheerfully complies. Pepito catches the treat, and realizes that wow, you are really in charge, if you can even order this would-be intruder to give him a treat

After chatting for a minute or two with Ralph, shut the door, walk over to waiting, quiet Pepito, and praise him to the high heavens.

Eventually, Pepito should learn that it's OK to alert you to dangers with some warning barks, but that once you say, "Quiet," his job is done.

TYPES OF BARKS

Dogs have different barks for different purposes. You can encourage one type over another. For example, instead of full-fledged frenzy with ear-splitting shrieks, maybe you'd prefer that your dog warned you of a stranger's presence with a softer, calmer, warning bark. Next time your dog is in crazy-bark mode, you'll probably notice that among the shrieks there are softer barks now and then, as the dog's perception of the threat waxes and wanes. When the barking is too wild, say, "Cha Cha, soft," and discourage her as discussed in this chapter. As soon as the barking gets more mellow, say, "Cha Cha, good soft. Good girl." She gets petting and a treat. With time she'll realize that loudness is unappreciated, while toning down her response gets a reward.

Please note: If you are also teaching your dog the "quiet" command, you must be sure to consistently use that command when you want her to be absolutely silent, but use the "soft" command when you just want the dog to tone it down. Don't mix up the two, because then your dog won't be able to tell which one you really want.

ONE TIME WHEN TLC DOESN'T HELP

Contrary to your every instinct, comforting a fearful dog can do more harm than good. Your pooch learns that good things come out of being scared—she gets your attention and TLC. A better approach is to act upbeat, and refocus the dog's thoughts on an activity like obedience training, agility work, or just goofing around with a game of chase or fetch. The more nonchalant you act, the more secure the dog is likely to feel.

Destructive Chewing

All dogs chew, and all dogs need to chew. It is essential to dental health and stress relief (see chapter 7, pp. 133–134). For puppies, it helps new teeth come in, reducing discomfort. But does your dog need to shred your favorite slippers? Or whittle the legs off your dining table? Or collect the sprinkler heads from your lawn? There's destructive chewing, and there's appropriate chewing. Without your guidance, your best friend can't know the difference. To a dog, that sprinkler head doesn't look much different than the plastic toy you gave her the other day. To learn what's OK with you and what's not, your dog needs your help.

First of all, dogproof the environment as much as possible to keep your pooch out of trouble. Make the garbage, laundry hamper, and other temptations inaccessible.

While learning the rules, dogs should never be unsupervised. Leaving a new dog home alone almost guarantees destructive chewing. Confine the dog in a crate, a fun and safe backyard, or a secure dog pen. Even when you're home, consider keeping your new pooch on leash, so that you can keep her close to you, or use the other indoor confinement methods described in chapter 4, p. 48.

If your dog starts chewing that magazine on the coffee table, say, "Leave it," and hand her a toy or chew, saying "Beegee, toy! Take it!" Then praise her when Beegee gnaws on that instead of on your reading material. Go through the same procedure every single time she tries to chew something inappropriate. Eventually she learns that while the toilet paper or the TV remote are off limits, dog toys are a lot more fun.

To satisfy her chomping urges, make sure Beegee has *appropriate* chew opportunities every day. See chapter 7, p. 134, for guidance on safe chewing options. And spend time with your new best friend, giving your dog enough exercise, playtime, and cuddling to make her too tired and contented for chewing mischief.

Digging

Digging is second nature to dogs. In the wild, they need this survival skill to catch earth-dwelling prey like gophers and moles for food. They also dig for shelter and safety—a cool place to lie in the summer and a warm den in the winter—and to create storage for bones or other highly prized items. Have you ever seen a dog who was given a toy or a treat carry it to a corner of the house and go through the physical actions of "digging" an imaginary hole with her paws, then "burying" it using her nose? Why does a dog do that? Because she's a dog. It's in the dog's genes. A dog cannot be anything but herself.

In our backyards, dogs might dig because of instinct or because they're bored or just because it's fun. It's a great stress reliever, like chewing, and provides good upper-body exercise besides.

Regardless of their canine companions' motivations, many humans dislike holes in their yards. Dogs, however, don't see the problem with the pits and craters they've designed. Isn't that how the ground is supposed to look?

Redirect your pooch's excavation energy. Try setting up a digging pit or area as described in chapter 11. Bury toys in it to entice the dog to dig there. Some people sprinkle cayenne pepper over their lawns or flower beds as a repellent. When your dog attacks the wrong place, lead her to the right place, using a chirpy voice. "Darly, dig here! Find the toy, Darly!" The second she sniffs the ground or begins to dig, praise her.

If possible, you might use inexpensive do-it-yourself fencing such as simple posts and chicken wire to keep Darly out of your landscaping until she gets the picture. Otherwise, don't leave her in the yard unattended. Every time she digs in the wrong place, it reinforces her belief that it's OK.

WELL, IT'S ONE WAY TO LOSE WEIGHT

Problem: Have you ever had the food on your plate disappear when you left the room for only a minute? Have you ever left a loaf of bread, a block of cheese, or your favorite oatmeal cookies on the kitchen counter only to find them missing seconds later? In those cases you might have heard an odd noise nearby—the happy thumping of a tail.

Dogs don't see themselves as thieves. According to canine etiquette, if the pack leaders leave food unattended, the lower-ranking pack members are permitted to eat it. If you correct your dog for trying to take your food when you are present, that makes perfect sense to the dog. But if you leave your food by itself, in your dog's mind, it's up for grabs.

Solution: Make any food you wish to keep completely inaccessible when you are not there to control the situation. You can either put it away, or confine your dog in a safe, reliable way so that she can't get to the food.

You might also turn it into a training opportunity. Recruit a human training partner. Leave some people food in a people spot like a countertop or table. Tie a string to a few shake cans and place them somewhere near the food (see the description of shake cans in chapter 8, p. 157). The string should be long enough to reach an adjacent room or closet where you'll be able to see your dog, but the dog won't be able to see you. The other end of the string is in your hand. As Penny starts to grab some food, pull the string. The noisy cans clatter to the floor and startle her. She starts to run away, but just then, your training partner comes in, silently and quickly inspects the food, then says, "Good girl, Penny, good leave it." Penny gets praise, petting, and a treat. After enough tries, Penny will learn that when she goes for the food, something bad happens; when she leaves it alone, good things come her way.

Resource Guarding

Dogs are intelligent and even selective about what they want. If they perceive something as valuable, they believe it must be valuable to others too. Surely everyone else in the world—dogs and humans alike—must cherish that old torn-up squeaky toy as much as they do. So they are willing to go to extremes to make sure it remains theirs. But dogs, just like the rest of us, have to learn to share.

When you notice your dog becoming especially enamored of a certain item, be it a food bowl, the crumbs she finds on the floor in the kitchen, or a toy, stay on the lookout for possessiveness. Signs include standing over the item protectively, stiffening the body, growling, or even snapping and biting.

Your first goal is to eliminate or at least limit the source of the problem. Don't leave your dog's food bowl out. As soon as she finishes eating, pick up the bowl and store it. Don't give the dog free access to those kitchen floor tidbits. Instead, while you're cooking, keep the dog tied near you to a ring on the wall or other stable object, or in a puppy pen portable enclosure, or keep her outside the kitchen with a baby gate. For a toy, you might try the "trade" game to teach the dog to give something up on command. While she's holding the toy in question, offer the dog a treat she can't refuse—whatever she likes best. The dog will have to drop the toy to eat the treat. Immediately take the toy and say, "Good drop, Dolly. Good girl!"

To prevent dogs from guarding resources from each other, which often results in fights, never leave them unsupervised around valuable items. Play games that reinforce pack order and strengthen their comfort and security around each other (see chapter 5, pp. 69–70).

Jealousy and Possessiveness of You

You and your pooch, Maple, are cuddling on the sofa. Your wife, Luisa, comes up to give you a hug, only to be met with a glower and a growl from your canine companion. Understandably, Luisa backs off and abandons her attempt at affection. Next time she tries it, a couple of days later, Maple snaps at her hand. The third time, Maple decides she needs to make her feelings more clear. She lunges and nips Luisa's nose.

Maple sees you as "hers," and Luisa as an interloper. Does this mean you have to choose between your dog and your wife? Let's hope not. Dogs carry in them nearly every human emotion, including jealousy and possessiveness of their friends. Maple doesn't hate Luisa; she just wants you all to herself. But you must stop your adoring pooch from becoming a dictator. Consult a professional trainer, who might suggest some of the following steps.

First, protect your wife. Confine Maple without isolating her. See chapter 4, p. 48, for safe, comfortable confinement options. Sometimes, place Maple in the confinement area even when your wife isn't home, so that the dog won't suspect Luisa's presence to be the cause for her "imprisonment."

Play games. In the food toss game, Maple sees that you're in control and that you want your wife to share your life and Maple's too. With Maple on a leash secured to a stable object, stand next to her. Invite your wife to approach. Luisa should look only at you, not at Maple. When Luisa is eight feet away, raise your hand in a "stop" motion and say, "Luisa, stop there please." Maple might try hard to stare her down, but Luisa should make absolutely no eye contact with her.

Instead, get the dog's attention with treats—her favorite kind. Move a treat slowly around so that Maple can track it with her eyes. Say, "Maple, look, a treat," and "Maple, sit." When the dog complies, say, "Maple, now Luisa will throw your treat." At Maple's eye level, move the treat into Luisa's waiting hand. She moves it up and down slowly, getting Maple's gaze to follow. When the pooch's mouth is turned upward, you say, "Maple, catch!" in a happy voice. Your wife looks at Maple, tosses the treat, and in that moment the dog begins to see Louisa as a food source. Also, the dog begins to get used to eye contact with her archenemy.

Attend obedience classes with Maple and get private lessons with a trainer. It might take consistent and diligent work over a long period of time before Maple can be trusted around Luisa, but as in many other such cases, Maple might finally accept the "interloper" as one of her pack leaders, and as a mate for you, her dearest best friend.

Neurosis, Phobia, and Separation Anxiety

Have you ever felt such fear that your stomach was all in knots? Have you ever had a panic attack? Have you ever been afraid of heights? Or of the dark? Does it comfort you to be near those you trust and love? Dogs can experience the same feelings.

Almost any sound, sight, smell, or situation can cause a dog to feel afraid and develop a neurosis or phobia. A burly rottweiler runs away from the sound of the toaster. A powerful Akita trembles at the sight of a shiny floor. It's about personality and past experiences, and it doesn't mean the dog is crazy. Many fearful canines are medicated with mind-altering drugs or killed. There might be other ways to help your best friend.

Your richest resource in these cases is time. It can be a great healer. The traumas that caused your dog's worries might eventually fade in her memory, as you provide positive experiences to replace them. But that's not always enough. In many cases, what you need to do is set up controlled situations in which you can slowly and gently desensitize your pooch to whatever it is that troubles her.

Let's say that bookcases terrify your dog, Anika. Perhaps a bookcase once fell on or near her. Now, she won't go into a room containing any tall, slender piece of furniture. (Yes, this sounds funny, but we've seen every pooch phobia you can imagine!) For this reason, Anika refuses to enter your living room, the pet store, or the vet's office. Hauling Anika into those places and forcing her to stay there will do absolutely no good.

Set aside a few minutes a day over a period of weeks or even months to work on the problem. Using a happy voice and Anika's favorite treats, entice her into the doorway of the room in question. On the first few tries, she'll probably just dart up long enough to grab the treat, then dart off. Make that doorway an appealing place with lots of treats and her favorite toy or chew. Sit there in a chair. Do happy talk. Sing. Anika will probably begin to linger there a little longer on each try. Every day, set your chair a few inches farther into the room and closer to the dreaded bookcase. To collect all the treats, toys, and petting you're dispensing, Anika learns, almost without noticing, to tolerate the presence of her imagined foe, the bookcase, and eventually to forget all about it.

One common form of neurosis is separation anxiety. It might seem touching that your dog can't bear to be away from you, but it's not healthy for you or for your dog. She might act out her misery in a variety of ways—barking, destructive chewing, escaping your property, self-mutilation such as chewing on a tail or a limb, or even aggression toward other family members and pets.

Again, time is on your side. It's a weapon you can use against your dog's anxiety, dividing time up into small amounts to get the dog accustomed to your absence. First, though, minimize your pooch's stress levels by giving her nutritious food and plenty of exercise, playtime, chewing opportunities, and cuddling with you.

Second, make sure that the space where you're leaving your best friend—whether it's a crate, a room, or the backyard—is safe, comfortable, and as interesting as possible (see chapter 5, pp. 62–65, on safety; chapter 8, pp. 153–156, on crating; and chapter 11, p. 216, on backyard fun).

Keep in mind that an extremely anxious dog can hurt herself, even in the softest of settings, for example by clawing at the door of a crate or chewing through the door of a room.

Third, habituate the dog very slowly to your absence. Of course, your life can't stop because your pooch has separation anxiety. You have to continue going to work, grocery shopping, and out with friends. But in between, with the following method, you can show your dog that your absences aren't always lengthy, and that you'll always come back.

After a long, brisk walk or a fun session of fetch in the backyard, place Anika in the area where you expect her to wait. Give her a special treat, such as a large biscuit, and use a matter-of-fact tone to say something like, "Anika, I'll be back." Leave for one minute. Don't come back in if she's barking or crying. Wait until a short break in her barking or crying—no matter how short—then burst in and say, "Good Anika! Good quiet!" Reward her with another special treat. This focuses her attention on the treats, instead of on missing you. Over a period of days or weeks, slowly increase the amount of time you're gone during these sessions. With enough repetition, most dogs get used to the idea of your coming and going. They realize some absences are short, and others are long, but they'll always have you back again. There are, however, tougher cases that require the help of professional trainers or veterinarians.

Chew Therapy
Stuffed Kong-type rubbery toys are great to distract bored dogs, or dogs suffering from separation anxiety.

A door is what a dog is perpetually on the wrong side of.
—Ogden Nash

DOMINANT, OR JUST A DOG?

Dogs are born into litters, designed to be members of a pack and to hold a place in the pack order—alpha or subordinate. True alpha or dominant dogs are rare. They know they are on top, and don't have to prove it. They exude confidence. Other dogs react accordingly, giving ground. The dominant dog also gives ground, sharing a favorite ball. She isn't angered by the wild, ball-chasing shenanigans of subordinate dogs, because she recognizes their need to play, and she values the unity and contentment of the pack. Also, the dominant dog knows that if she really wanted the ball, the others would surrender it.

You might think you have a dominant dog. Maybe your puppy leaps up and grabs at your hands and clothes. What you are witnessing is your puppy's prey drive, not dominance. Puppies mouth, nip, and bite each other, then move into your home and continue exploring the world with their mouths. As a puppy matures, genetics, instinct, and early experience shape her behavior. If the puppy lacks human intervention—in other words, training—she might begin to explore dominance.

Maybe the dog begins to push you to pet her by nudging or pawing at your hand. You respond by petting the dog. She shoves ahead of you through doors and on stairways, and you move aside. She growls near food or toys, and you back off. The blueprint you've encouraged becomes engrained. The dog stops obeying well-known commands. The nudging for rubs progresses to growling if you do not obey. The dog resists handling by you, the veterinarian, and the groomer. In the house she will not move out of your way. You must go around her or the growling intensifies to snapping.

If the dog wasn't a dominant puppy, what happened? This type of dog is highly intelligent and possibly insecure. During the months when she was searching for her rank within a pack, the dog simply responded to the situations you and your family unknowingly set up.

Remember: She's a dog, thinking like a dog, responding to those situations just like a dog would do with other dogs. She's looking for her path, and your job is to guide her.

Aggression

All dogs, regardless of breed—from the cutest Chihuahuas to the sweetest Labradors to the gentlest Great Danes—have the potential to be aggressive. Aggression is an emotional and sometimes explosive response to many factors. These can include protection of territory, protection of family, protection of resources, self-defense, social status, sexual drive, fear, anger, pain, irritation, and hunger. Humans also act aggressively for the same basic reasons. Fortunately, many of us learn to control and restrain our emotions, and to make the right choices for our behavior. That is exactly what we need to teach our dogs—to make better choices.

When a dog exhibits aggression toward humans or other pets, your best first step is to contact a professional trainer for advice. If you adopted the dog from a shelter or rescue organization, contact them immediately, report the trouble, and ask for help. They should try to work with you to find solutions. (Also, see chapter 3, pp. 33–34, for information on discerning if the aggression is appropriate or inappropriate.) In general, a trainer might propose ideas such as the following:

Establish Trust and Authority

First and foremost, your dog must believe that you can and will deal with threats to protect the pack. Quite often, dogs exhibit aggression because they feel that if there is a threat, you are not capable of dealing with it, and therefore they must stay alert and ready to step in (see chapter 8, pp. 143–144, for more on trust).

Aggression in Public

Socialization is key. Getting your dog accustomed to other people and other dogs in a variety of controlled situations is one of the best ways of overcoming aggression. Take the dog for leashed walks, where she can see, hear, and smell humans and dogs of all kinds, without being close enough to harm them. Instead of letting your dog bark and snarl—thus reinforcing the negative behavior—find a quiet corner of a busy parking lot and distract the dog with obedience training, games, and her favorite treats.

Depending on the extent of your dog's problem, you might have to do this for weeks, months, or even years. At first your dog probably won't do very well, since her attention will still be riveted on other things. Persevere with a peppy tone and attitude. Keep it interesting and challenging. Show your dog that giving you her attention and participation will bring a lot more fun, praise, and treats than growling and lunging at passersby. This is a slow process, and nothing happens overnight, if ever. But the goal is to take the dog's focus off the feelings that make her aggressive, and redirect them onto *you* and the great fun you can have together. Over time you might be able to safely move closer to the triggers of the dog's aggression—other people, dogs, or the world at large.

Aggression with Visitors

At home, before company arrives, put the dog on leash. Practice just walking around the house. When the doorbell rings and the dog starts barking, remain calm as you talk to your friends through the door. Then put your dog in her crate in the room where you'll visit with your guests (see more on crate training in chapter 8, pp. 153–156). Let them in, and ask them not to stare at the dog. Ask them to completely ignore her , even though the dog is now barking savagely. Show them to the sofa or chairs and ask them to sit. Make a big production out of it, so that your dog clearly sees that you are in charge, and that you are controlling the "intruders," so that she doesn't have to.

The dog might stop barking, looking confused. Go directly to the crate and praise her profusely, as if she had just given you a million dollars. Reward the dog with her favorite treat. If she hasn't stopped barking, go to the crate and say, "Quiet." Still barking? Rattle a shake can, or tap it loudly against the crate door, if necessary, to startle the dog. The split second the dog is silent, *immediately* praise her heavily and give her a treat. Be careful using the shake can—remember to stop rattling it as soon as the dog is quiet.

The idea is to show the dog that when you are relaxed and comfortable around visitors, she can be too. She can let down her guard and not worry about protecting you. Over time, as you repeat the exercise above, your dog should get to the point where she becomes quiet in response to your command, and rests peacefully in her crate while you visit with company. Eventually you might be able to tie the dog securely to a piece of heavy furniture or a ring on the wall when your guests visit. Make sure the dog cannot slip out of her collar or otherwise break free and come near your company. Instruct your guests to stay well away from your dog and completely ignore her while you proceed with your visit, now and then praising and rewarding your dog for her good behavior.

Aggression with a Household Member

First of all, keep your dog physically away from that household member. Immediately contact the shelter or rescue group where you adopted the dog, report the situation, and ask for help. If you rescued the dog from the streets yourself, you'll need evaluation and advice from an experienced trainer/behaviorist.

There are many dogs with horrible upbringings or bad genetics. Some of them are difficult or impossible to change. There are also dogs that are misunderstood and with the right training can be helped. After receiving guidance from professionals, your task will be to decide if you have the time and energy needed to reeducate your dog, and if your family can get along safely with her in the meantime.

Aggression with Other Dogs

Quite often, a dog that is "dog aggressive" got that way because at some point she was attacked or hurt by another dog. Your primary goal is to teach your pooch that not all dogs will hurt her, and that the dog can actually have a lot of fun with other dogs if she gives them a chance. Socialization is vital in this case. Find as many opportunities as you can to put your dog in controlled situations in the vicinity of other dogs. Your dog and all the other dogs must be on leash. If your dog starts barking and carrying on when she is 100 feet away from another dog, stay 101 feet away, and praise her to the sky for being calm. Do that enough times, over a period of time, preferably accompanied by treats, and you'll be able to move within ninety-eight feet of other canines, then ninety-five, and so on. Eventually, with guidance from a trainer, your dog might be able to walk within sniffing distance of a fellow pooch.

Always assume the worst—that your dog will attack the other dog—so that you'll be prepared to restrain her if needed. But expect the best, so that you don't "telegraph" your tension.

Stay light on the leash. Don't pull it tight. Make sure it has a little slack. Act normal and upbeat. Chatter pleasantly: "Good girl, Lulu, good quiet! Wow, look, there's another dog. Cool, huh? Hi, doggie, how are you? This is Lulu. Good girl, Lulu, good quiet. Lulu, you're so good, you get a treat! Want a treat?" Thus Lulu learns that the presence of another dog is superb. It means happy talk, praise, and cookies.

At some point, you might tie Lulu's leash to something secure, put her on the "wait" command, and give her a treat—her favorite kind. You stand just a few feet beyond the point where she can reach you. A training partner brings his or her mellow, trained dog up to you, holding the leash and making sure the dog does not approach Lulu. You greet them both cheerfully. You instruct the other dog to sit. You give him praise and a treat. You instruct Lulu to sit. You give her praise and a treat. Go through more obedience commands for both dogs with praise and treats.

Sooner or later, Lulu will probably realize, "Hmm. My human is in control of that other dog. Maybe I can chill, and just follow the commands, and eat those scrumptious treats." With enough time, she might be able to play this game side by side with other dogs—with all dogs always on leash and under careful vigilance. Perhaps, some day, she'll be comfortable and calm enough that you can let her sniff other dogs, and vice versa. Then there might come a day when she can be safely off leash with other canines.

In any case, your goal is to get Lulu's attention on you, and on the fact that you're in charge, and on what a wonderful world this can be.

DO NOT GET BITTEN

Never put yourself, other people, or pets in danger with an aggressive dog. If you see signs of inappropriate aggression in your pooch, contact a trainer or rescue organization immediately for guidance.

CANINE AGGRESSION—HARD AND HAZARDOUS

Canine aggression can be awfully stressful. It puts you, your family, other people, and other animals at risk—not just physically, but also financially in terms of possible medical or legal bills, should your dog do some harm. Also, it can be a hard nut to crack. Once aggression is engrained, it can be very difficult to reverse.

If you have an aggressive dog, keep in mind that her recovery will be a process. For some dogs it takes longer than for others. And some of them never come around. They might improve a bit, at least to the point where you can walk down the street without creating a public spectacle of snarling and snapping. But no matter how hard you work, your best friend might never lose her suspicions and anger, and you might never be able to fully trust her around factors that set her off.

Tragically, there are highly aggressive dogs that must be euthanized if they pose an unmanageable risk to humans and other pets. Some people advocate isolating such dogs so that they don't have to killed. Isolation is not much of a life for a member of this highly social species.

That being said, for most aggressive dogs there can be significant improvement or even a "cure." Tens of thousands of success stories attest to it. With the help of reputable, experienced trainers, most dogs come around.

PUGNACIOUS PUPPY PUPILS

Not all dogs work and play well with other dogs. This can be because of many factors, including a lack of socialization in puppyhood or having been attacked, which only has to happen once to turn a dog permanently against other dogs. Sometimes, a pooch can receive a lasting bad impression in puppy kindergarten, of all places.

> On the first night of puppy obedience school, Ronan chased Tippy under a chair. Ever since then Tippy has been afraid of all dogs.
>
> What should have happened instead:
>
> The instructor, having evaluated all ten students, noticed that Ronan, the biggest, heaviest pup in the bunch, was a bully. Before he had a chance to terrorize Tippy, a shy creature about a third his size, he was redirected to play with the outgoing, assertive puppy Sonya, who had been chasing him to play. Every time Ronan lost interest in Sonya and zeroed in on Tippy, the instructor showed Ronan's human how to step in front of him, and walk straight into him, causing him to turn back and become interested in Sonya again. Tippy's family should also have stepped in front of her, to show her they would not let the bully jump on her.

HOW TO BREAK UP A DOGFIGHT

Never get between fighting dogs! *Never* grab their collars! They are so absorbed in combat that they might not notice who they're biting. Try to remain calm. It's always safer to have a helper. Make sure you have leashes ready.

The Water Treatment: Turn on a water hose full blast, aiming straight into the dogs' faces. Even after they separate, continue blasting both dogs. Interrupt their intentions and behavior by distracting them with the forceful use of your voice. Use their names, and give them familiar commands like "sit" or "down," allowing you to gain some control. Separate them with something large and physical such as a garbage can or open umbrella. Try to get one dog inside a door, exercise pen, yard, or house.

The Can Treatment: Get your shake can (see chapter 8, p. 157). Shake it vigorously, scolding them in deep, ominous tones. They should momentarily stop fighting. If you have a helper, get the person to corral one dog while you leash the other and remove her immediately. If you are alone, continue driving the dogs apart with the cans, and try to herd one into a separate area. Caution: Do not throw the shake can. If it breaks you'll lose your secret weapon.

Coprophagia (Eating Poop)

Coprophagia is the eating of excrement, commonly called *poop*. Many dogs exhibit this behavior. You might either have one in your own home or know someone who does. To us humans, it's a behavioral problem. But the poop-eating dogs would disagree. What compels so many of them to this disgusting habit?

Preference

Dogs living with cats are drawn to the litter box by the aroma of "tootsie rolls." Kitties eat strong-smelling canned fish and liver. How can a pooch resist?

Solution: Make the litter box inaccessible to the dog. Perhaps keep the box in a bathroom or laundry room, with a cat-sized pet door installed in the door.

Housekeeping

After labor, dog mothers eat their puppies' afterbirth, then keep their dens clean by eating the puppies' poop, even as it's coming out. A dog in an environment where feces have accumulated might be compelled to do some tidying up—by snarfing it up.

Solution: Scoop the poop!

Play

There are breeds that instinctively like to pick up things to carry. If there is nothing there but feces they will carry it, and even play with it.

Solution: Remember why you got a dog? You wanted a best friend, not a lawn ornament. Make more time for her. Exercise the dog so she'll be tired, not bored. Also, make her environment more interesting to alleviate boredom when she's alone (see chapter 11, p. 216).

Instinct

While we wear deodorant and colognes to mask our natural scents, dogs prefer to smell like roadkill or garbage. They're quite delighted to rub and roll in it . . . and then, naturally, eat it.

Solution: Reduce the dog's access to this "perfume."

Fear

Some dogs punished for defecating in the house learn to eat the "accidents" as a way of hiding them, so that you won't get mad.

Solution: Make sure your pooch has adequate opportunities to do her business outside. Assign all dog care chores so that it's clear which family member should be letting her out on those busy mornings. Make sure everyone agrees to their jobs and that they're responsible enough to carry them out.

Stress

A dog who never would have considered sampling stools might do so in response to a big change or upset in her life or routine.

Solution: Think ahead to changes in your life that might affect your dog—a move, a different work schedule, a new family member (especially pets!)—and try to smooth the transitions. Introduce all changes as slowly as possible and provide extra exercise and cuddle time, showing your dog that her status in the pack and her well-being will be preserved.

Health

Talk with your vet about health issues to consider, including the following:

- Your dog food might lack the minerals or vitamins the dog needs, so she's constantly ravenous (see chapter 7, pp. 115–118, for more information on proper nutrition).
- Two feedings and some healthy snacks are generally better than one meal a day. They're easier on digestion and mental state, giving the pooch some

thing to look forward to, so that she's not as tempted to "help herself."
- Because of intestinal parasites or other medical problems, the dog's not getting the full nutrient value from her food, or it's not being fully digested. Stools smell like the food and even have a similar consistency. Thus the dog finds it appealing.
- Because of a medical problem, the dog is lacking digestive enzymes.

However, all that said, some dogs are quite determined poop-eaters, and the only solution is constant vigilance of the guilty parties.

Why Bother to Train and Learn?

Every day, people take time out of their busy schedules to train with their dogs and make change happen—both for themselves and for their canine companions. And those dogs, too, rise to the challenge. There's a certain heroism in that. Change is rarely easy. Instead, the people could just dump the troublesome pooches and get new ones. The dogs could dig in their paws and refuse to try. Why do any of us bother?

From the canine point of view, we might surmise that because dogs are instinctively pack oriented, they are driven to meet expectations and fit in. Furthermore, twelve thousand years of selective breeding have made them love us. Most dogs want desperately for humans to love them back. And if it takes passing up that oh-so-chewable Oriental rug, they will make the effort to stay in our good graces.

From the human point of view, it would be all too easy to just return a pooch with a behavior problem and get a different one. Many people do that, and sometimes it's a valid course of action. Then why do others persevere with "problem" pooches?

One main reason, of course, is simple—love. When you give your heart to a best friend, it's awfully hard to take it back. Also, many folks realize that no pooch is without her problems. Just as we humans all have our faults, so do dogs. There's no such thing as perfection when it comes to living beings.

But there's yet another, often unsung reason for going through the not inconsiderable hassles of training. It's the light in your pooch's eyes when she "gets" it. Turning the corner on a stubborn behavior issue can be hugely satisfying, especially since poorly behaved dogs are often not happy ones. In helping a dog learn safer, more companionable ways of interacting with the world, you're building her confidence and opening a whole new world of fun and freedom to you both.

Finally, here's one of the best reasons to stick it out through a dog's misdeeds: The typical canine's calculation of quid pro quo is lopsided. More than likely, whatever gift you make to your dog—attention, teaching, patience, understanding, and love will be repaid a thousandfold.

It is scarcely possible to doubt that the love of man has become instinctive in the dog.

—Charles Darwin

Bandit before.

Bandit after.

Happily Ever After True Story Number Nine:

Bandit

• •

As the pinecone rolled away, the puppy scuttled after it, his roly-poly body sliding pell-mell across the trash-strewn yard. His caramel-colored fur was soft and baby fine, the hairs as short as eyelashes. His oversized eyes tracked the pinecone, which lay perfectly still. The puppy pounced. One clumsy paw thumped the pinecone, driving it away. As the puppy dove after the pinecone, the scruff of his neck was grabbed. He yelped and went still. The hand was attached to an old man's arm, and he swung the puppy away from the toy, carrying him to a small clearing.

Roughly, the man clamped a collar around the puppy's neck, then snapped a chain to the collar. The chain was attached to a tree that grew next to a dilapidated doghouse. Next to the doghouse was a cracked bucket. Dirty water puddled in the bucket. The man shuffled off in the direction of a house. The puppy scooted after the man, but sat down hard when the chain yanked him back. As the man disappeared behind a stand of pine trees, the puppy leaped up, his bright eyes straining to catch a glimpse, his body straining to break free. After tugging and pulling didn't work, the puppy began to whine. He howled, his high-pitched puppy voice echoing through the forest.

Sometimes, the man would come back. Without a word, he would drop food on the ground and pour some water into the bucket. He rarely touched or spoke to the puppy. And soon, the puppy stopped straining against the chain and his voice quieted too.

When the man stopped coming, the puppy began to starve. One night, as the temperature dropped well below freezing, the puppy lifted his head and began to howl. But his voice was deep, not at all like a puppy's. And his skeletal body was that of a dog. A dog that was six years old.

It was the howl that saved him. Someone heard him and then people came. They unhooked the chain and took him away from the clearing. He was brought to a house where many other dogs lived. There he was fed. He drank some water. He found a soft blanket and curled up, making his body into a tight ball.

"I've never seen a large dog able to make himself so small," said Lynn Gartland, Bandit's new mom.

For half a dozen years Bandit had been chained outside in the Colorado Rocky Mountains, enduring extremely cold temperatures along with wind, snow, and ice. Any dog living in those circumstances would develop coping mechanisms in order to stay alive. Bandit's ability to turn himself into a "curled-up snail" was his way to keep the cold out and to conserve what little warmth his body made.

Lynn and her husband, Tim, learned about Bandit when the local newspaper featured his story. They already had five rescued dogs on their thirty-five acres of land, and they were not looking to adopt anyone else. "We didn't need another dog, but Bandit needed a home, so we decided to adopt him."

Because Bandit had never socialized with dogs or people in his entire life, it was something of a surprise to Lynn and Tim to see how respectful Bandit was toward the other five dogs. He did not act shy, nor was he overly rambunctious. Even during meals, although he vacuumed up his kibble, Bandit never showed food aggression.

Each day Tim takes the entire pack for a six-mile walk around the property. Bandit's urge to run through the trees competes with his need to stay indoors with Lynn, causing him great decision-making anxiety.

"As Tim and the other dogs are walking down the driveway, Bandit will dash back and forth through the dog door to check on me," Lynn reports. "I just pet him and tell him what a good boy he is, then he runs back outside to catch up with the others."

Whether he is underfoot or "in your face," as Lynn says, Bandit just wants to be close to something living, preferably Tim.

"Tim was sitting in his chair the other day and Bandit jumped up and landed on his lap!" she said. And there he stayed, all sixty-five pounds of him. "He has filled out, his coat is beautiful, and he's so thrilled to be alive that, to him, every minute of the day is fun."

10.
Home Sweet Home: Finding a "Forever" Family for Your Rescued Dog

You've Rescued a Dog but Can't Keep Him: How to Hunt Up Just the Right New Home for Your Friend in Need

Kellie: Chasing Little Green Squirrels

We are at the grassland with the boy. The shaggy dog and I are jumping on him and he is grabbing our heads and kissing us. Then he throws a round green thing. I look at it. He picks it up and throws it. I look at it. How nice that he's enjoying the round green thing. There's a squirrel! I must chase it! Where'd he go? Squirrel is gone. The little green thing is just lying in the grass. I think I'll sniff it. Hmmm. Pick it up. Toss it. Why look at that. It bounced away and I pounce on it. Got it! The boy is excited. Wait! He grabbed my little green thing. His hand sent it flying! It is bouncing on the grassland. Just . . . like . . . a . . . little green squirrel! I chase it! A squirrel that can't run faster than me! Boy, make it run away again! And with a huge smile on his face, he does. And I fly after the little green squirrel.

Maybe you risked your life saving a panicked pooch from speeding traffic (although we don't recommend it!). Or perhaps your neighbors, who left their dog outside in drenching rainstorms and frigid temperatures, finally came to their senses and surrendered their neglected dog to you. (Being a courteous complainer can save a life!) However it happened, you now have an animal in your care who is completely dependent on the decisions you make about his future. But you are aware of one thing that is enormously clear: You cannot keep the dog.

You've weighed your choices and have decided to try to find him a new family.

In reading this chapter you might feel a bit rescued yourself. We are here to help with a step-by-step process you can follow or modify as you see fit.

You might feel overwhelmed by this responsibility. Take heart. Loving homes are out there. The creativity and perseverance that flow out of your caring spirit can lead you to them.

> Properly trained, a man can be dog's best friend.
>
> —humorist and writer, Corey Ford

Adoptability Assessment

Before you start trying to rehome your rescue, make an honest assessment of your chances for success. Ask your vet, trainer, and local shelter or rescue organization for opinions. Give some thought to these questions.

- If I was looking for a dog to adopt, what qualities about this one would be attractive to me? (He's calm and great with kids.) Which ones would be unattractive? (He's got thick fur that needs frequent grooming.)
- Is he a large dog? Is he over the age of five? Both of these can make the dog harder to place.
- Is the dog of a breed that many people consider dangerous (for example, pit bulls, rottweilers, Dobermans)?
- Is there anything about his health or behavior that would make me reluctant to adopt the dog? Can those conditions be corrected?
- Are there any health issues that will narrow the field of potential adopters? (If the dog needs medication several times a day, someone must be available to give it.)
- Are there any behaviors that will narrow the field? (If the dog is a brilliant backyard escape artist, you might need a home where he's never left outdoors unsupervised.)

Is Your Rescue Unadoptable?

Unadoptable—a dog labeled with this word most likely will never be placed in a home. Instead, these dogs face humane euthanasia. Therefore, it is a label that must never be mistakenly used.

The sad fact is that a certain number of dogs in the homeless population, after being health checked and temperament tested, will be deemed unadoptable. Foster homes and kennel space in shelters are at a premium. Although deciding to euthanize an unadoptable dog can be emotionally devastating, the reality is that if you have to do so, you're giving another needy dog a chance at a life and a future. The home that would have gone to the troubled dog can go to a different homeless pooch instead.

Some unadoptable dogs can be helped through intervention, such as professional behavior/training or specialty veterinary care. If you have the resources and time to provide these services to your rescue, then follow your heart with a clear head. In the end, you still may face the fact that your rescue cannot be rehomed.

Here are some characteristics that could make a dog unadoptable:

- Confirmed history of biting and aggression toward people and animals
- Confirmed diagnosis of a fatal illness
- An elderly dog suffering from severe effects of old age

As difficult as it may be, do not shield yourself from the facts a temperament test or a veterinary exam may reveal. You have a serious decision to make and your emotional state will be taxed. If you must euthanize your rescue, acknowledge your sadness. You have every right to feel pain, disappointment, anger, and grief. Contacting a pet loss support group can be very helpful during this time. Check with your local shelter. Here are some recommended Web sites: http://www.pet loss.net and http://www.superdog.com/pet loss/counsel.htm.

Checklist—Preparing Your Rescue for Placement

Before you offer your rescued pooch for adoption, meet these goals:

Vet exam

Vaccinations

Spay/neuter

Microchipping

Treat as many of his health issues as possible.

Put all the dog's health records and vet receipts into his Doggie Dossier (as described in chapter 5, pp. 60–61).

Expose the dog to as many new experiences, people, animals, and environments as your time allows.

Correct as many of his behavior problems as possible.

Keep a Doggie Diary noting the dog's health, behavior, likes, dislikes, amusing moments, and so on, to include in the Doggie Dossier.

Decide on your adoption policy.

Decide on your adoption fee.

Decide which supplies and services you will offer the adopter—for example, crate, bowls, training, pet sitting, and so forth.

At Our Best—Tips on Preparing Your Rescue for Placement

As you go through the checklist on preparing your rescue for placement, here are some tips that might help:

Health

According to your available time and budget, you have addressed some or all of your rescue's health needs, including spay/neuter. You've kept your receipts and copies of the medical records and placed them in the Doggie Dossier. It is imperative that you share any and all medical information about your pooch with prospective adopters. Most of them will deeply appreciate the time and money you have spent on their new family member. In the "Adoption Fee" section on p. 188, you'll learn how you might (or might not) be able to set the fee to an amount that allows you to recover some of the money you've spent—money that has not only made your rescued dog more adoptable but made him feel better too.

Behavior

All along, you have been carefully observing your rescue's behavior, jotting down notes whenever possible. You have exposed the dog to a variety of people, animals, and situations to see how he'll react. You have worked to improve his problem behaviors through gentle but firm and consistent training.

Will you be able to eliminate every single naughty habit? Will you be offering a flawlessly behaved dog for adoption? Highly unlikely. None of us humans is ever perfect, and neither are pooches. Chances are that the dog might still be a destructive chewer or an obnoxious barker or a kitty chaser.

Your first job before offering the dog for adoption is to give him a sense of security and well-being. This will give the dog the ability to relax so that he can begin to learn. You'll accomplish this simply by providing regular meals, comfortable shelter, daily opportunities to exercise and play, and of course, plenty of your company and love.

Your second job in the behavior department is training. You might have time and resources to take the dog through a full obedience class or hire a professional behaviorist for private instruction. Or you might only be able to read a book about training and teach the dog some of the basics. In general, the more training a dog gets, the more adoptable he becomes. Even a few simple commands can be impressive. Watch the prospective new family's eyes light up when they see the dog sit, stay, or lie down at your word. It demonstrates that their new pooch will be an apt pupil for their own future efforts.

Your third job, behaviorwise, is to thoroughly list and describe any remaining unwanted behaviors to interested adopters. Full disclosure is key. Just as in health matters, you want the dog's new family to know everything you have noticed about his temperament—good and not so good—*before* they make the decision to take him home.

Imagine this dog and all his personality quirks in someone else's living room. What problems might they encounter? What information can you provide to help?

You might worry that such honesty will scare away adopters. You're absolutely right. Someone might own a home full of pricey antiques that one tooth mark could ruin. That's not a good match for your Jaws. Another prospect might live next door to a crotchety neighbor who can't stand the slightest bit of barking. That's definitely not the home for your Luciano Pavarotti.

Anyone who expects to live with a perfect dog is dreaming. If your honesty scares someone away, good riddance. Your pooch deserves a guardian who's going to love him along with his flaws while patiently, lovingly encouraging him to be better. After all, isn't that what best friends do?

BASIC DOGGIE MANNERS

Your rescue's chances for adoption skyrocket if you help him achieve these basic manners: walks on leash fairly well without pulling, doesn't mouth or jump on people, is friendly and confident—not suspicious and skittish, gets along reasonably well with other dogs.

Grooming

Think "first date." And first impressions. You want your rescued canine to exude health and vitality, and of course, to look irresistible. Even the homeliest of four-footers can sparkle after a bath and a brush-out.

Whether you scrub the dog down using the hose in your driveway or treat him to a day at the doggie spa, the end result will plump up his chances for adoption. Make sure the dog's nails are trimmed, the ears are clean, and that he's sharing his skin with no fleas or ticks. If the dog's type of coat requires clipping, try to get that done. Overall good grooming will show interested adopters that you care about this pooch and that they should too.

A canine senior citizen, or one with medical problems, might not be able to glow quite as much as a young and healthy dog. But certainly being clean and pest-free will help the dog feel perkier and thus allow his natural charm to shine through.

Setting the Rules—Your Adoption Policy

Before you begin looking for a new home for your rescued dog, set your adoption policy. Thinking things through in advance can help streamline the process and take out the stress.

Every adoption policy should contain certain standard elements as well as some that are tailored to your dog's personality and health needs. This section will help you design the right policy for your rescue.

Spay/Neuter

Again, we strongly urge spaying or neutering prior to adoption. As discussed in previous chapters, this procedure helps your rescue stay safe and healthy, and it is essential to reducing the horrors of pet overpopulation. Once the dog is in the new owner's possession, it's difficult to enforce any requirements, so it's best to perform the surgery before the dog leaves your custody.

However, if the pooch's health or your time limitations prohibit surgery, you might stipulate in the adoption agreement (see p. 189) that spaying/neutering must be done within a certain period of time. As an incentive, you can offer a reimbursement for the cost of the surgery.

Adoption Application

Anyone interested in adopting your rescue will need to fill out an application. You must get accurate answers about the adopter's home, family, other pets, and attitudes toward dog ownership—in writing. Sometimes people take what they write more seriously than what they say. It will help you stay organized and on top of things if you have prospective adopters' information on paper at your fingertips. And it allows you to compare various applications more easily.

Create the application in advance, perhaps using the sample we've provided below as a guide, and add any more questions you'd like to ask.

LAYING DOWN THE LAW

The sample adoption application and adoption agreement contained in this chapter are based on similar documents used by California-based private rescue organizations. Please note that in both samples we included some legalese, such as the disclaimer clause in the application—as sample language *only*. We are not lawyers and do not intend to give you legal advice. If legal issues and liability are of concern, you might wish to consult an attorney in your state about your own adoption application and adoption agreement. Usually legal disputes do not arise from dog adoptions. Unfortunately, though, that's not to say it won't happen in your case.

Sample Dog Adoption Application

Dog's Information (*Rescuer to fill this in*)

Name of dog:

Breed, color, weight, and age:

Rescuer's Information (*Rescuer to fill this in*)

Name:

Home address, city, state, zip code:

Home phone number, cell phone number, and e-mail address:

Adopter's Information

Name:

Home address, city, state, zip code:

Home phone number, cell phone number, and e-mail address:

Age:

Questions—Adopter, please answer these questions as fully as possible, using as much space as necessary. Thank you for your time and interest.

References—Please provide names, phone numbers, and addresses of two nonrelatives who know you and your home well. May we call them?

Do you rent or own your home? Please describe—apartment, townhouse, condo, single-family home? How long have you lived there?

If you rent, please provide a letter of approval from your landlord to keep a dog indoors. Please also provide the landlord's telephone number. Do we have your permission to call your landlord to check on his or her approval?

Who is your veterinarian?

Is the dog going to be a gift? If so, explain:

What are your feelings about spay/neuter?

What interests you about this particular dog?

What dogs and other pets have you had in the past? (breed, weight, age) How long did you have them? What happened to them?

Do you currently have any pets? Please describe (breed, weight, age).

Are they up-to-date on vaccinations and health care? Spayed/neutered?

Why do you want another pet?

Have you ever owned more than one pet at the same time? Have you ever owned more than one dog at the same time? Are you prepared for the increased work, commotion, and expense of having multiple pets?

How do you think any current pets will react to having a new dog in the home?

What training methods have you used in the past with your dogs?

What did you do, specifically, when you had behavioral issues with your dogs?

Are you willing to attend dog-training classes with your new dog?

Are you familiar with crate-training dogs? Would you be willing to find out more about crate training and possibly implementing it with a new dog?

When was the last time you brought a new dog home?

What do you remember about the first several weeks of transition after you brought the dog home? How did it go? Do you feel ready to sign on for that again?

For the first week after adoption, are you going to be able to lighten your schedule enough to give this pooch a lot of extra care and attention? How many hours a day will you be spending with the dog during that week?

Sample Dog Adoption Application (continued)

Where will the dog stay when you are not home—indoors or outdoors? If outdoors, where? If indoors, where?

How many hours a day will your dog be alone?

Describe your typical day on a weekday. On a weekend?

How will your dog be cared for when you are out of town?

Do you have a fenced yard? If so, describe your fence.

Are there locking gates? Do you keep them locked?

Do you have an outdoor kennel? If so, describe material, top, base, surface.

Do you plan to let your dog off leash anywhere other than on your property?

How much car traffic is there on your street?

Is your front door secure so that a dog cannot escape? Are the screens and windows in good repair?

How do you plan to exercise your new dog?

If you have a pool or live near a body of water, how do you plan to keep your dog safe from drowning?

Number of adults in household? Ages?

Number of children in household? Ages?

How do you plan to teach your child(ren) about respect and care for this dog?

Is there anyone in your home who disagrees with the plan to adopt a new dog?

Who will be responsible for the care and exercising of the dog?

Does anyone in your family have allergies to dogs?

Is everyone in the family willing and able to give the new dog a lengthy adjustment period?

What changes in your life are you anticipating in the next year? In the next five years? (For example, new baby, grandchildren, new job, moving, remodeling)

Are you willing to pay an adoption fee for this dog?

Will you allow us to perform a home check, during which we will visit and inspect your home and yard for dog safety and comfort?

Will you allow us to perform follow-up visits and phone calls?

Disclaimer—There is no guarantee made, express or implied, that any person requesting to adopt a dog through me (*Rescuer's name*), will automatically be approved. All adoptions are subject to acceptance based on a review process that requires collecting information from references and visiting the applicant's home. Decisions on placing dogs in adoptive and foster homes are based solely on the judgment of (*Rescuer's name*), and adoption applications may be denied for various reasons. (*Rescuer's name*) reserves the right to refuse adoption to anyone without disclosing the reasons, and to make all decisions regarding placement or final disposition of any rescued dog in his/her care whether in, or being placed in, a foster or adoptive home or other facility.

I certify that all information in this adoption application is true and correct, and I understand that false information may void the application. Signature(s) and date:

The Adoption Fee

To ensure that your dog is going into a caring home where he will be valued as part of the family, it is best to charge an adoption fee. It might range from $150 to $300. We recommend that you factor in such out-of-pocket costs as the vet exam, vaccinations, microchipping, spay/neuter, medications, obedience classes, food, and supplies.

However, don't count on being able to recoup your expenses with the adoption fee. Rescuing dogs is almost always a bad financial investment—but a sound moral one.

Should anyone dispute the idea of paying an adoption fee, this implies that the applicant cannot afford to care for a dog. Also, animals that are offered "free to good homes" have been known to be sold to research labs for experiments or used as bait to train fighting dogs. If applicants refuse to pay, tell them to go away.

Fully Fenced Yard

If the adopter has a yard, it must be fully fenced with material tall enough and strong enough to contain this particular dog, and all gates must have locking mechanisms. If your rescued pooch is a tunneler or a climber, the adoptive family might have to take measures to make sure their new pooch doesn't escape. (See chapter 5, pp. 62–64, for more information on escape attempts.) If the adopter does not have a yard, there must be a feasible plan for frequent on-leash potty breaks and exercise.

Allowed Indoors

Dogs should only be placed in homes where they'll be allowed to live primarily indoors with the rest of the family (see chapter 5, p. 59).

Children in the Home

Puppies should never be placed in homes with children under five years of age. Learning how your rescue interacts with children will help you determine whether his new home should include children, and if so, what their minimum age should be.

Mandatory Return

If the adopter decides at any time and for any reason that he or she cannot keep the dog, the dog must be returned to you. This is critical. Otherwise, the adopter might get rid of your rescue in an irresponsible or even cruel way.

Home Check

You must visit the home of the potential adopter to make sure it meets all the criteria you have set. Seeing the residence for yourself will assure you that it offers the safe, comfortable environment your rescued dog deserves. If any adopters object to this part of your policy, thank them for their time, scratch them off the list, and move on (see pp. 195–199 for more details on the home check).

Adoption Agreement

Every adoption should be carried out under a written agreement. Even if the adopter is a friend, neighbor, coworker, or relative, an agreement on paper will help prevent misunderstandings. It will ensure that you both agree to mutually acceptable terms. Below you'll find a sample adoption agreement you might use as a guide in creating your own.

Sample Dog Adoption Agreement

Dog's Information (*Rescuer to fill this in*)

Name of dog:

Breed, color, weight, age:

Rescuer's Information (*Rescuer to fill this in*)

Name:

Home address, city, state, zip code:

Home phone number, cell phone number, and e-mail address:

Adopter's Information

Name:

Home address, city, state, zip code:

Home phone number, cell phone number, and e-mail address:

Agreement (*Adopter to read, initial, and sign where indicated*)

I agree that the animal is being adopted for myself and will not be sold, adopted, or given to another party. _____ (*initial*)

I agree that the animal will not be allowed off the premises of my home without proper supervision. When the animal is off the premises, he/she will be held on a secure leash and wear a proper ID. _____ (*initial*)

I agree that this dog is to be a companion animal, not a guard dog. The dog will live primarily inside my home, not outdoors. _____ (*initial*)

I agree to care for the animal in a humane manner and be a responsible animal guardian. This includes supplying adequate food, water, shelter, attention, and professional medical care. _____ (*initial*)

I agree that if at any point I cannot keep the animal, I will return him/her to the original Rescuer, and that I will not request a fee beyond a refund of the adoption fee I paid. _____ (*initial*)

I understand and agree that the Rescuer makes no guarantees about the animal's health and that the Rescuer is not responsible for future medical care and costs required by this animal. _____ (*initial*)

As of this date, the following health issues have been noted: (*Rescuer to list health issues here.*)

I understand and agree that the Rescuer makes no guarantees about the animal's temperament and is not responsible for future damages or injuries caused by the animal. _____ (*initial*)

I give the Rescuer permission to phone me at my home at any reasonable time to ensure that the animal is being properly treated and cared for. _____ (*initial*)

I agree to allow the Rescuer to visit my home throughout the lifetime of the dog to ensure that the animal is being properly treated and cared for. Visits will be arranged by appointment. _____ (*initial*)

I agree to keep the Rescuer informed of my current home address and phone number. _____ (*initial*)

I understand that the Rescuer follows a strict adoption policy. I have read, signed, and agree to comply with the adoption policy provided in a separate document. _____ (*initial*)

I agree that all statements I have made on this form are true. If it is found that any statements I have made on this form are not true, the adopted animal can be confiscated.

Adopter's signature and date:

Driver's license number:

License plate number:

Rescuer's signature and date:

Follow-Up Visits

After you place your rescued dog in a home, you must perform follow-up visits to check on the animal's well-being (see pp. 201–202 for details).

Customizing Your Adoption Policy

Every pooch is unique, with his own needs, strengths, and weaknesses. While setting your adoption policy, consider the following:

Health

If your rescue has special health needs, make sure the adoptive family has the time, financial resources, and willingness to meet them. For example, maybe the dog will always require medication three times per day. Will someone in the adoptive family be available to give it to the dog? Maybe he has bad teeth that need daily brushing at home and yearly cleanings at the vet's office. Will the new family be able to keep up with that? An older dog might sometimes experience incontinence. Will the dog's new caregivers love him enough to clean him, mop up the mess, and to realize that it's not the dog's fault?

Behavior

Sadly, even if a prospective adopter has fallen crazy in love with your rescue, and vice versa, they might not be right for each other. You could be asking too much of both dog and adopter by placing your rescue in a home where the cards are already stacked against them both. For example, if your rescue is guilty of toy guarding and the possible new home has young children, placing the dog there could be a recipe for disaster. If your macho rescue has a pattern of aggression toward male dogs, World War Three could result from placing him in a family that includes another male canine.

Certainly, there are exceptions. It could happen that an interested adopter fully comprehends the difficulties posed by your rescue's behavior problems yet is truly committed to diligent training. Such an adopter might be too good to pass up.

The Extras

Here's where your understanding of your rescue come into play. Of course, any home that provides love and proper care is a good home. But just like the rest of us, your rescue has unique personality traits that make him what he is. Will the people in the new home be able to appreciate, indulge, and even enjoy those traits? For example, maybe you've rescued a Labrador mix that trembles at the sight of the ball he prays you'll throw. Your customized policy for that dog should aim for families who will have fun playing frequent games of fetch in the backyard or at a nearby off-leash dog park. On the other paw, when you throw a ball, what if your rescue just yawns and moseys up to you for an ear rub? Then make sure that his new family won't mind the lack of athleticism.

THAT PERFECT PREVIOUS POOCH

Be on the alert for signs that interested adopters want their new dog to be like their previous one. If they say things like, "Our old dog was an Australian shepherd mix and that's why we want another one," mention to them that all dogs are different, and that your rescue's personality might not resemble that of the Aussie mix they had before. Also, if their previous pooch was a calm, cooperative senior when he passed away, ask them if they remember what life was like when he was young and rambunctious like your rescue. Are they ready to tolerate all that energy again?

SAMPLE DOG ADOPTION POLICY

A summarized form of a sample adoption policy that you can use to inform prospective adopters about your multi-step adoption process is found below. You may customize it as you like. Also attach a copy of the Dog Adoption Agreement as well as the Dog Adoption Application. Thus, prospective adopters are fully informed up front about your careful screening process.

YOU MIGHT HEAR COMPLAINTS

Some people—prospective adopters, relatives, or others—might ridicule or criticize you for following a careful adoption policy and for being "picky." Things we have heard include (among others we won't repeat): "You'll never find a home better than mine. Let me have the dog before I change my mind," and "This is just a dog you're adopting out, not a child!" All par for the course. There is probably no dog rescuer in the world who hasn't been hassled at some time or another. Welcome to the ranks!

PACKING YOUR DOG'S BAGS— THINGS TO GIVE ITS NEW FAMILY

To strengthen the relationship you are creating with the adopter, and as a sign of goodwill, consider offering supplies and services. Possibilities include a dog

Dog Adoption Policy

Prospective adopter has read and understood the Dog Adoption Policy below and the Dog Adoption Agreement attached. (Adoption Agreement does not need to be signed until the end of the screening process.)
Signature and date:

Spay/neuter—Rescued dog will be spayed/neutered before entering the new home. Or, if that is not possible, Adopter will spay/neuter as soon as possible after adoption, as per prior agreement.

Adoption application—Must be filled out in full.

Telephone interview—A half-hour conversation during which Rescuer and Adopter will ask each other questions to see if it might be a good match.

Initial meeting—A one-hour meeting at a public place that will include the Rescuer, the Rescued Dog, the Adopter, and all residents of the Adopter's home, including other dogs.

Home check—A one-hour visit by the Rescuer, a Helper, and the Rescued Dog at the Adopter's home for the purpose of assessing the future safety and well-being of the Rescued Dog.

Some basic requirements—Dog to live indoors. Fully fenced yard or several on-leash walks and exercise sessions per day. No children in home under a certain age.

Dog Adoption Agreement—Please read the attached agreement. You do not need to sign it at this time. If you are selected as the adopter for this dog, you will be asked to sign the agreement.

Adoption Fee—Adopter will pay to Rescuer an Adoption Fee of $_____. (*Rescuer to fill in the appropriate amount.*)

crate, dog bed, bowls, brush/comb, bag of food, treats, toys, vouchers for vet exams, pet store discounts, and training or boarding coupons/discounts.

You might consider offering free future boarding in your home, if your schedule allows, up to a certain number of days per year, and by prior appointment only. Or you might offer free walks and play dates, with the same stipulations. One advantage of such services is that they give you an easy opportunity to check on the dog and, of course, enjoy a little time with your rescue now and then!

Must Love Dogs—How to Advertise

There are many ways you can get the word out that you have a dog available for adoption. Refer to the Doggie Dossier that you created for your rescued dog. Using that information, write an ad or press release that will inspire that special someone to come calling. Put it into the form of a flyer and include a cute photo of your dog. Don't forget to mention any special talents or funny quirks—the dog's an awesome Frisbee catcher or he loves cuddling up with your pet rabbit. Post it in veterinary hospitals, grooming shops, pet supply stores, doggie day-care businesses, dog parks, supermarkets, shoe stores—wherever a friendly proprietor gives permission.

Your local shelters and private rescue organizations might be willing to post your flyer in their offices or on their Web sites and to help you get the word out in other ways. Some could be too overwhelmed with their own rescue efforts to provide you with a lot of assistance, but they might have some time to at least advise you.

If your rescue shows signs of having a pedigree in its background, you can contact breed rescue groups for help in rehoming the dog. Find them by performing an Internet search using the name of the dog's breed and the word "rescue" as key words (for example, "German shepherd rescue" or "cocker spaniel rescue"). Some breed rescue groups will even help you place a dog that is a mixed breed if the dog shows some clear characteristics of the group's specialty breed.

Then there's the Internet. Become a member of an animal companion group by searching for the phrase "dog homes" on Yahoo, MSN, or Google, or create your own group on these Web sites. There, you can post and send out information about your rescue to people who are interested in adopting dogs.

Also online, many Web sites provide matchmaking services between people and companion animals. For example, Petfinder.com and Craigslist.com are both popular and widely accessed sites.

If you feel creative, make your own Web site starring your rescued dog. Do a search for "create a Web site." You will find many Web-site hosting services that will guide you step by step in creating and publishing your own site. Then promote your site using the suggestions and links from your Web hosting company.

The power of your voice can be the best resource of all. Tell every person who crosses your path (especially if your rescue is with you) that you have a dog who is looking for a new home. Talk not only to groomers, veterinarians, and boarding kennel staff, but also to everyone else—your dentist, pastor, insurance agent, and mail carrier. Ask them to keep their ears open in case they hear of anyone wanting to adopt a dog. You may find that you are only a few degrees of separation from the perfect adopter.

Be Picky—Screening Applicants

Your public relations and advertising skills have been so successful that your telephone is ringing off the hook with people clamoring to meet your rescued dog. Now is the time that your character-judging skill kicks in. In order to figure out who will have the privilege of adopting your rescue, you need to gather some specific information.

The Adoption Applicants

When someone expresses interest in adopting your rescue, be polite and upbeat. Take the time to answer all questions applicants might have about their possible new pooch. At this point, you don't need to ask them many questions. After you've answered the applicants' questions, ask them to fill out your Dog Adoption Application. If for any reason they don't like the idea, then you know right off it's not the kind of home your rescue needs. Cooperation and honesty between you and the adopter are essential.

Explain that you follow a strict adoption policy and send a copy of it to them along with the Dog Adoption Application, as well as the Dog Adoption Agreement for their review.

Once you receive the completed adoption application (and the signed adoption policy copy), review them thoroughly.

Good signs: Thoughtful, thorough answers and a sense that the applicants are trying their best to respond with the information you seek.

Red flags: Inconsistencies between different pieces of information. Anything that sounds too good to be true, such as a statement that an adopter has one hundred fenced acres. The previous pet had to be rehomed for a minor reason or died young and unnecessarily or "ran away." The applicant has pets but no vet. Statements like, "I've trained many dogs—they just need to know who's boss," and long work days that don't allow much time with the dog. The applicant wants a dog as a companion to another dog. Other pets are not spayed and neutered. The applicant has a purebred but doesn't know much about the breed. The applicant is giving the dog as a gift. The applicant is not willing to give references.

If an application passes your inspection, contact the prospective adopter and politely ask to schedule a thirty-minute telephone interview at a time that will be quiet and convenient for you both.

The Telephone Interview

During the phone interview, the first thing to do is relax. It might feel as though you're prying, demanding details about someone else's life and character. In a way, you are. But you have spent time, money, and perhaps risked the wrath of family members to save this needy pooch, all for the sake of ensuring his future safety and happiness in just the right forever home. A careful screening process is your best chance to do that.

The adopter might feel a little nervous too. These feelings of discomfort on both your parts are normal. You might break the ice by acknowledging the awkwardness of the situation, and joking that you must sound like the Fido FBI. After a little shared laughter, the two of you can discuss how it's all for a good cause. The Fido in question needs the right home, the adopter needs the right Fido, and your job is to make that match. The type of adopter you want for your rescue will appreciate the fact that you are being careful for both their sakes.

Have the filled-out adoption application in front of you so that you can refer to it. Have a notepad and pen too, so that you can make notes during the conversation.

Go through the adoption application. Make positive comments about answers that made you feel good about the adopter. Follow up on any questions whose answers might have been unclear or unsatisfactory. See how able or willing the applicant is to make changes at home or in lifestyle to accommodate your rescue's needs.

Although you must always be courteous, don't be shy about asking your questions. Listen patiently and attentively to the answers. Beyond the words you hear, there are subtle cues that can help you make your decision. A person's demeanor can give you clues to personality and lifestyle. Listen to the tone of the adopters' voices when you ask about the security of their backyards or the ages of their children. Are they confident and forthcoming or do they sound defensive and annoyed? Are they patient with your questions or do they rush through answers and seem to want to get off the phone? Do they show interest by asking meaningful questions? Do they express logical concerns about the dog's temperament and behaviors?

One of the most important areas you should explore with potential adopters is how willing they are to work on the problems that will almost certainly arise once the dog is in their home. You'll get a feel for their problem-solving abilities when you ask how they dealt with training past animal companions. If you detect a sense of humor, it could come in handy during those dreaded moments like messes on the Oriental rug, a gnawed pair of Ferragamos, or an escape attempt that almost gives everyone heart attacks.

When interviews go well, tell the applicants that you see them as possible matches. Ask if they're feeling the same way. If so, ask them to meet you and the pooch for an in-person initial meeting of about thirty to sixty minutes. Arrange the meeting for a time and public place that's easy and convenient for you both. Ask them to bring along all family members, including dogs, who live in the house (see pp. 195–196 for more details).

Make it clear that the initial meeting is an opportunity for you all to get to know each other better. You feel they are great candidates, but you are not yet agreeing to let them adopt the dog. At the meeting you will not be making a decision. Suggest that they shouldn't either. You should both take twenty-four hours after the meeting to digest what you learned and felt. Suggest also that they let their family members know about this policy, so that there will be no misunderstandings or disappointments.

YOUR SAFETY FIRST

As you search for a new home for your rescue, you will probably be dealing with many strangers. Protect yourself. You won't be doing yourself or your rescue any favors by putting yourself at risk.

Never invite prospective adopters to your home or give them your home address. For any in-person meetings, arrange to rendezvous at a busy public place—for example, a park or a shopping mall parking lot. Do *not* take children with you. Tell someone else where you're going and what time you plan to be back.

When you perform the home check, don't go alone. Take along a helper—a willing friend or relative. Do *not* take children with you. Again, give someone the address of where you're going and what time you plan to return.

Follow the same safety procedures when you deliver the rescue to his new home.

Initial Meeting

Make sure that the potential adopter has brought along any family members, including dogs, who live in the house. This way you can observe how everyone reacts to your rescue.

Before the meeting, let your freshly groomed rescue have a potty break. Read the sidebar below, "Checklist—Things to Observe during the Meeting." If the adopter has a dog or dogs, read the tips on introducing dogs to each other in chapter 5, pp. 68–70.

During the meeting, keep your rescue on leash and ask that the potential adopters leave their pooch(es) in the car nearby for a few minutes. This way they can first meet the rescue without the added chaos of doggie introductions.

Try not to talk much. Of course, if the prospective adopters have questions, go ahead and answer them. But mostly this is your time to observe.

It's also time to give the possible adopters a chance to get to know the pooch who might become a lifetime member of their family. Don't be defensive or try to explain his every move. They're either going to feel comfortable with the dog or they're not. There's not much you can say to affect their feelings and you wouldn't want to do that anyway. Adoption is an entirely personal decision—the adopter's privilege. This is the adopter's opportunity to make that very important decision. Chatter and explanations from you would only get in the way.

While the pooch and the family are interacting, make mental notes of what you're seeing and hearing. Let the impressions sink in so that you can recall them later while making your decision.

After fifteen minutes or so, ask them to bring out their own dog(s) on leash. Follow the instructions in the sidebar "Building Relationships with Canine Family Members," pp. 68–69, on introducing dogs to each other in chapter 5.

At the end of the meeting, thank the possible adopters for their time and tell them that you'll be contacting them the next day, after you've given your decision some thought. Ask them to do some careful thinking too on whether this is the right pooch for them. Remind them that if you both continue to feel positively about the adoption, there will be one more step—the home check.

CHECKLIST—THINGS TO OBSERVE DURING THE MEETING

Understandably, the prospective adopters might be excited and perhaps a little nervous about meeting their possible new pooch. But do they approach the dog calmly and confidently? Are they somewhat dog savvy? Or are they jittery and frightened? Adopters who are fearful of dogs might misinterpret normal future behaviors as aggression.

How do the adopters speak to and touch your rescue? Are they gentle and loving? Or do they shout commands, roughhouse, or try to outmuscle the dog?

Is there kindness and genuine concern in their eyes toward the dog? Or is this just an impulse thing—with only excitement for themselves and nothing for the dog?

Do they think they know all there is to know about dogs and dog training, or are they interested in learning more about the dog and how to best care for him?

Are all the adults participating? Or does one of them talk on a cell phone the entire time, barely acknowledging the pooch's existence?

How do they react if the dog leaves a paw print on their stylish shoes? Are they horrified? Or do they seem more focused on how adorable those furry paws are?

Do the children speak softly to the dog, petting his head with care and concern? Or do they shriek and wrestle?

How do the adopters treat their own dog? Does the dog look healthy and well cared for? Does he seem happy and confident?

How do your rescue and the adopter's dog(s) react to each other?

How is your rescue taking this meeting? Is the dog displaying behavior that's normal for him? Some dogs are always shy around new people. Others are too boisterous. Look for anything out of the ordinary. Does the dog seem unusually reticent, fearful, aggressive, or agitated? If so, does this get better during the meeting or grow worse? Do the prospective adopters do anything to ad-

dress the behavior, such as squat down so the dog will feel less threatened or speak more softly so as not to overexcite him?

WILL THE DOGS GET ALONG?

If the prospective adopter already has dogs, and if they seem friendly, and if after completing the screening process, you decide this is the right new family for your rescue, consider arranging several get-acquainted dates for the dogs before the adoption. The first dates should all take place on neutral ground and on leash at a park or parking lot, away from either dog's home. Eventually you can allow the adopters to take the dog home with them for a few hours of visiting, working up to a day, then overnight, only when the dogs are happy and comfortable together. Remain available for any advice or help the prospective adopter needs. Agree to accept your rescue back if things don't work out.

HOW TO SAY NO TO AN ADOPTER WHO ISN'T RIGHT

This can be one of the most difficult parts of rescuing a dog. It's even worse if the interested party is a friend or relative. No one likes to feel rejected, and who among us likes to be the rejecter? But for the sake of your rescued pooch, you have to be prepared to be just that.

To say no, some rescuers make up excuses like, "The dog's owners found us and want him back." Others believe that diplomacy is the best policy. They simply tell the prospective adopter that they feel it's not the right match. If the adopter presses to hear why (which the adopter usually does—wouldn't you?), the diplomatic rescuer says something truthful but tactful such as, "You're a very active person. I think you'll need a pooch who could keep up with you better than Fluffy could" (instead of, "You're so high-strung that you would drive this dog crazy").

No matter what comes out of your mouth, you're almost certain to cause disappointment or even anger. To keep things as calm as possible and to preserve your own emotional energy, we have a few ideas.

Stay nonconfrontational. Don't criticize. Even if the spouse acted like Godzilla, don't say, "Your husband was too rough with Roxy." Even if the children were hellions, don't say, "Your kids didn't stop fighting long enough to say hello to the dog." Even if you caught the adopters in a boldfaced lie, don't accuse them of dishonesty. Even if the adopters' dog smelled like it hadn't had a bath in years, don't accuse them of neglect (see chapter 4, pp. 42–43, for information on confronting a neglecter or abuser).

Most important, when you have to say no, don't feel guilty. From the beginning you informed the adopters that your adoption policy was strict, and that it was designed for the benefit of both your rescue and the potential adopters. Keep the conversation as short as you can, thank them for their time and interest, and refocus your energy on your big mission—finding your rescued pooch the right forever home.

The Home Check

After the twenty-four-hour thinking period, if all the information you've gathered still leads you to believe you've found the right family, you have one more job to do—the home check.

Contact the candidates and ask if they'd like to continue with the screening process. If they're still interested in adopting your rescue, ask when you, a helper, and the rescue can visit their home for the home check, and make an appointment.

Take along a copy of the Home Check Checklist on pp. 198–199, as well as a pen and notepad to jot down your impressions.

Arriving for the home check, thank the prospective adopters for allowing you to visit. Be polite, friendly, and never pushy. Remember that you and your helper are guests in their home—not storm troopers. As the dog's rescuer, you have a right to ask questions and request to see various parts of the home, but as the home's residents, they have the right to refuse. However, if you sense dishonesty or a lack of cooperation, your decision about that family might be made right there on the spot.

During the home check, keep your rescue on a leash, and request that they confine any pets while you're touring the home so that you can concentrate.

This is your chance to see firsthand the yard where your rescue will play and the room where he will sleep. You'll see all the family members your dog will grow to love in their own environment.

Think in terms of the word *safety*. This is especially important if the adopter has never had a dog before. Follow the checklist and be thorough in your inspection.

If you feel this family is a great match but just needs to correct a few safety lapses, you might offer ideas. For example, that box of chocolates on the coffee table could be deadly to a dog that devours it. That puddle of antifreeze on the garage floor could kill the dog who laps it up. The latch on the side gate is loose, making it easy for a dog to slip out.

On the other hand, if there are major issues, you might have to rule this adopter out. For example, maybe on the adoption application and in your telephone interview the adopter said the dog would be sleeping on a dog bed in his or her bedroom, but while in the home you see that their current pooch sleeps out on the back patio. The adopter explains that the current dog is an "outdoor" dog, but the new dog will be the "indoor" dog. Immediate disqualification! First, it's probably not true—your rescue will most likely end up on the patio too. Second, if it is true, how terribly unfair to the current dog. All dogs deserve to live as part of the family.

If no major issues crop up, and if after you've made your tour you're still feeling positive about this family, it's time to introduce your rescue to the resident dog(s) on that dog's home turf. This can be tricky. See chapter 5, pp. 68–70, for tips on introducing dogs to each other. Next, refer to chapter 5, p. 71, for tips on introducing dogs to cats and other pets, and have your dog meet all the pets in the home.

After the home check, have everyone contemplate the decisions at hand. For twenty-four hours, you should evaluate everything you have learned about the potential adopters and their family and pets. During the same time period, the adopters should think about the dog they've met, and imagine him living with them for the rest of his life.

Home Check Checklist

Both indoors and out, you are evaluating your rescue's future health and safety. Even the most well-meaning and responsible dog owners sometimes overlook hazards in their homes. For more details on dogproofing a home, see chapter 5, pp. 62–66.

Below you'll find some sample questions to consider. You might add more of your own, according to your rescue's needs and personality. If the answers are not obvious, don't hesitate to ask the prospective adopter about them.

Outdoors

Is the fence strong and tall enough to contain your particular rescue? For most medium and large dogs it should be six feet tall. For smaller dogs, take into account the dog's agility and escape inclinations.

If your rescue is a fence climber, is the fence material of a type—wood, concrete, or vinyl—that the dog can't scale?

If the dog is an under-the-fence tunneler, will the family be able to secure the bottom of the fence (as described in chapter 5, p. 63)?

Do the gates shut and lock properly?

Is the yard generally tidy and well kept? Does it contain any items that could be harmful if chewed or eaten? Any poisonous plants?

Where will the dog go potty? Where will he play? Is there a recreational digging area where the adopters wouldn't mind doggie excavations?

How close are the neighbors?

Indoors

Do all the doors, including screen doors, shut and lock properly?

Are all the windows and screens in good repair?

Is the house generally tidy and well kept? Do you see any items that could be harmful if chewed or eaten? Are electrical outlets and electronic equipment out of reach?

In which rooms will the dog be allowed? Are there any the dog won't be allowed in?

Where will the dog eat meals? Where will he sleep?

Where do the other pets eat and sleep? Do they have clean water available?

Relationships and Interactions

Are the potential adopters really comfortable with your visit? Do they make excuses for things?

Do all the family's pets look healthy and well cared for? Are they spayed or neutered? Wearing IDs?

How do the humans interact with the pets? Are they treated like family members?

How do the pets behave? If there is misbehavior, how is it dealt with? Does the adopter believe that the new dog will "train" the current dog, or vice versa?

How do the humans interact with each other (adults with adults, as well as adults with children)? Does the family seem generally happy together? Mutually respectful, or tense, chaotic, or rude?

If there are children, are they fearful or welcoming with the dog?

Do the adults supervise the children with the pets? Do the adults expect the children to be responsible for the care of the pets?

If there are other companion animals, how do they react to your rescue?

Overall, remember that your gut feeling can be important, coming from information that you're taking in but perhaps processing on an unconscious level.

The Big Day—Your Rescue Goes to His New Home

Based on the adoption application, telephone interview, initial meeting, home check, and your gut feelings about the adopter, you now get to decide—is this a match? Or should you continue the search? If what you've learned has made you wish *you* could move in with this adopter, give yourself some credit. Because of your thoroughness, patience, and concern for your rescued dog, *you* have found someone who will give the dog the life he deserves.

Call the adopters with the happy news. After the twenty-four-hour thinking time, would they still like to welcome this pooch into their family? If so, arrange a time to deliver their new family member to their home.

Pack up any items you've chosen to give the adopter. One thing you should definitely try to provide is a bag of the food your rescue is used to eating. This will help prevent the diarrhea that might occur with a sudden diet change. Also make sure to provide at least a one-week supply of any medication or medical equipment the dog needs. Change any IDs on the dog so that they contain the adopter's contact information. That will be one less thing the adopter has to do during the hectic first days. If you have found this book or any other dog care guide helpful, consider giving the new family a copy as an adoption gift.

Sit down and write a one-page reminder sheet—a list of the most important things you feel the adopter should remember during the transition period (see the sidebar "Sample Reminder Sheet for Adopters," p. 200).

Put the reminder sheet and your rescue's Doggie Dossier into a large envelope marked on the outside with the pooch's name and your name and contact information, so that the new family can reach you easily at any time with their questions.

Give your rescue one last, good brushing—and a big hug.

As you drive the dog toward his exciting future, why are you choked up? Is that a tear streaming down your cheek? You have invested a lot of love in this dog. You stepped out of your safe life to save a life. You inconvenienced your family members and other pets to give this dog a haven until his future could be settled. You used your hard-earned money to make sure the dog was healthy and well fed. You devoted your valuable time to search for, scrutinize, and choose the best new family. Go ahead and cry. (We do it every time!)

As the old saying goes, busy hands are happy hands. After your rescue is tucked into his new home, take your mind off his absence by turning your attention back to the people, pets, and responsibilities you might have ignored a bit while you were absorbed with the rescue. You might even take some time to write letters to government officials, reporting to them about all the time and money you've just devoted to a problem that could be eliminated by better public policy.

Most important, give yourself a pat on the back. Keep positive thoughts in the forefront by remembering that your rescued sweetie is starting a new life—all thanks to your hard work, dedication, and love for a helpless animal.

> His ears were often the first thing to catch my tears.
> —Elizabeth Barrett Browning about Flush, her cocker spaniel

SAMPLE REMINDER SHEET FOR ADOPTERS

- Feeding details: amount, times of day, brand
- Medication: names, amounts, times of day, how to administer
- Health: instructions for any special care
- Potty: tips, such as, "If the dog starts whining and staring at you, it means he needs to go potty."
- Exercise: how much and what kind of exercise the dog needs; for example, "He is accustomed to two miles of brisk walking per day."
- Play: for example, "The dog loves it when you throw the little green frog toy."
- Other tips, such as, "Don't leave the dog in the kitchen alone with food on the countertops. Block its access to the room with the kitty litter box or else he'll 'snack.' The dog is afraid of big trucks. If he hears one when you're out walking, he might try to bolt."

LONG-DISTANCE ADOPTIONS

You might locate just the perfect home for your pet—five states away. Maybe the interested adopter is your uncle's college roommate. He has always wanted a Gordon setter mix, and you're sure that your older rescue's mellow temperament will fit into this retired adopter's lifestyle.

If the potential adopter can't come to meet the dog, and you can't afford the time and money to go there and perform the home check, look for reputable rescue organizations in that area that might be able to perform those in-person screening tasks for you. Internet searches should turn up groups in the possible adopter's town or nearby. If you don't have Internet access, call your local shelters and private rescue organizations, explain your predicament, and ask if they can help you find phone numbers for those other groups. *Do not* adopt out your rescue to anyone—no matter how fabulous they sound—without completing the screening process.

LEAVING ON AN AIRPLANE

You've thoroughly screened an out-of-town adopter who's great, but neither of you can make the drive. Here are tips on flying your dog to a faraway home:

- Ask your vet if your dog is healthy enough for plane travel. The airline might need a letter from the vet to that effect, as well as copies of vaccination records.
- Make sure your rescue is crate trained well before the trip (see chapter 8, pp. 153–156).
- Ask the airline for all the details you need to arrange for flying the dog to his destination. This should include any documents and information you need to provide and what type and size of traveling crate the airline requires. Make sure you find out everything the airline requires up front to avoid last-minute glitches.
- Airlines that have written guidelines and rules for canine travel prove they are not only qualified to transport dogs, but that they have taken the time and energy to consider the needs of traveling animals.

- Coordinate and communicate an organized plan so that the adopter knows exactly what time the pooch's flight arrives, where in the airport to pick him up, and what documentation the adopter will need to show airport officials.
- If either you or the adopter is able to accompany the dog on the flight, some airlines allow smaller dogs within certain weight limits to travel in the cabin, confined in a crate that fits under the seat.
- For dogs traveling in the cargo hold, they must be at least eight weeks of age, healthy, and not aggressive or easily distressed. Most airlines require a letter from a veterinarian attesting to all of the above, as well as to a rabies vaccination.
- *Do not* sedate your rescue so that his body can regulate itself better in the cargo environment. Make sure the travel crate meets the airline's standards and is large enough for your dog.
- Clearly mark the crate with the words LIVE ANIMAL—THIS SIDE UP. Also include your contact information and the adopter's contact information.
- Try to book a nonstop flight, and consider the weather. A good airline will not allow animals to travel under extreme weather conditions.

Follow-Up Visits

About a month after the adoption, phone the adopter and ask for an appointment for the first follow-up visit. Most adopters welcome the chance to show off how healthy and happy the pooch is with them. Just keep in mind that there aren't many people these days who aren't terribly busy, so be accommodating and understanding if you have to work around their schedules.

However, if the adopter is evasive or combative, that's a huge red flag. In that case, remind him or her that follow-up visits are included in the signed adoption agreement, and keep insisting that they must be performed.

During the follow-up visit, your main goal is to see how your former rescue is adjusting to his new family and environment and vice versa. It's also time to enjoy a few hugs and kisses with your old pal and, if all goes well, to take delight in witnessing a marvelous happy ending!

Under the adoption agreement, you are entitled to make further follow-up visits over the years. Using your own judgment of how the adoption is going, you might opt to visit more or less often. Stay in regular phone or e-mail contact with the adopters. Check in now and then to ask how your pooch and his family are doing. Ideally, you have forged a lifelong partnership and friendship. Maintain and nurture it for everyone's benefit.

DOGGIE ADOPTION AND THE LAW

It's difficult to enforce the adoption agreement. You'd have to drag the adopter to court, and even then the outcome would be difficult to predict. The main reason to have the agreement in writing is to make it clear up front to the adopter that you're serious about your stipulations. Maintain that tone of seriousness in your conversations if you encounter resistance to any of them. Ultimately, if the adopter reneges on anything, you'll have to contact a lawyer and explore your options. Let's

hope it doesn't come to that. Fortunately, it usually doesn't.

Trouble in Paradise—Problems with the Adoption

It would be unusual for your rescued pooch to settle right into his new home without a glitch or two. Be prepared for phone calls from the adopter regarding something naughty the dog did or a health problem that has cropped up. Welcome those calls. The fact that the adopter feels comfortable enough to ask you for support and advice, or even just to vent a little, is a good thing.

Even if the problem seems minor and you feel annoyed that the adopter can't figure it out, put a lid on it. Remember that the two of you are linked in a partnership to provide the rescued pooch with loving care. Put yourself in the adopter's shoes. Remember how stressful those first transitional weeks can be. Using all the knowledge and skills you gained during the rescue process, reach into your reserves of patience, pull on your thinking cap, and do your best to help.

There are limits, though. You cannot solve all problems for the adopter. At some point, the new owner will have to step up to the plate. If the calls begin taking up too much of your time, gently refer the adopter to other sources. Have handy phone numbers for:

trusted veterinarians

after-hours emergency veterinary hospitals

reputable trainers, boarding kennels, dog walkers/pet sitters

schedules for obedience classes in the area

dry cleaners, tailors, carpet and upholstery cleaners (for those oopsies)

Alternatively, maybe during your follow-up visits you find that your rescue is not being properly cared for or that there are safety lapses that haven't been fixed. In those cases, offer gentle suggestions and request that the adopter address the problems. Do not become angry or confrontational. Keep the adopter as an ally, if possible. Most people want to do the right thing by their pets, and if you offer help and encouragement instead of badgering and criticism, they might respond better.

However, if none of that works, read on.

TOP TEN REASONS PEOPLE GIVE UP THEIR DOGS

The National Council on Pet Population Study and Policy finds that people relinquish their dogs to shelters for ten common reasons:

1. Moving (7 percent)

2. Landlord not allowing pet (6 percent)

3. Cost of pet maintenance (5 percent)

4. Too many animals in household (4 percent)

5. Owner having personal problems (4 percent)

6. Inadequate facilities (4 percent)

7. Having no time for pet (4 percent)

8. Pet illness(es) (4 percent)

9. No homes available for litter mates (3 percent)

10. Biting (3 percent)

Irreconcilable Differences—If Your Dog Is Returned to You

No matter how hard you worked to screen for just the right home and then to offer support and advice to the adoptive family, sometimes an adoption can go awry. When you least expect it—perhaps months or even years after you deliver your rescue to the new owners—you might get that call saying that for whatever reason, the family can no longer keep your rescue. Or during your follow-up visits, you might find that the dog is not receiving proper care and your requests and suggestions for improvement go nowhere.

First, even if you are seething, try not to show anger. If the adopter has contacted you wishing to return the dog, that is in accordance with your adoption policy. Be grateful. The alternative might be that your dog would be abandoned in the streets, or worse.

In cases where the adopter is providing good care and is able to do so for a while longer, offer to work with the adopter on finding a new home for the pooch. Often, adopters wish to help with this process. Plus, it reduces confusion and stress for the dog, as he will only have to make one transition instead of two.

If it's a case where you have decided to ask for the dog back because he is receiving poor care, it might be easier than you think to accomplish. Many times if a dog is not properly cared for, it means the owners have lost interest and might be grateful for the chance to get the dog out of their hair. Other times, though, especially if an owner's ego kicks in, it can be extremely difficult to remove the dog from the home. You would have to contact an attorney and perhaps your local government animal welfare department for help. If a government agency becomes involved, it might take the dog into its own facilities and not relinquish him to you. This can all be a nightmare. Here are some ideas on how to make it go more smoothly.

If you have to ask for the dog back, do so nonconfrontationally, using as much tact as you can muster. Be supportive and understanding. Here's a sample dialogue:

Mikey is a real handful. I remember how hard he was sometimes for me to manage. But you did a really good job of teaching him to fetch. I bet if you had more time in your busy life right now, you could teach him a lot more. I know it's hard to give up a dog when you've put in so much work on him. I'm concerned for both you and Mikey. Probably neither of you is happy with the situation where you don't have time to give him enough potty breaks. That kidney infection he's developed could turn life threatening.

I have some time in my life right now so I could take care of him. Let's arrange a time for me to come pick him up. Later when things calm down for you, you'll have time for a dog again.

Sound mealymouthed? Groveling? Does it gall you to have to be nice to someone who has neglected sweet Mikey so badly? Even if you have to deliver your speech through clenched teeth, remember that you're doing it for Mikey.

Whether the relinquishment is voluntary or at your demand, try to get the adopter to provide some vital information when you get the dog back:

What are the reason(s) for returning the dog?

What measures did they take, if any, to correct the problem(s)?

Do they have any positive feedback about their experiences with this dog?

What, if anything, would have helped them to keep the dog? (for example, a taller fence, no other pets, owner at home more?)

Once you get your rescue back, rejoice! The bright side of having your rescued dog in your care again is simply that he is safe and not in danger of being euthanized in an animal shelter. The dog is not a frightened, starving stray scavenging for food in trash bins. He is safe with you, and that's a reason for celebration!

But the fact is, you still can't keep him, and you must still find the dog a new home. The difference this time is that you are now an experienced dog rescue/dog advertising/dog placement guru. If your reputation has spread, soon people will be coming to you with their questions about what to do with the dogs and animals they have rescued. So get back in the saddle or office chair. Pull out your files, forms, and art supplies. If you were honest in your Adoptability Assessment on p. 182, there's more than likely a home out there somewhere for this dog, and you are the expert who is going to track it down. Even more good news is that you have some additional information about your rescued dog now, based on what the former adopter told you.

Sometimes, a returned dog may show disturbing behaviors or bad habits developed in the adoptive home. It is a good idea to tackle them immediately. Refer to chapters 8 and 9 for help on behavior issues. Consulting with a professional dog behaviorist or trainer can also be a good course of action.

The bottom line is, don't despair. Unless your rescue is deemed vicious by a professional behaviorist, you need not feel defeated. You have accepted this animal into your life and have taken on the responsibility of ensuring that he has a future. For that, you are to be commended.

Just make sure not to wear yourself out. If you've given rehoming your best shot but feel you've come to the end of your available time and resources, remember that there are many good, responsible animal shelters and rescue organizations that could take over in finding a new home for your pooch in need.

Whatever the outcome of your efforts, the authors of this book thank you for working hard to save a life.

My little dog—a heartbeat at my feet.

—Edith Wharton

Dolly.

Happily Ever After True Story Number Ten:
Dolly

• •

With his tail wagging in anticipation, a "customer" walked into the shop and began to nose around the merchandise. As he perused a shelf filled with delectable treats, the "shopkeeper" fell into step behind him. The customer gently touched the pretty bags and almost picked one up, but thought better of it after realizing he was being watched. They moved to the next aisle with calendars, books, and knickknacks. On the floor was a box of meaty-looking dog chews. The customer briefly looked over his shoulder at the

shopkeeper. Their eyes met. The customer could not help himself. He grabbed one of the chews and made for the front door.

"Oh, it happens all the time!" Stan laughed as he reached down to pet Dolly, his five-year-old, mixed-breed shopkeeping partner. "Most of our customers are dogs, so the shoplifting is to be expected." Canine thieves flock to Dolly's Treasures, a pet supply store "owned" and operated by Dolly. Stan and Karen Fox like to think they too manage the business, but Dolly is too quick for them, confronting each new customer first.

Although Stan and Karen signed the papers and stocked the shelves so the shop could open its front doors, if it were not for Dolly, the store would never have materialized. Karen said, "When Stan retired from his job at Hewlett-Packard, I told him he was too young to stay home. Well, he wasn't about to leave Dolly at home alone again, so he said he needed a job where she could come with him."

"We adopted Dolly from a woman desperate to 'get rid of her,'" Karen explained, using her fingers like quotation marks. "It was her loss, because Dolly is the smartest, most talkative dog I have ever known." In the shop Dolly proves her natural saleswoman abilities by declaring how delicious the dog treats are. To an inquiring customer, Dolly deftly sticks out her tongue, then says, "Yum, yum!"

One day in December, Santa Claus came to the shop so dogs and cats could have their picture taken with him. Dolly had never been busier. She hustled from one end of the store to the other, greeting and inspecting the line of dogs and people, making sure the candy cane dog treats were plentiful, sniffing Santa's boots for unmentionables—the work never ended.

That night at home, Dolly headed straight to her bed. Although she was worn out, it was for a good cause. All the money raised from photos with Santa went to the local humane society.

Looking back, Karen and Stan know they saved Dolly from being surrendered to the animal shelter. By supporting their local humane society, they hope to help homeless dogs, any one of which could have been Dolly. Standing behind the shop counter surrounded by doggie merchandise, Karen said, "Dolly is such an inspiration to us. She helped us create this wonderful store. She helps us give back to the community. Dolly is really our own little treasure."

11.
Finally, the Good Stuff: Having Fun with Your Rescued Dog
After All the Hard Work You've Done to Help Your Friend in Need, Now It's Time for Both of You to Reap the Rewards! Friends Who Play Together, Stay Together

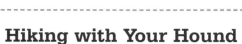

Kellie: Life's a Beach

I am in the car with Abby, and I'm feeling just fine. Good things happen when Mom opens the car door—like now! This place smells different. Abby looks confident. I'll just follow that fluffy tail. Whoa! Ears up, eyes darting. What in the rawhide is that? It looks like water, but it is so noisy! And it's moving and crashing. Abby is rolling in the soft, grainy ground. Sniff, sniff—she's covering herself with a heavenly smell! Digging . . . digging. . . . Got it! Abby chomps on it. Now Mom's got it and won't give it back. Guess she knows a good horse pie when she sees one!

Friendship—you and your dog. You saved her life, and now she's a big part of yours. Enjoy!

The great pleasure of a dog is that you may make a fool of yourself with him and not only will he not scold you, but he will make a fool of himself too.

—Samuel Butler

Hiking with Your Hound

For many pooches and their people, the sight of a hiking trail makes the tail wag and the heart soar. It means tranquility and excitement amid nature's beauty, a revitalizing workout, and—for the inquisitive nose—a whole world of pleasures.

Before stepping out on a hiking adventure, there are a few steps at home you'll want to take. Check paw pads for wounds and abrasions. If you find any, treat them, and put off the trip to another day. Even minor paw injuries can worsen easily and take a long time to heal, so it's best to baby them. After you get home, perform another check. And in between, while you're on the hike, if your dog starts favoring a leg or licking a paw, take a look to see what's wrong. A sprain, cut, or scrape means you'd better head back to the car, treat the wound, and complete the hike some other day.

It's not a bad idea to carry a small doggie first-aid kit containing gauze pads, tweezers, and topical wound ointment and bandages, or keep one in the car.

In dog off-leash areas, tie a colorful bandanna around your pooch's neck so that she's easier for you to spot.

Carry about eight ounces of water for your dog for every hour of the hike. Snacks for longer hikes or on the way home would be much appreciated by your hiking partner. Caution: During strenuous exercise, and for about an hour before and after, don't give your pooch large amounts of water all at once, as this can cause bloat (see chapter 6, pp. 89–90). Offer small amounts more frequently.

To avoid trouble on the trail, pass up the ones with jagged rocks or anything else that might injure paws. For snow hiking, use dog booties to prevent ice balls from developing between toe pads. A path overgrown with weeds, shrubbery, and overhanging branches is a great place to meet foxtails, ticks, and snakes.

In an area with sensitive or dangerous wildlife, keep your canine on leash, and stay alert to avoid encounters. Wild animals will most likely avoid dogs, but the following species seem to have a higher rate of run-ins: snakes, porcupines, and skunks.

Know how to identify harmful plants, and watch where your dog puts her nose.

Don't forget to use poop bags. As with all litter, pack it in, pack it out.

Right after the hike, perform a thorough tick check on both yourself and your dog.

Now that you're both prepared, get out there, drink in the fresh air, and enjoy the happy sound of your pooch panting!

DOGGIE DEPTH PERCEPTION—OR LACK THEREOF

Dogs possess very little depth perception. Pooches have been known to chase birds or butterflies straight off cliffs, falling to injury or death. In any area with steep terrain, keep your pooch securely on leash.

WARNING TO WEEKEND WARRIORS

It's hard to have fun when you're in pain. That's why it's a good idea for both you and your dog to work up slowly to any new activity. A five-mile hike or a high-impact agility training session is not the best way to start your recreational program together if neither of you has been that active before. Start off with less strenuous and shorter periods of exercise, see how it goes, and then build up over time.

Remember that even young, energetic, bouncing-off-the-wall pooches can't always handle unaccustomed types and amounts of physical exertion. It could cause sprains, ligament tears, or even bone trouble.

Your doctor and your veterinarian are the best advisors on exercise levels for you and your furry friend.

STAYING TOGETHER

Travel and outdoor activities present more opportunities than usual for you and your dog to lose each other. You're often in unfamiliar territory and easily distracted by new sights, sounds, and alluring new smells. Keep an extra sharp eye on your canine companion. Remember to securely shut doors on cars, RVs, and hotel rooms. Make sure collar tags and other IDs are up to date. Include your cell phone number, and possibly the number of a friend or relative who can be reached when you're not at home to take calls.

THE POOCH BACKPACK

With your vet's okay, your dog might be able to shoulder her own hiking supplies. To most dogs a backpack feels very similar to a dog collar. Generally, they can carry up to 25 percent of their body weight. Items to store in the pack would be bottles of water, poop bags, and treats. Also include a small doggie first-aid kit containing gauze pads, tweezers, topical wound ointment, and bandages.

Introduce your dog to her pack well in advance. Fill it with scrunched newspapers and a few treats, then head out for a walk. During the walk, offer your dog treats from the pack. The next time you grab the pack and snap it onto your dog's back, she'll know it's time for a hike and a snack.

GOOD MANNERS IN THE GREAT OUTDOORS

With this list, you and your dog can contribute toward changing the negative stereotypes many people have about dogs in the wilderness:

- Always keep your dog leashed unless the area allows off-leash pooch walking, *and* your dog is reliably well behaved under your voice command.
- Always pick up after your dog and dispose of this poop in trash bins.
- Never let your dog chase wildlife. A deer crashing through the underbrush is a good moment for "sit, stay" training.
- Hike only on trails where dogs are allowed (fewer nasty looks from fellow hikers).
- Practice a code of silence; barking can disturb wildlife and other hikers.

WHERE TO HIKE WITH YOUR DOG

The following are general guidelines; always check before going, to be sure pets are allowed and to learn about leash requirements.

National parks—Dogs are not allowed on trails; only where a car can go.

National monuments—Some allow dogs, some do not.

National forests—Dogs are allowed.

National grasslands—Dogs are allowed.

National recreation areas—Dogs are allowed.

National seashores—Dogs are most often not allowed.

National lakeshores—Dogs are usually allowed, especially along the Great Lakes.

National historical parks—Dogs are usually allowed.

State parks—Dogs are usually allowed but must be kept on a nonretractable leash.

Oceans of Fun

Offering sand, seagulls, and rolling waves, a beach can be a pooch playground. At designated off-leash areas, your dog can swim, chase a Frisbee, mingle with other pooches, or partake of a picnic lunch. (Of course, you stashed snacks for your dog in that basket!).

Where there's sun and unprotected skin, there's sunburn. Even dogs can get pink from the sun's rays. Rub sunblock onto your dog's ears and nose every thirty minutes.

While enjoying the seashore or the lakeshore, use the same water safety precautions you would use for children. For example, don't assume your dog knows how to handle rough surf or currents. When conditions are dicey, keep the leash on.

If previously your pooch was a landlubber but shows an interest in entering the water, you might want to accompany her. Start in a shallow area where the waves won't knock you both over. When the water lifts your dog, hold her rear end up, because beginning dog swimmers don't always use their back legs. Once the dog is paddling with both front and back legs, you'll know she is swimming. She'll be using a whole set of different muscles, so don't let your dog overdo it the first time.

A dog in the water will drink the water, salty or not. Usually the worst result is temporary vomiting or diarrhea. Don't let your dog drink excessive amounts. And if tummy troubles persist past one day, consult your vet.

Wash your dog after any dip in the ocean, as the salt can dry out the coat and skin.

Meanwhile, hang ten with your four-pawed friend!

BEST BOATING BETS FOR YOUR POOCH

Beforehand, give your dog a potty break on land.

Strap on a doggie life vest. These can be purchased online or at marine stores.

Never tie up your dog on board a boat. If the boat flips over, the dog can't swim away.

Keep your pooch protected from the sun to avoid heat exhaustion.

Bring a small area rug so that paws can have relief from hot or slippery decks.

Keep fishing supplies, such as hooks and bait, safely away from your four-legged sailor.

Before motoring out, let first-time canine boaters get accustomed to the feel of floating. Once you start the engine, keep the dog calm and reassured by petting and talking to her in a cheerful voice. As the boat enters rougher waters, notice if your dog is getting motion-sick—drooling or bowing her head. If this becomes a problem, your vet can offer a medical solution, or you can refer to chapter 5, pp. 56–57, where car sickness is discussed.

Road Trips with Rover

Most dogs love car rides. And most of us enjoy driving with agreeable passengers. Perfect match! Seeing historic places, scenic landscapes, or funky slices of local life can be a blast with an enthusiastic travel mate like your pooch. Maybe the dog can't quote poetry while the two of you gaze at a dazzling sunset, but she's there, experiencing the quiet moment in her own way. Namely, "How fast can that sparrow fly away from me once I pounce?"

On road trips, you don't really want your dog chasing birds. Make sure she is properly leashed, preferably not on a retractable one. While they may be fine in your own neighborhood, such restraints might not provide the control you need under more exciting circumstances. Of course, always have those poop bags on hand. While traveling, your dog's elimination routine might get disrupted, so it's a good idea to never be bagless.

If your dog is not used to riding in the car, acclimate her in advance. Go for short drives and work up to longer ones (see chapter 5, pp. 56–57, for tips on motion sickness).

Be cautious about leaving your dog in the car alone. Even in the shade, interior temperatures can become deadly in a matter of minutes. And vandals or thieves might harm the dog in your absence.

Always keep plenty of water bottles in your car, so that even when you are out in the middle of nowhere, you can both stay happily hydrated.

If your trip involves overnight stays, make sure to research and reserve your bed beforehand. More and more hotels accept pets these days.

Well before the trip, get your pooch used to eating meals in places other than home. Some dogs can be picky about dining in unfamiliar settings. Take your dog for car rides, and then stop to feed her in a parking lot, or at the park, or at a friend's house.

DOGGIE AUTO SAFETY

A doggie harness or restraint device, the equivalent of a seat belt, protects the driver from distraction by the dog and protects the canine passenger from sudden braking or impact. Fitting around the dog's chest and shoulders, it attaches to the existing seat belt system in your car. Purchase one online or through pet stores.

Your pooch probably loves sticking her head out the window while you drive, but she might get a lot more than fresh air. Eyes, mouth and ears become targets for insects, gravel, and all sorts of other debris.

THE SAME BUT DIFFERENT

Like many people, most dogs relish travel. And, like us, they love the excitement of new experiences but appreciate familiar comforts in between. A little advance planning can help the trip go more smoothly for both of you.

When you're packing your bags for a trip, remember to pack for Pookie too. Bring along plenty of the food and treats she's accustomed to eating, bowls for food and water, supplements, medications, toothbrush/toothpaste, crate and bedding, brush, towels (in case of rain or swimming), a doggie first-aid kit, a de-skunk kit, cleaning supplies including enzymatic stain and odor remover, and a few favorite toys and chew items. A helpful Web site on traveling with your best friend is www.tripswithpets.com.

While traveling, try to stick to your normal routine as much as possible, with feedings, potty breaks, and exercise at around the same times as at home.

HOTEL PET ETIQUETTE

Never let your dog run freely on the hotel property. Keep her leashed.

Before the trip, train your dog how to use and enjoy a crate. Hotel managers appreciate pet owners who bring their own crates, and are more likely to agree to allow your dog to stay as a guest. Plus it gives your dog a snug, familiar spot of her own.

Don't leave any uninvited guests behind—make sure your dog is flea- and tick-free.

Dogs should be kept off of beds and other furniture.

For easy cleanup, place food and water bowls on tile or vinyl floors, or on newspapers or plastic sheeting.

Don't leave your dog unattended in the room. She might think of things to do there that she wouldn't do at home—chewing, barking, jumping out the window . . .

Try to find an area off the hotel property for bathroom breaks. Always scoop the poop.

Go for frequent walks to prevent in-room accidents. Bring cleaning supplies in case one should happen. Don't try to hide oopsies. If you can't clean them ef-

fectively yourself, ask for help from the front desk and offer to pay for any permanent damage.

Tip cleaning staff a little extra as a thank-you from the canine guest (helps build goodwill and overcome negative perceptions about doggie travelers).

For more information on where traveling dogs are welcome, here are some helpful Web sites: http://www.petswelcome.com; http://www.dogfriendly.com; http://www.takeyourpet.com.

SKY TRAVEL

Prefer flying to driving? Most dogs can handle plane trips. See the "Leaving on an Airplane" sidebar in chapter 10, pp. 201. Just make sure your destination is dog friendly. Hawaii and Great Britain, for example, quarantine arriving canines. But maybe learning the hula or curtseying to the queen wasn't on your dog's list of things to do anyway.

Camping: Canines Communing with Nature

If your favorite five-star hotel turns up its nose at four-legged guests, consider "ruffing" it. Many campgrounds welcome dogs. And there are some where people wouldn't dream of staying without their canine family member. These camps offer specialty experiences geared for what dogs enjoy most.

Imagine a place where dogs take turns running through an agility course. Where they splash and play in their own swimming pool or on their own lakefront beach. Where the restrooms have tubs specially designed for doggie baths. Where evenings are spent snuggling by the campfire and nibbling biscuits.

Furry visitors just need to be well behaved around other campers and their pets. If your pooch is a wildlife aficionado (one that gives chase!) keep her safely leashed. And since campers camp because they enjoy the outdoors, they would probably rather hear the twitter of birds than the baying of your dog.

If your pooch is ready to commune with nature respectfully, she is in for a treat. Check out the listing of canine campgrounds below, and you may never check into that five-star hotel again.

CAMPGROUNDS FOR CANINES

This Web site gives pet-friendly campground contact information state by state: http://www.campingpet.com. Also try http://www.dogfriendly.com for a list of pet-friendly campgrounds.

Games and Tricks

Maybe one of the reasons we find dogs so irresistible is their similarity to children. They find joy in simple things and they love to play. When you take a few moments to play a game with your dog, or teach her a new trick, you not only make her day, but you also steer her away from unwanted behaviors, and you deepen your relationship. Your dog's attention focuses on you instead of on that sofa cushion she would love to shred. You communicate and encourage. The dog learns to respond and enjoy herself at the same time. And the more fun your dog has (especially with you), the better companion she becomes.

Playing can involve almost anything that you and your pooch both like: a quick chase around the kitchen table or some friendly keep-away with a toy. You can also try more structured games or tricks that exercise your pooch's mind, as well as her body.

Below you'll find some great possibilities to get you started. First, you need to establish some basic obedience commands such as "sit," "stand," "stay," "come," and "drop it." This is all in good fun, but after enough practice you could stage a show for friends and family. And if you've rescued your pooch with the intent to rehome her, knowing a couple of tricks can make the dog all the more appealing to adopters.

Simon Says: This game teaches your dog to respond to your commands regardless of the circumstances. It will also entertain you, the canine performer, and anyone watching. Simply think of commands that your pooch is good at, and give them in a variety of strange ways. Turn your back to the dog and say, "Sit." Touch your toes and say, "Down." Hop side to side and tell your dog to come. You'll get a workout in the process.

Happy Hunting: Hide treats in areas of the backyard where you want your pooch to hang out instead of any off-limits areas. Bring your dog outside and ask, "Where's the treat?" Lead the dog to one of the more obviously placed treats, still asking, "Where's the treat?" When she finds the yummy, give the dog lots of praise. Keep leading her to the vicinity of other yummies until the dog starts searching on her own. Soon your dog will associate the "approved" part of the yard with good things like happy hunting.

Hide-and-Seek: This game reinforces important commands that keep your dog safe: sit, stay, and come. Put your dog in a sit-stay in an area of your house or yard where you can easily hide from her. Now go hide. Call your dog by saying, "Scooter, OK, come!" When your dog finds you, it should be all hugs, kisses, and praise.

Toy Identification: This game develops your dog's intelligence and impresses family and friends. You will need to schedule some rehearsal time before the big show. Start with your dog's two favorite toys. Make up names for them, such as "Fuzzball" or "Monkey." Hold up one toy and say her name. Encourage your dog to take it in her mouth. Then remove the toy and give your dog a treat. Repeat this over several sessions until your dog recognizes that toy's name. Do the same for the second toy. Over time, you can introduce more toys.

Next, put your dog in a sit-stay. Place the two toys a few feet in front of the dog. Say, "Scooter, get Fuzzball!" Even if Scooter just nudges the correct toy, give him lots of praise. As you continue practicing, and with proper rewards and praise, your dog can learn to identify and pick up several different toys.

Will Wag for Love: This trick demonstrates the fact that your voice—no matter what you're saying—can be like music to your dog's ears. Have the dog do a sit-stay and stand in front of her. Using your "happy" voice, the one that your dog loves best, say any kind of silly word, such as the name of a fruit or vegetable. Pretty soon, "broccoli," "onion," or "cucumber" will elicit hip swaying and tail wagging.

Yes, I Agree: This trick helps your dog tune in and pay attention to you. Sit in a chair directly in front of the dog. Have her do a sit-stay. Holding a treat, say, "Yes," and raise it over the dog's forehead. She should lift her chin, looking up at the treat. Then move the treat below her nose. The dog should point her nose downward. Now say, "Yes," and slowly move the treat up and down in front of the dog's face. Her head should follow suit. Soon, you'll be able to say, "I am smart and good-looking, yes?" And of course your dog will agree with you.

I Bow To You: Have your pooch do a stand-stay. Kneel in front of her, and say, "Bow," while at the same time placing your hands and a treat between the dog's front paws. Keeping her rear extended, the dog will lean her head down for the treat. Practice until you no longer need to kneel. Soon you will be able to stand and bow back to your dog!

The Old Standby—Fetch: People often assume that all dogs know how to fetch. Not so. But many dogs who are clueless on retrieving can learn what they've been missing. Begin by praising your dog whenever she shows interest in the ball or takes it in her mouth. Then tell the dog to "drop it," and when she does, reward the dog again with praise and a treat. Once your dog has mastered "drop it," and is still showing interest in the ball, toss it a few feet away. If the dog brings the ball to you, reward her. Even if she picks up the ball, then drops it immediately, reward her. If you can urge the dog to take a step toward you with the ball in her mouth, reward her lavishly. Repeat until your dog gets the idea that coming toward you—and preferably *to* you—with the ball is a profitable thing to do. With repetition and patience, eventually the dog might master this skill that didn't come naturally.

RAINY DAY FUN

On days when the weather prohibits outdoor activities, you and your pooch don't have to get cabin fever. Try playing games and learning tricks such as the ones described in this chapter. That gives your dog a mini vacation from boredom.

If conditions permit driving, make a trip to a local pet store and stroll the aisles, letting your dog sniff to her heart's content. The excitement alone gives her a bit of a workout to tide the dog over till the weather clears up.

DANCING WITH YOUR DOG

Does the sound of music get you clapping and your dog's toes tapping? Get ready to boogie down. Dancing with dogs is not only fun for both of you—it's a sport! Called Musical Canine Freestyle, it encourages responsible pet ownership through choreographed dance using music, costumes, and athleticism. Teams of people and dogs develop and execute dance routines that appeal to an audience and judges. Performances are evaluated on good synchronization between dog and person, difficulty of choreography, dog's overall enthusiasm, and costuming. Along with lots of applause, these teams reap many rewards: fitness, friendships, and a stronger bond between person and dog.

Or if you and your dog simply want to strut your stuff on the dance floor at your cousin's upcoming wedding, a few wiggles, weaves, and whirls is all you'll need to steal the show.

Many videos on the market might help get you started in the wonderful world of dancing with your dog. Moves include your pooch weaving backward through your legs, walking on her hind legs, and jumping over or through your arms.

For more information, you can go to http://www.worldcaninefreestyle.org/ or http://www.caninefreestyle.com/.

Agility Training

If you want to get in shape and get off that diet, agility training could be the answer. And bring your dog too! Agility is a sporting event where you guide your off-leash dog through a course that's about one hundred eighty yards long. With your help, the dog will navigate a series of obstacles including tunnels, seesaws, tire hoops, weaving poles, jumps, and hurdles.

Since your dog will need to know some basic commands such as "sit," "stay," "down," and "come," agility training is enjoyed best after she has completed some obedience work. If your dog knows off-leash heeling, better yet. And those who like to fetch are well on their way to picking up the finer points of agility.

Most breeds and mixes are able to participate in agility training. First, consider your dog's age and level of fitness. Agility is encouraged for dogs between the ages of six months and ten years. If your dog is overweight, has hip or joint pain, or is a senior citizen, have your veterinarian give her an overall health check. On that note, what is *your* level of fitness? Expect to be jogging through the course, so if it's been a while since you tied on your running shoes, you should consult your doctor first.

If you are a competitive type who likes to play to win and race against the clock while spectators cheer—and if your dog is outgoing and adventurous—the two of you might have the right stuff. To find an agility group near you, contact the United States Dog Agility Association online at http://www.usdaa.com or by phone at 972-487-2200.

A FUN BACKYARD

In many backyards, there's nothing to keep a pooch company except boredom. This can lead to obnoxious boredom barking and many other unwanted behaviors. Try not to leave your dog alone for long periods, but for those occasions when she is on her own outdoors, doggie play equipment can make things more interesting. You'll enjoy playing there with your dog too.

A pooch's fantasy backyard could include made-for-dogs products such as Doggie Drencher, tire jumps, seesaws, tunnels, and chutes, all available online.

You can hang things like rope toys, tug toys, or old tires attached to bungee cords, and in turn attach them to something stable, such as a sturdy tree limb. The objects should be just barely within the dog's reach to present a challenge.

Fill a dog-size metal tub with water for splashing or with sand for digging. In both cases, bury the tub to a level that allows the dog to get in and out easily.

Every dog's backyard should include a digging area—either the metal tub or a bigger plot—where the dog won't get in trouble for excavations. Even in a small yard you can find a few square feet somewhere. If you want, you can surround it with wood or plastic edging. For better drainage mix in sand, up to about 50 percent. When Chico starts to dig in a place where you don't want holes, say, "Chico, no dig," then lead him to his digging area, and say, "Chico, dig." To demonstrate, do a little digging yourself. If the dog's still not interested (the gophers or intriguing smells are in the other parts of your yard), bury toys or treats in the approved sector. Issue lavish praise when the dog unearths them.

Caution: For safety reasons, it's best to use play equipment made especially for dogs rather than trying to make it yourself. Also, some strong chewers can destroy equipment and hurt themselves in the process. For wobbly puppies, use ramps with rails.

ROTATING TOYS

To keep your dog more interested in her toys, rotate them. If the dog has ten toys, give her only three or four each day. Their occasional absence makes your dog's heart grow fonder of them.

Search and Rescue (SAR) Teams

Whether it's for an earthquake, tornado, or bomb attack, SAR teams are among the first to respond to disaster. The work these dog-and-person teams do can be dangerous, heartbreaking, and rewarding.

To begin you must have a current CPR and American Red Cross Emergency Response card. Things you learn include map and compass use, radio communications, wilderness survival skills, tracking, and helicopter safety.

SAR dogs can be of any breed, but the most successful tend to be working, herding, sporting, or hound dogs. A sensitive nose is a must. They must be able to pick up a scent and stick with it no matter how much it intermingles with other scents in the area. Dogs who enjoy playing and who respond to rewards are especially sought after for SAR training. They must be well socialized and have undergone basic obedience training. Since rescue missions might be in forests, rocky terrain, or the rubble of fallen buildings, agility training for both you and your dog is helpful. Knowing how to swim is also a plus.

Handlers must be physically fit, enjoy working outdoors in a variety of weather conditions, and be especially fond of interacting and communicating with their dogs. Training can take up to two years. Handlers are financially responsible for their own uniforms (the dog wears a special jacket too), equipment, vehicle, and gasoline.

To learn more about SAR, try contacting these organizations: Search Dog Foundation, 888-459-4376 and SAR-Dogs, www.sar-dogs.com.

THE NOSE KNOWS

Dogs possess a phenomenal sense of smell. Have fun and let your dog use this miraculous talent. You can participate in organized tracking and "scent work" with groups all over the country, or play "nose games" at home, as follows.

Put a leash on Dexter and have him sit and stay, or have a partner hold the leash as you say, "Dexter, wait."

Show him his favorite toy that smells strongly of his mouth. Tie a string on it, and slowly drag it across the floor. Turn your back as you remove the string and place the toy under a chair. Ask Dexter to "find it." If the toy has a name, use it. On leash, encourage Dexter to follow his scent to the toy. Lavish praise upon him when he finds it.

Cut a hot dog (nitrite-free) into twelve pieces. While Dexter watches, lay a trail, placing pieces about two feet apart. Have a favorite family member or friend hide behind a bush in the yard or an open closet in the house with a small piece of hot dog to toss to Dexter when he gets to the end of the trail.

Therapy Dog Team Volunteering

Are you the nurturing type who is drawn toward helping others feel better? Has your dog never met a stranger? If you and your dog are looking to spread some goodwill and affection, consider becoming a therapy dog team. These teams generally visit patients in hospitals, convalescent homes, mental health centers, juvenile detention centers, and abused children's shelters.

Studies show that animals, especially those trained for therapy, can be a calming and healing presence. Patients with dementia, when visited by dogs on a weekly basis, show an improvement in their apathetic state, becoming more interested in the people around them. Pets visiting nursing homes help relieve loneliness and increase socialization among the residents. When four-footers are in a facility, more laughter occurs, and residents tend to talk more easily with each other and the staff. Those with pets in their lives tend to struggle less with depression. A therapy dog sitting in a classroom during reading lessons can motivate beginners to practice reading aloud.

Animals are successful therapists because they make us feel safe without judging. Animals don't care if a person has a fancy hairdo or not. When the touch of a human is awkward or simply not wanted, a dog's soft muzzle or silky coat can feel pleasant and non-threatening. The power of touch can awaken even the most reserved or crabby among us. And for those who have been abused, having an animal to hug and hold can provide that physical contact that all humans need.

Does your dog gravitate to bedsides when someone has the sniffles, or gently snuggle its nose in your lap when you're having a bad day? You might have a natural therapist in your midst. Even some less calm pooches can learn to settle down and provide comfort. If you decide to tap into that big heart of your dog's, here are the steps you need to take before you visit your first patient.

Do an online search of "pet therapy" or "animal-assisted therapy," or ask your local animal shelter or librarian to help you find a pet therapy organization near you. These groups offer the classes and tests necessary for certification for you and your dog. For a small fee, many organizations provide you with help, such as accident insurance, special leashes and equipment, and support group meetings with fellow therapy dog teams. Among other requirements, your dog needs proof of vaccinations and visible signs of good health, such as a glossy coat, proper weight, and no signs of fleas or ticks.

You, the human member of the team, also have responsibilities, such as being neatly groomed and friendly, keeping your voice low and soft, and most important, keeping a close eye on your dog to make sure she is calm, comfortable, and well behaved.

Doing this important work not only improves the lives of others; it also solidifies the friendship between you and your dog.

> Isn't it wonderful how dogs can win friends and influence people without ever reading a book?
>
> —E. C. McKenzie

IS YOUR DOG PREPARED FOR THERAPY WORK?

Did your dog pass a general dog obedience class, where she has learned sit, stay, down, and come?

Is she familiar with stairs and elevators?

Can the dog walk on linoleum and carpeted surfaces?

Is she comfortable around wheelchairs or someone using a walker or a cane?

Does your dog know not to jump on people?

Is your dog well behaved at the veterinarian's office and the groomer's?

Is your dog healthy and insect-free?

Is your dog gentle when accepting treats?

Does your dog have any sensitive areas where she does not like to be touched?

Is your dog friendly toward children and other dogs?

Does your dog tend to growl or bark for any reason?

Special Events That Make a Dog's Day

Many animal welfare organizations host events to raise money for their programs, and offer terrific entertainment for you and your pooch.

One of the most popular is the dog walkathon. Make sure your pooch has current vaccinations, is not aggressive with others, and is equipped with a proper collar and leash. Wear comfortable walking shoes, and have extra poop bags on hand. (You can make a friend for life by handing a bag to that embarrassed someone who forgot to bring some.)

Animal rescue organizations usually take full advantage of holidays with Halloween costume contests, photo opportunities with Santa, and pet carnivals. Show your support of both the event and the nonprofit organization by signing up in advance and by spreading the word to all your dog's friends. Bring your bucks, because some events offer baked goods, toys, nail clipping, or tooth brushing (for your dog!). The comical contests feature categories like best tail wagger, dancer, kisser, and person/dog lookalike.

If the event is well publicized, often the local media show up. Imagine your dog on the evening news or on the front page of your local newspaper. And when the two of you tiredly head home, it's gratifying to know that the money you spent on a day of fun will help other dogs who are still waiting to find their forever homes.

Party Animals

Does your dog have a pooch pal, or a whole pack of them? Do they get along well enough to gather in your house or backyard without engaging in World War Three? Do you enjoy spending time with your dog's buddies and their people? Then throwing a pooch party for just one guest or for an entire group can be a terrific treat for all concerned, while building your best friend's social skills. Whether the occasion is your dog's birthday, or the day she became a member of your family, or nothing in particular, you can invite four-footed friends and their folks to eat, romp, and make merry.

Most dogs are foodies, so here's your chance to shine in your pet's eyes, while filling her nose with tempting aromas. Invest in a couple of books on cooking for canines and create festive foods to please both pets and their people. You can make a Fido favor for each guest by filling affordable dog bowls with treats and toys. Wrap each in an oversized poop bag, and nothing goes to waste!

Undoubtedly, the partying pooches will invent their own games, but if you want a few moments of human-dog interaction, here are a couple of group game ideas:

Hold the Potato: Have all the dogs leashed and lined up next to their handlers. Each handler has a spoon with a potato balanced on it. The hand holding the spoon must also hold the leash. "On your mark, get set, *go*!" Everyone races to the finish line. If someone drops the potato, either the dog can pick it up in her mouth, or the handler must pick up the potato, balance it on the spoon, and resume the race. The winner is the first one to cross the finish line with their potato either on the spoon or in the dog's mouth.

Simon Commands! While the dogs and their handlers walk around in a big circle, "Simon" stands in the middle of it, giving commands that start with, "Simon says." Handlers pass on each command to their dogs. Those who don't follow through—or do so when Simon didn't say, "Simon says"—are eliminated. The last one standing wins!

SOCIALIZING SAFELY

Whenever you host canine guests in your home, put safety first.

First, remember that your dog and her pals might act very differently in your home than they do on the street or at the dog park. Territorial and resource-guarding issues can suddenly make longtime pals go ballistic. If your dog and the others have never been together in your home before, it's best to introduce them slowly to the idea, in short sessions over time and under close supervision. Always make sure that there is mutual respect and that no dog is picked on or harassed.

Decide which rooms or which backyard areas you can make totally doggie safe, and keep all others blocked off. Your pooch is familiar with your home and its unique rules, but maybe the other pooches aren't. Try to predict what could become a disaster. For example, put away your treasured breakables and chewables—that crystal vase, the throw your Aunt Bess crocheted, or the rain boots and that bag of heavenly scented chicken manure by the tool shed. And is there anything heavy and precarious, such as the TV or the marble planter, that could be knocked over by rambunctious playmates?

Indoors or out, make sure there's no way for pooches to sneak away. Keep all exterior doors and gates securely locked and do frequent head counts.

Keep decorations simple. Dogs don't care much about frills, unless they can be ripped up, chewed, or eaten. Something as innocent as string on a balloon can tangle up the intestines and kill. Less is more when it comes to decor.

Most important, *never* leave dogs unattended.

Park It at the Dog Park

With few outdoor places to play, city dogs treasure off-leash time. An official dog park, where freedom reigns, can be a destination of delight for urban dwellers.

It's also a good place to socialize your pooch—getting her accustomed to other canines and humans—and for you to make friends and network with dog-friendly folks. Together you laugh about your dogs' wild antics, commiserate over naughty behaviors or health issues, and exchange advice and information. Also, your dog can serve as a great ambassador for the rescue cause. That couple who have always bought pedigreed Labradors might decide to adopt next time, now that they've fallen in love with the frisky Lab you found at the local shelter—the one who faithfully fetches every ball you throw, and is the only dog in the place that comes when called. (Another life saved!)

If you live in a community that is full of concrete and sparse on room to roam, you can start the ball rolling for an off-leash park. Check with the parks and recreation department to see if anyone else has expressed an interest. Ask the staff if they'll help you. To convince them of the virtues of pooch parks, point out the items listed in "Tips on Starting a Dog Park" below. You might add that dog parks aren't just places for dogs—they provide recreation and build a sense of community for human citizens too.

If your area already boasts off-leash spaces, don't neglect them. Contact local officials to let them know how much you enjoy the parks. Organize or participate in fundraisers, weekend cleanups, or anything needed to keep the parks up and running.

Tips on Starting a Dog Park
(Reprinted with permission from the Marin Humane Society, Marin, California)
Community Benefits:

Socializes and exercises dogs in a safe environment

Promotes responsible pet ownership

Provides elderly and disabled owners with an accessible place to exercise their companions

Enables dogs to legally run off-leash

Promotes public health and safety

Provides a tool for realistic enforcement of dog control laws

The Ideal Dog Park Is Designed to Include:

Concern for the environment

One acre or more surrounded by a four-foot to six-foot fence

Entry is double gated

Shade and water

Adequate drainage

Parking close to site

Grass area; routine mowing

Covered garbage cans with regular trash removal

Pooper-scooper stations

Benches

Wheelchair access

Safe location, not isolated

Regular maintenance

Things to Consider Before Developing a Dog Park:

Appropriate site selection

Noise

Maintenance and health concerns

City support

Traffic

Supervision of park

The Role of a Dog Park Group:

Raise funds for amenities

Monitor use

Cleanup

Serve as communications liaison with city, neighborhood, and dog owners

For more information about dog parks, visit http://www.dogparks.com.

DOG PARK SAFETY AND ETIQUETTE

Dog parks can be paradise when pooches and their people play by the rules. However, with dogs being dogs and people being people, it's not always fun and games.

Some dog parks have volunteer groups that oversee their operation.

A primary role is making sure the park is safe and clean for pooches and people. Volunteers monitor the park during the busiest hours. Whether or not a park has monitors, owners should watch their dogs closely and practice common sense and courtesy.

Be cautious with treats or toys in dog parks. They can cause fights.

Don't take young children to the park. Dogs might not always watch where they're running or mind their manners with little people.

When dogs are crashing around having a grand time together, they might not notice that you are in the way. Carry a shake can (described on p. 157 in chapter 8) so that if they start heading at you full tilt, you can rattle it to make them veer away.

Sometimes, dogs zero in on a more timid dog, and harass or even gang up on her. Never let your pooch pick on others. If another dog looks intimidated or is not initiating play, redirect your dog's attention to you or to a more willing playmate. Conversely, if another dog is pestering your pooch, and yours looks frightened, don't assume that they can work it out for themselves. It is your job to protect your best friend. What's the point of visiting the park if it's no fun for Fido? Ask the dog's owner to distract the bruiser away from your dog, and move to another part of the park. If necessary, you might have to visit the park at times when the bully isn't there.

The best way to prevent dogfights is by close observation and quick preventive action. Should you notice a rising problem between dogs, immediately distract the dogs with a toy or whistle. Should a fight erupt, *never* put yourself between the dogs (see chapter 9, pp. 176–177, for information on how to break up a rumble).

A well-equipped dog park will have several trash cans and bag dispensers available. For regular users, it is a good idea to help with cleanup by pitching in and picking up. Should you see someone miss his or her dogs' elimination moment, you can tactfully let the person know the dog's business is ready for cleanup.

At the End of the Day, Cuddle

Take a moment to look back and remember life before your dog entered it. Fewer towels to wash and bills to pay. Cleaner floors and greener lawns. As you and your pooch cuddle together on that sheet-covered sofa, perusing the half-gnawed newspaper, and sharing a bagel (her loving gaze hypnotizes you into giving her half), you realize that the dog is no longer just your rescued dog. You belong to her as much as she belongs to you. Your bond will last a lifetime. You are family. Licks and kisses.

The dog is the god of frolic.
—Henry Ward Beecher (1813–1887)

Jan, B-Lady, and Sugar Bear.

Carlos Rebollar

Happily Ever After True Story Number Eleven:

B-Lady, Magoo, and Sugar Bear

· ·

B-Lady, Magoo, and Sugar Bear—three very different dogs who walked through the doors of a shelter at different times over the years but had something in common: They were unlikely to walk back out. They were all stray dogs, unclaimed by owners. And for various reasons, none of them were adoptable. Who would rescue them?

"Twenty years ago, I came home from a three-month hospital stay. An accident had paralyzed me from the waist down, and I was having a hard time bouncing back." Jan Nelson felt unimportant and despondent. In a wheelchair, she knew she could never walk her dogs again. Carlos, her partner, took over the walking duties but also encouraged Jan to volunteer with him at the Santa Cruz, California, SPCA where he was a board member.

"The wheelchair made me so self-conscious," she remembered, "but at the shelter I just zeroed in on the animals and forgot about anyone staring at me." Soon Jan realized she was in her element. Saving the lives of dogs became a way of saving herself. She quickly became a regular fixture with a volunteer job as Purebred Rescue Liaison. One day while touring the dog kennels, Jan noticed a golden retriever sitting quietly in her kennel. There was a cantaloupe-size tumor growing between her shoulder blades, yet she seemed oblivious to it. She stood up and beamed at Jan, her tail wagging and her brown eyes sparkling. Jan and Carlos debated whether they should adopt the dog.

They realized she would need extensive medical treatments, and even then her life could be short. To Jan and Carlos, the risks were worth it.

Worried that she had waited too long, Jan called the shelter to ask that they reserve the dog for her. The woman at the other end put the line on hold while she checked to see if the dog was still there. As Jan sat with the phone pressed to her ear, she whispered, "Oh please, let her still be there, because if she's gone, I don't know how I'll get over this." Then the music playing through the receiver gave her hope. It was Gloria Estefan's "Always Tomorrow." Jan listened as the words told her to always try to make a difference, never give up, and summon inner power day after day. Then the shelter employee's voice broke into the song to say, "Oh yes, she's still here."

Jan and Carlos named their rescue "B-Lady." She quickly became a favorite to all who met her. During many vet visits, she charmed and delighted doctors, staff, and fellow patients. But despite surgeries to remove the tumor, it returned. After two short years as part of the family, B-Lady had to be humanely euthanized.

"I had been in a wheelchair for ten years before I started volunteering at the shelter," Jan said. "I couldn't even go into a restaurant. B-Lady helped me get back into the community, making me realize I had something to give." And although B-Lady was gone, the shelter dogs kept reminding Jan they needed her.

Magoo was a young, black, nearly blind cocker spaniel "who should have never been born," according to a veterinary ophthalmologist who examined him. Magoo was brought to the shelter by a young woman who saw him toddling along a lonely stretch of highway on the Pacific Coast.

When Magoo was eligible for adoption, no one showed any interest in him. So Jan convinced the shelter's public relations department to feature him on their televised pet-of-the-week segment. Still, not one inquiry. But Jan didn't give up. After finding a foster home for Magoo, she made an appointment for him with an eye specialist.

In the veterinarian's office parking lot, Magoo leaped out of the car and promptly bumped right into a telephone pole. Jan remembered saying, "Oh no! Poor thing!" But then he just looked around, as if to say, "Hey, I'm OK!" Jan was overwhelmed by how undaunted he was. "Right there in front of me was this little dog teaching me about coping with a disability." To this day, Jan wishes she could thank the woman who noticed Magoo and rescued him. Jan would tell her, "You have no idea what a difference you made by that one simple act."

Sugar Bear was a dog who had never been noticed. She was brought to the shelter as a stray, three-year-old shepherd mix. Her kennel was at the end of the line of kennels, so she was almost invisible among the many adoptable dogs. Jan visited with Sugar Bear and realized that with her quiet, shy personality and her bland color and markings, she was a dog that was going to have a tough time finding a home. So Jan decided to focus her attention on placing Sugar Bear. But as the days passed, the dog was always passed over.

Then something happened. A twelve-year-old shelter volunteer became frightened when Sugar Bear raised her lip, showing her teeth. The staff had no choice but to deem Sugar Bear unadoptable, and she was placed on the euthanasia schedule. Jan was devastated. "We had already taken home three dogs that year. Carlos and I thought a fourth in one year was too many, so I prepared to say good-bye."

Through her years working at the shelter, Jan had said good-bye to many dogs. But it never got easier. She spent the last afternoon petting and talking to Sugar Bear. Then she left and grieved into the night. For three days, Jan stayed away from the shelter. When it was time to go back, she prepared herself to specifically visit Sugar Bear's kennel to meet the new occupant. She stopped her wheelchair in front of the kennel gate, and there, looking at her through the wire mesh, was Sugar Bear. "If I could have jumped up in the air I would have!" Jan said, "She was still slated for euthanasia, but I didn't care; she was coming home with me."

Now, all these many years later, Jan looks back to that moment of locking eyes with Sugar Bear as one of the happiest moments of her life. She has come full circle from enduring the effects of a terrible accident to realizing her life still matters. B-Lady, Magoo, Sugar Bear, and countless other dogs would agree.

If I can stop one heart
from breaking,
I shall not live in vain:
If I can ease one life the aching,
Or cool one pain,
Or help one fainting robin
Unto his nest again,
I shall not live in vain.

—Emily Dickinson

Resources

Recommended Books

Bonham, Margaret H. *The Complete Guide to Mutts: Selection, Care and Celebration from Puppyhood to Senior.* Howell Book House, 2004.

Crisp, Terri, and Samantha Glen. *Out of Harm's Way: The Extraordinary True Story of One Woman's Lifelong Devotion to Animal Rescue.* Pocket Books, 1996.

Donaldson, Jean. *The Culture Clash: A Revolutionary New Way to Understand the Relationship between Humans and Domestic Dogs.* James and Kenneth Publishers, 1997.

Foster, Ken. *The Dogs Who Found Me: What I've Learned from Pets Who Were Left Behind.* The Lyons Press, 2006.

Giffin, James M., MD, and Liisa D. Carlson, DVM. *Dog Owner's Home Veterinary Handbook.* Howell Book House, 2000.

Lane, Marion S., and The Humane Society of the United States. *The Humane Society of the United States Complete Guide to Dog Care: Everything You Need to Keep Your Dog Healthy and Happy.* Little, Brown and Company, 2001.

Langbehn, Jenny. *97 Ways to Make Your Dog Smile.* Workman Publishing Company, 2003.

Leigh, Diane, and Marilee Geyer. *One at a Time: A Week in an American Animal Shelter.* No Voice Unheard, 2003.

Martinez, Rita. *Rescues Are Special* (booklet). Vizsla Rescue Fund, Inc. Available at vizslarescue@comcast.net.

McConnell, Patricia, PhD. *The Other End of the Leash.* Ballantine Books, 2002.

Mehus-Roe, Kristin, ed. *The Original Dog Bible: The Definitive Source for All Things Dog.* Bowtie Press, 2005.

Owens, Paul, and Norma Eckroate. *The Dog Whisperer: A Compassionate, Nonviolent Approach to Training.* Adams Media Corporation, 2007.

Palika, Liz. *Purebred Rescue Dog Adoption: Rewards and Realities.* Powell Book House, 2004.

Pitcairn, Richard H. and Susan Hubble Pitcairn. *Dr. Pitcairn's New Complete Guide to Natural Health for Dogs and Cats.* Rodale Books, 2005.

Sife, Wallace, PhD. *The Loss of a Pet: A Guide to Coping with the Grieving Process When a Pet Dies.* Howell Book House, 2005.

Singer, Peter. *In Defense of Animals.* Blackwell Publishing, Inc., 2005.

Sternberg, Sue. *Successful Dog Adoption.* Howell Book House, 2003.

Recommended Web Sites

(In addition to those mentioned in the book)

www.animalbehavior.net

www.capeanimals.org

www.dogwise.com

www.drsfostersmith.com

www.ken-foster.com

www.nikenossecondchances.com

www.pawprintmag.com

www.peacelovepets.com

www.pet-abuse.com

www.petfinder.com/shelters/underdogrescue

www.pet-loss.net

www.petpopulation.org

www.petsincredible.com

www.thepoodlepreserve.org

www.saintsrescue.ca

www.southernanimalfoundation.org

www.vrescuefund.org

About the Authors

Katerina Lorenzatos Makris (aka Kathryn Makris) has written seventeen young adult novels for major publishers and a teleplay for CBS-TV. Her articles have appeared in *National Geographic Traveler*, *Travelers Tales*, *San Francisco Chronicle*, *Mother Jones*, *Veggie Life*, and many more publications. An essay about a year exploring Greece with her mother won first place—and airfare for a trip around the world—in the Book Passage travel writing contest. As a wire service reporter and radio talk show host her interviews included Sissy Spacek, Colonel Harland Sanders, Ralph Nader, the Reverend Jesse Jackson, Senator Bob Dole, Ted Danson, President George H. W. Bush, and Benji the dog.

At age ten Katerina fostered homeless cats and founded the Kindness Club, a group of kids writing letters to city officials about animal welfare issues. Later she volunteered at a shelter, and in recent years she and her husband have rescued and rehomed dozens of canine friends in need. She is developing the Artemis Project to help abused and abandoned hunting dogs in Greece.

Raised in Florida and Texas speaking Greek and Spanish, Katerina now thrives on Southern California's mix of cultures with her husband, sea kayak, flamenco shoes, and seven ex-street dogs.

Shelley Frost is the author of *Throw Like A Girl: Discovering the Body, Mind, and Spirit of the Athlete in You*. Through her Make-A-Movie Workshops, Shelley has written and produced more than fifty movies involving hundreds of children. Shelley has also written numerous articles on animal topics for various publications including *Vegetarian Times*, *Animals Agenda*, *Pawprint*, and *Animals Voice Magazine*.

Shelley has produced numerous children's videos including *Kidstuff with Dick Clark*, *Real Girls*, *Real Sports*, *Little Patriots*, *Tot Talk Around the World*, and *Babymugs!* which garnered Shelley a guest spot on the *Oprah Show*.

Born and raised in the San Francisco Bay Area, Shelley has volunteered and worked for local animal welfare organizations for twenty-seven years. Currently she is producing a documentary about one man's efforts to decrease pet overpopulation in Mexico.

Shelley lives with her husband Kevin, her thirteen-year-old son Bret, and Kellie and Abby, her two adopted Mexican daughters . . . I mean dogs.

Index